Exploring Ireland's
Wild Atlantic Way

DISCLAIMER

The activities described in this book have risks and can be dangerous, and many of the sites featured are in remote locations. The authors and publishers have gone to great lengths to ensure the accuracy of the information herein, but they cannot be held legally or financially responsible for any accident, injury, loss or inconvenience sustained as a result of the information or advice contained in this book. Swimming, jumping, diving, cycling, climbing, walking, sleeping outdoors or any other activities at any of these locations is entirely at your own risk. The inclusion of an area in this guidebook does not mean you have a right of access.

Mapping contains OpenStreetMap 2018 © OpenStreetMap contributors available under the Open Database Licence from www.openstreetmap.org /copyright.

Front cover: Dunmore Head, Kerry (see page 84) | Richard Creagh.
Back cover: Photos by Richard Creagh, David Flanagan, Conor Ryan (wave) and Grace Smith (castle - CC BY 2.0).

Boyeeghter Bay, Donegal (see page 209) | Gwen Clarke

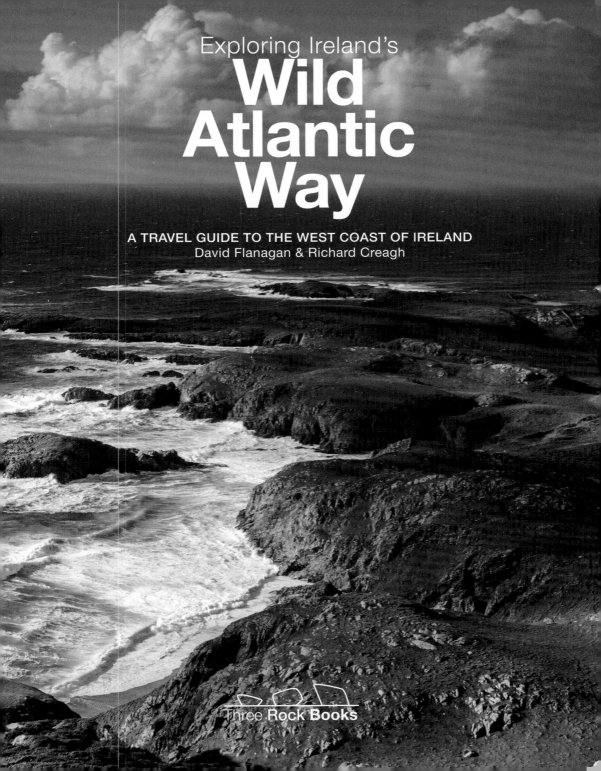

Exploring Ireland's
Wild
Atlantic
Way

A TRAVEL GUIDE TO THE WEST COAST OF IRELAND
David Flanagan & Richard Creagh

Three Rock Books

Sea cave, Garrylucas, Cork (see page 43) | RC

CONTENTS

Cliff jumping, Loop Head, Clare (see page 100) | RC

INTRODUCTION

The Atlantic coast of Ireland is an amazing place, a land full of contrasts. Beaming sunshine one minute, thick cloud and rain the next. Deserted islands and packed pubs. Calm bays and raging open sea. Barren moorland and fertile grassy plains.

It's easy to understand why it has been so popular. Until recently most tourists gathered in a select few areas that had the benefit of strong marketing to back their natural beauty. But the west coast of Ireland has always had more going for it than just a handful of destinations. You could spend your whole life in this part of the world and you wouldn't find everything it has to offer. Between the scenery, the people, the heritage, the food, the music and the wildlife, there is something for everybody.

The Wild Atlantic Way is a 2500km touring route along Ireland's west coast. It was created in 2014 by Fáilte Ireland, and has encouraged visitors to explore all corners of the coast, including areas that were often overlooked in the past.

This book will be of interest to anyone planning to visit the Atlantic coast of Ireland.

Whether you live in Ireland and are looking for ideas for weekends away or you are visiting from abroad, you will find plenty of useful information between its covers.

The book's focus is on the outdoors, on getting out into the fresh air, the wind, the sun and the rain, and exploring and discovering Ireland's greatest asset - its natural beauty. And it's while walking, cycling, swimming, climbing, fishing and paddling that you will encounter Ireland's second greatest asset, its people.

We have detailed hundreds of points of interest along the coast, from the world famous attractions to the hidden gems.

Don't fall into the trap of trying to see too much. Choose an area and linger there rather than rush from one destination to the next. Like a lot in life, the more you put into getting to know a place - its locals, its wildlife, its weather and its seasons - the more you will get out of it.

Hopefully this book will encourage you to get outside, stretch your legs, arms and mind, and visit the wilder parts of Ireland that most people never experience.

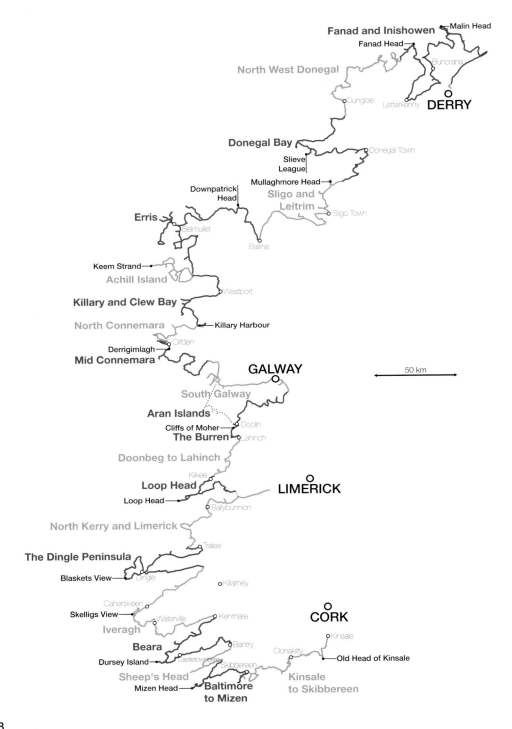

Fanad and Inishowen — Malin Head
Fanad Head
North West Donegal
Buncrana
Dungloe
Letterkenny
DERRY

Donegal Bay
Slieve League
Donegal Town
Mullaghmore Head
Downpatrick Head
Sligo and Leitrim
Sligo Town
Erris
Belmullet
Ballina
Keem Strand
Achill Island
Westport
Killary and Clew Bay
North Connemara — Killary Harbour
Derrigimlagh — Clifden
Mid Connemara
GALWAY
South Galway
Aran Islands
Cliffs of Moher — Doolin
The Burren — Lahinch
Doonbeg to Lahinch
Kilkee
Loop Head
Loop Head
LIMERICK
Ballybunnion
North Kerry and Limerick
Tralee
The Dingle Peninsula
Blaskets View — Dingle
Killarney
Cahersiveen
Skelligs View
CORK
Iveragh
Waterville
Kenmare
Kinsale
Beara
Bantry
Clonakilty
Dursey Island — Castletownbere
Old Head of Kinsale
Skibbereen
Sheep's Head
Kinsale to Skibbereen
Mizen Head
Baltimore to Mizen

50 km

8

The signs that mark the route of the Wild Atlantic Way | RC

FINDING YOUR WAY

This book is organised by county (with two exceptions - Sligo and Leitrim form one chapter, as do Limerick and Kerry). Most counties are also further divided into sections, and at the start of each section there is an overview map. These maps are accurate and to scale, and designed to give a sense of how places are positioned relative to each other. If you plan on exploring the back roads you will also need a digital or paper map.

As the Wild Atlantic Way is a linear route we had to document it in one direction. There is no best direction to travel the route, it all depends on your plans and interests. We opted for south to north as this means the passenger in a car travelling north will have the best view of the coast.

THE WILD ATLANTIC WAY

The Wild Atlantic Way route has over 160 official discovery points, of which 15 have been designated as signature discovery points. They are:

- Old Head of Kinsale, Cork (see page 43).
- Mizen Head, Cork (see page 54).
- Dursey Island, Cork (see page 63).
- Skelligs View, Kerry (see page 74).
- Blaskets View, Kerry (see page 86).
- Loop Head, Clare (see page 102).
- Cliffs of Moher, Clare (see page 110).
- Derrigimlagh, Galway (see page 139).
- Killary Harbour (south), Galway (see page 146).
- Keem Strand, Mayo (see page 162).
- Downpatrick Head, Mayo (see page 173).
- Mullaghmore Head, Sligo (see page 188).
- Slieve League, Donegal (see page 195).
- Fanad Head, Donegal (see page 212).
- Malin Head, Donegal (see page 219).

These represent some of the best known and most popular sights along the Way but they are by no means the only things worth seeing.

NAVIGATING

The route taken by the Wild Atlantic Way is very well signposted and quite straightforward to follow. However if you want to deviate to explore then you will need something to help you find your way.

The traditional option is a road map, which can be bought in any petrol station, but the more modern alternative is a satnav or smartphone. Even if you aren't using the phone network while in Ireland it's possible to download the maps of the areas you are planning to visit either in advance or when you get Wi-Fi access. You will then be able to use your phone to navigate even when you have no signal.

To do this go to Google Maps on your phone, search for the areas you are interested in and select download.

Fáilte Ireland has produced a very useful smartphone app that gives details of places to see, where to sleep and eat, and worthwhile festivals and events. It uses your phone's GPS to show your position on a map and is a handy alternative to downloading the maps for yourself. It also works off-line so you won't incur any data roaming charges or be dependent on a phone signal. Download the app from www.wildatlanticway.com/pages/the-app/.

Throughout the book you will see numbers in square brackets - these are longitude latitude coordinates in decimal degrees. If you enter them into any satnav or map website (such as Google Maps or Bing Maps) they will pinpoint the relevant location. A digital file, which can be loaded onto your smartphone or satnav device, containing all the locations in this book is available from www.threerockbooks.com.

Annagh Strand, Achill Island, Mayo (see page 163) | Janusz Sowa

INFORMATION FOR VISITORS

GETTING HERE

The three main airports in Ireland are Dublin, Cork and Shannon. While Dublin is the busiest, Cork and Shannon are better suited to those travelling to the west coast. Cork Airport is only a 30 minute drive from the beginning/end of the Wild Atlantic Way and Shannon Airport in Clare is a good option if you want to go straight to the mid-west of Ireland.

There are various other smaller airports where it may be possible to fly to, depending on where you're coming from. These include Knock in Mayo, Farranfore in Kerry and Carrickfinn in Donegal.

It's also possible to travel to Ireland by ferry. There are regular sailings into Dublin from Holyhead (Wales) and Liverpool (England), and into Rosslare (the southeast corner of Ireland) from various ports in South Wales. Car ferries also run from Roscoff and Cherbourg in the north of France to Cork and Rosslare.

GETTING AROUND

Public transport in Ireland, particularly in rural areas, is limited. Buses and trains can be expensive and unless you're moving between the cities, journeys often involve multiple transfers. Getting to some rural areas is impossible by public transport.

Car hire offers the flexibility to explore at will and can be good value. But be warned; many first time drivers in Ireland are initially taken aback by the narrow, winding roads. So take it slowly, remember to

11

Doughmore in summer, Clare (see page 108) | RC

stay on the left and if you're unsure just pull in to allow traffic pass, provided there's room to do so.

Hitch-hiking is still relatively easy in rural areas, where the roads are small and people are generally more open to helping out. The potential dangers needn't be stated here, but if you're stuck for a lift, it might be worth sticking out your thumb.

WHAT TO BRING
The best thing you can bring to Ireland is a good set of waterproofs. Both a hooded jacket and trousers will probably be well used on a holiday in Ireland, especially if you plan on spending time in the outdoors.

A pair of sturdy, waterproof walking boots will also serve you well. Though most of the walks described in this book follow paths and tracks, you will still encounter mud, puddles and uneven ground. Bring warm clothes and long sleeves, even in summer. A nice summer's day can still be chilly, especially if there is a sea breeze.

And while the sun is never that strong it's easy, particularly on windy days, to underestimate its strength. So use sunscreen.

ACCOMMODATION
For the most part there is plenty of accommodation available along the Wild Atlantic Way, from basic campsites to five star hotels. We have mentioned most campsites and hostels as well as some other unusual places that we think might be of interest. If you want to research B+Bs, guesthouses or hotels then Trip Advisor is a good starting point.

FOOD AND DRINK
The food industry in Ireland has improved hugely in the past decade, and there are plenty of world class restaurants all over the country. Most pubs also serve very good food. In general, more touristic towns will be a bit pricier, but they'll also have more on offer, so shop around if you're on a budget.

Vegetarian options can be quite limited in most of Ireland, especially outside the cities, and vegans should be prepared to arrange most of their own meals.

If Ireland is famous for anything other than its scenery it's the pubs and the beer and spirits that it produces. Guinness is world famous, but there are plenty of other local variations of the black stuff available (especially in Cork). Ireland's craft brewing industry has really taken off in the past few years and many towns now have micro-breweries with locally-made beers and spirits. From Dingle to Donegal there are new craft beers coming to the market every other month, adding to the growing list of artisan produce for which Ireland is renowned.

Winter storm at Clogher, Kerry (see page 88) | RC

MONEY

Ireland uses the euro currency, meaning that if you're coming from most places in Europe you won't need to change money before you get here. Larger towns will have ATMs but many smaller villages won't, so be sure to carry some cash if you're planning on staying somewhere rural for a few days.

WEATHER

Nobody comes to Ireland for a sun holiday. The weather is famously mixed but isn't actually as bad as it's made out to be. Expect a lot of change. If you're lucky you'll get a settled spell. If you're unlucky you'll get wind-driven mist for days on end. The most likely scenario is a bit of both.

Good waterproofs and a sense of humour are your best defence against bad weather. The best thing to do is to not let the weather dictate your trip too much. Getting in the sea is a great way to spend some time on a rainy day, and most land-based activities can be just as much fun in the rain as they are on a nice sunny day if you have the right attitude.

WHEN TO VISIT?

SUMMER

The weather during an Irish summer can be glorious and miserable and everything in between, and all on the same day. By the middle of June the daylight lasts for more than 17 hours, giving both early birds and night owls a chance to see some sun, should it appear.

When the weather is nice in the summer, the west coast of Ireland is an amazing place to be. The hedges are filled to bursting with wildflowers, the mountains go green and even the sea can feel warm (on a good day). There are few finer pleasures than lying out on a sun-warmed rock after an invigorating swim in the Atlantic. Maybe, cooking freshly caught mackerel over a driftwood campfire could top it off.

Anybody not familiar with higher latitudes will savour the sun as it hangs near the horizon, and dusk lingers long into the night.

While the main tourist hubs can be packed at this time of year it's not that hard to escape the hordes. The islands are best in summer; away from it all but still lively.

WINTER

While summer is the most popular time with tourists that doesn't mean it's not worth visiting at other times of the year. Though the winter tends to be cold, wet and windy, the same conditions can be found at any time of year, and at least in winter you will be expecting it. The days are quite short (about 8 hours of light in early December) but the rawness of a breezy hillside walk or mind-numbing surf in mid-winter will appeal to some. And a warm fireside and

The main road across Inishnee Island, Galway (see page 135) | DF

quiet pint is all the sweeter after time outdoors in the cold, dark months.

Stargazing in rural Ireland is best during the long, dark nights of winter (if you're lucky enough to get clear weather). Whale watching along the south coast has traditionally been best at this time of year, but again, the weather conditions don't always allow for trips. The sea can be particularly ferocious in winter, and is worth seeing in its own right (from a safe position). The low light and mixed weather of the darker months might appeal to photographers too.

Come in the winter if you want to avoid the crowds, but plan well as some accommodation and activity providers will be closed.

SPRING

March and April occasionally have some of the best weather of the year in Ireland. The first high pressure system after the winter is sometimes the most stable of the year, giving weeks of settled weather. That said, there is no real predictability with the Irish climate and anything can happen at any time of year.

Spring tourists will avoid the summer crowds, and enjoy a time of year when the landscape is coming to life again after winter. This can also be a great time of year for the outdoor enthusiast; temperatures are pleasant for walking, the days aren't so long that the sun wakes you in your tent at 5am, and the dreaded midges (tiny, infuriating biting insects) haven't come out yet. During the month of May the woodlands come alive with wild garlic and bluebells, making for pretty scenes. The sea thrift that thrives along most of Ireland's coast is at its best in the early days of summer, adding colour to the sea cliffs. Seabird colonies are well and truly established by the middle of spring, giving birdwatchers plenty to look at.

AUTUMN

Autumn is a good time of year for fishing and foraging. Nearly every ditch and hedge on the west coast is laden down with blackberries in September, making a great addition to porridge or an evening stroll. The inshore mackerel season lasts well into autumn, and experienced foragers will find fungi in the forests.

Many rural communities have harvest festivals in August, with all sorts of activities on offer. The sea is at its warmest in September, and the first swells of winter often produce stellar surf before the wind starts howling.

PLACE NAMES

Irish place names have a mixed heritage. The vast majority are anglicised versions of old Irish names, translated phonetically from their original forms. While some places have a name that isn't derived from Irish, the majority do. This leads to a lot of similarities between certain place names, as the original names are almost all descriptive of features that can be found anywhere. After centuries of the language evolving the origin of many place names is uncertain.

Toponymy, the study of the origins of place names, is a fascinating subject that can reveal a huge amount about the history, culture and landscape of a place. If interested in this it's worth checking out Logainm (www.logainm.ie), a vast bilingual database of the place names of Ireland.

Some familiarity with the more common words that occur in place names will give an extra insight into a trip along the west coast.

Below are some frequently used place name elements that you may see on your travels.

Bally	From the Irish word Baile, meaning town or place e.g. Ballyferriter - Ferriter's Town (Ferriter being a surname).
...beg	Usually seen at the end of a name, from the Irish word Beag, meaning small e.g. Killybegs - The Small Cells (of a monastic settlement).
Bun	From the Irish word Bun, meaning foot of or end of (usually a river) e.g. Bunbeg - The Small Mouth of the River.
Derry	From the Irish word Doire, meaning oak wood e.g. Derrymore - The Big Oak Wood.
Gort	From the Irish word Gort, meaning field e.g. Gort na gCapall - Field of the Horses.
Inish	From the Irish word Inis, meaning island e.g. Inishmaan - Middle Island.
Kill	From the Irish word Cill, meaning church, or sometimes from Coill, meaning a wood e.g. Killarney - Church of the Sloes (the sloe being the fruit of the blackthorn tree).
Knock	From the Irish word Cnoc, meaning hill e.g. Knockmore - The Big Hill.
Lis	From the Irish word Lios, meaning ring fort e.g. Listowel - Tuathal's Ringfort.
Rath	From the Irish word Ráth, meaning circular fort e.g. Rathmore - The Big Ring Fort.
Roe	From the Irish word Rua(dh), meaning red e.g. Carraroe - The Red Quarter.
Slieve	From the Irish word Sliabh, meaning mountain e.g. Slieve League - Mountain of the Flagstones.
Tra	From the Irish word Trá, meaning beach. e.g. Tralee - Beach of the Lee (a river).

Paddleboarding on Carrownisky Strand, Mayo (see page 152) | RC

A pub in Milltown Malbay, Clare (see page 109) | RC

Croagh Patrick, Mayo (see page 84) | Dale Simonson

White Strand, Malin Head, Donegal (see page 219) | Harvey Futcher

Inis Tuaisceart, The Blasket Islands, Kerry (see page 86) | RC

FIVE ESSENTIAL EXPERIENCES

No matter where you go on the west coast of Ireland there are some experiences every visitor should seek out. Rather than focussing on specific places we have compiled a list, in no particular order, of experiences that can be found almost anywhere along the Wild Atlantic Way.

1 CLIMB AN ICONIC MOUNTAIN

A large portion of the Atlantic coast is mountainous and while modest by international standards, many of the mountains rise directly from sea-level, offering a tough challenge to hikers.

Some of them have been sites of pilgrimage for millennia, and though the motives for going to these sacred summits may be different in this day and age, there are plenty of reasons to keep the tradition alive.

Some of the mountains are outside the scope of the casual hiker due to steep, difficult ground but they will be of great interest to experienced walkers with good navigation skills. Others have well worn paths to the summit and should be within most people's ability in all but the worst weather. If you pick your day well the summit views will be well worth the effort. Here is a list of suggestions:

- Brandon Mountain, Kerry (see page 90)
- Diamond Hill, Galway (see page 145)
- Croagh Patrick, Mayo (see page 157).
- Knocknarea, Sligo (see page 183).
- Slieve League, Donegal (see page 195).
- Errigal, Donegal (see page 211).

2 VISIT AN ISLAND

A visit to most of the Irish islands is like a trip back in time. That's not to say that the islands are backward places - almost all enjoy the conveniences of the contemporary world, but they have retained a relaxed pace of living that most other places have exchanged for the rush of modernity.

Many of the islands are strongholds of the Irish language, and visitors are just as likely to hear people speaking Gaeilge as they are English in places like Cape Clear, the Aran Islands and Tory Island. They generally have vibrant traditional music scenes, and folklore is better remembered in these places than most others.

Most of the islands are dependent on tourism more than any other industry. So there are plenty of facilities on the most popular islands, and visitors can enjoy the feeling of being somewhere truly different without forgoing some creature comforts.

And for the hardier amongst us, there are plenty of islands with little or no facilities that are truly great places to get away from the rest of the world.

No matter which island you visit be sure to spend the night. When the day-trippers have all gone you'll get a real sense of the way life is lived on these remote Atlantic outposts.

3 A NIGHT IN THE PUB

Ireland is rightly famous for its pubs. Even in the smallest communities you can often find two or three different bars and they are the focal point of every town or village. It's very possible that some visitors will spend every night in a pub, chatting to locals, listening to traditional Irish music, or just sitting beside the fire enjoying a meal or a nice pint of Guinness. Whether you want to experience the buzz of a crowded bar or enjoy a drink in a quiet corner you will have plenty of choice.

After a day outdoors there is no better way to wind down in the evening, and no better place to meet people. In recent years the standard of food offered in pubs has improved significantly so they aren't just for night time visits. Some places are better than others for music but it's pretty easy to find live music in the summer time.

4 WALK THE COAST

You will never be far from the coast in Ireland, and the variety of seaside landscapes is one of the country's major attractions. Some places have huge cliffs and rocky headlands while other areas are fringed by vast sandy beaches.

A walk along the coast is the best way to see these sights at close quarters, as well as a whole lot more. There are secret sheltered coves that are perfect for a swim. Marine wildlife could appear at any moment. There are sea caves, arches and all sorts of impressive natural architecture. And there is the sea itself, and all its moods.

No doubt these places are great on sunny days but the coast is worth a visit at any time of year. You'll have a renewed appreciation for the roof over your head after a walk in some wild, wet weather. And on a fine evening there is no better place to watch the sun go down than along the west coast of Ireland.

See page 21 for more information about walking.

5 PUSH YOUR COMFORT ZONE

Ireland's reputation as a destination for outdoor activities is growing fast. With a great diversity of terrain Ireland is the ideal place to try a new activity. Watersports such as surfing, kayaking and paddleboarding offer a unique perspective on the coastline, while land-based activities such as mountain biking, rock climbing and caving allow you to visit places you might never get to see otherwise.

Dunmore Head, Kerry (see page 84) | RC

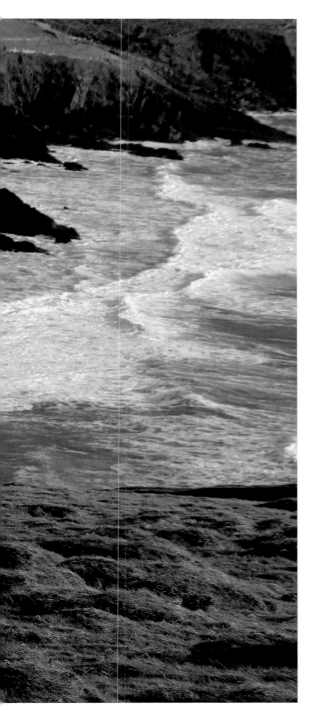

ACTIVITIES

Ireland's Atlantic coast is a paradise for those who enjoy the outdoors and this guide has a strong emphasis on activities that can be done along the Wild Atlantic Way.

WALKING

There is an endless variety of walks along the Atlantic seaboard, from short gentle strolls along sandy beaches to long days out on mountains that slope down to the sea. While some of those harder walks are only suitable for experienced hikers, there is no shortage of options for people looking for leisurely strolls in beautiful places.

You can walk miles and miles of beaches in Cork and Kerry, explore the rocky shorelines of Clare, get lost on the quiet country boreens of Connemara, or range over huge, rugged sea cliffs in Mayo and Donegal.

The rural nature of the west of Ireland means many of the roads are quiet, and ideal for walking. These small roadways are often lined with grass down the middle and bordered by high, verdant hedges that bustle with wildlife in summer. Much of the coast in these quiet corners is untended by farmers, leaving a wild and open border between land and sea that is ripe for exploration.

The majority of the walks described in this guide are signposted trails that are easy to follow and suitable for people of average fitness. Marked routes are thankfully becoming more prevalent, and the Irish Trails website (www.irishtrails.ie) is a brilliant resource for walkers looking for suitable routes in all areas of the country. As well as detailed maps and route descriptions there is feedback from people who have walked the trails, offering first-hand information to others.

Good footwear is recommended for off-road walking in Ireland. The damp climate and soft ground mean paths are often wet and muddy.

Almost all the land in Ireland is privately owned, from the tops of the hills to the high tide mark, and walkers must respect the rights of the landowners. Ignoring their requests could result in the loss of access, so please observe any signs you see while out walking, be they about trespassing, gates or dogs. Much of the west of Ireland is farming land and dogs can stress livestock, especially sheep. Please avoid bringing dogs where the signs say so. Park carefully, making sure not to obstruct gates, take all litter home and leave places as you would wise to find them.

TICKS

If you're walking off the beaten track in Ireland it's important to be aware of ticks. These tiny spider-like creatures feed on the blood of animals and

Wild camping, Loop Head, Clare (see page 100) | RC

occasionally humans. A small minority of them carry Lyme Disease. Wearing long sleeves and tucking trousers into socks can help prevent them coming into contact with your skin. Check yourself for ticks after walking in long grass, woodlands, ferns or any other wild green places, or if you've been in contact with animals. See www.ticktalkireland.org for more information.

MIDGES
Midges are tiny flying insects that can be a nuisance on calm, humid days between May and September, especially near lakes, rivers and bogs. And while they don't carry disease, their bites are very annoying. As they are blown away by even a gentle breeze and the west of Ireland is generally windy you needn't worry about them too much. But it's no harm to have some insect repellant to hand, even though it often achieves very little.

MOUNTAIN SAFETY
Ireland's mountains may be modest in height but the weather in the hills is especially fickle and can quickly change for the worst. Most of the walks described in this book follow well-marked trails in low-lying areas where help is never far and conditions are unlikely to become life threatening. But some walks are more serious treks into the mountains, and those without sufficient skills and equipment can quickly become wet, cold, lost and in serious danger.

If you are venturing into the mountains be sure to plan your route (including possible escape options), wear suitable footwear, carry a map and compass (and know how to use them), extra food and warm and waterproof clothing with you.

Always let somebody know where you're going and what time to expect you back. In case of an emergency dial 112 or 999, but be warned that many mountainous areas have poor phone signal.

MAPS
Ireland is covered at a scale of 1:50,000 by the Discovery Series of maps published by Ordnance Survey Ireland (www.osi.ie). They are designed for hikers and have plenty of detail. If you are planning on spending some time in a particular area then it's well worth getting the relevant map.

CAMPING
Camping is a great way to experience the great outdoors, and while the weather in Ireland may be unsettled it shouldn't put you off spending a night or two in a tent. There are few greater pleasures than waking up to the early summer sun on a quiet coastal headland or sitting around a driftwood fire before bedding down under the stars.

Details of campsites are mentioned throughout the book, from basic sites to plush glamping destinations

Cycling the Green Road on Inishbofin, Galway (see page 143) | DF

for those who like a bit of luxury. Nowadays many campsites also provide accommodation for those without their own equipment, with basic tents, canvas yurts and wooden pods offering rustic shelter all along the coast.

And in spite of the fact that virtually all land along the Irish coast is privately owned, wild camping is still an option once it's done with good sense.

Remote beaches and upland areas away from roads are the best options. Most landowners, once approached with respect, will be happy to suggest a place to camp that won't be in anybody's way.

Discretion is essential when wild camping; pitch your tent late, take it down early and don't make too much noise. If you are planning on lighting a fire choose suitable ground and minimise its effect on the landscape. And remember to take all your rubbish away with you.

CYCLING

Travelling by bike is the ideal way to explore an area. It allows you take in the landscape yet still cover enough ground to get around. Views race by while driving and it's all too easy to miss things when rushing past in a car. On the islands especially, cycling is a healthy, enjoyable way to discover your surroundings - most of the popular islands have bike rental.

Many of the towns along the Wild Atlantic Way also have places to rent bikes, and just like with the walking trails, signposted cycle routes are starting to pop up here and there in Ireland. While some may be more suited to triathletes, the majority cover much shorter journeys and won't leave your legs hanging off by the end.

The Great Western Greenway (see page 161) in Mayo is a relatively new cycleway and is already a major success. No doubt other similar initiatives will be rolled out in the coming years as the outdoor tourism industry gathers pace. However you aren't limited to these established routes - with the aid of a map and some imagination you will find miles of quiet roads to cycle all over the west coast, whether you are looking for challenging hill climbs or flat byways.

Remember that traffic (including bikes) travels on the left side of the road in Ireland. Helmets are strongly recommended, as are lights (required by law) and a high visibility vest. Many main roads in Ireland are quite narrow by international standards, so cycling on them is best avoided in summer especially when tour buses and extra traffic is more likely.

A perfect summer day at Coumeenoole, Kerry (see page 84) | RC

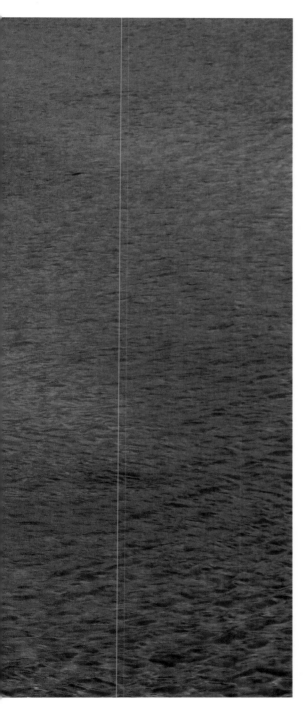

SWIMMING

There are thousands of quiet coves, open beaches, mountain lakes and safe harbours along the Wild Atlantic Way, and many would say that a trip to the coast is not complete until you have had a dip in the sea.

Even though the water won't be at tropical temperatures it's far from freezing in the summer, and a dip in this corner of the Atlantic is always invigorating. With cheap wetsuits now widely available there is little excuse for not diving in. In Ireland's changeable weather, getting into the sea is a perfect wet weather option, as being wet becomes something to do rather than avoid.

Many of the most popular beaches have lifeguards in the summer. In general they will be present at weekends in June and September, and daily in July and August, but this isn't always the case. The Irish Water Safety website (www.iws.ie) has plenty of information on lifeguards, water quality and beaches with Green Coast and Blue Flag awards.

WATER SAFETY

Ireland's Atlantic coast can be a dangerous place. It's prone to unsettled weather, with high winds and rough seas common even in the summer. If you plan on taking to the water be sure to check the sea conditions, the forecast and the tide, no matter what activity you're pursuing or what level of experience you have. Heed warning signs and if you're unsure just stay on land. Things can go wrong very quickly when the sea is involved, so be vigilant.

Be especially careful near cliff edges. Some softer sections of coast are easily eroded and the tops of some cliffs can be undercut at the edges, with little but air beneath a thin cover of soil.

Always be conscious of rogue waves near the sea. Whether you're fishing, taking photographs or just having a look, be sensible and don't stand with your back to the ocean.

In case of emergency dial 112 or 999, and raise the alarm as soon as possible.

Irish waters are home to about half a dozen species of jellyfish, the majority of which pose little problem to swimmers. Two species are worth being wary of; the lion's mane and the Portuguese man o'war. The former can cause severely painful stings and contact with the latter can be potentially fatal. However the chances of an encounter are very low. Unless you've been specifically warned about a certain case you shouldn't be deterred from getting into the water.

Another hazard to be aware of is the weever fish, which buries itself in the sand at the low tide mark leaving its dorsal fin exposed. If stood on it can cause considerable pain that can last for weeks. Weever fish are quite rare but it's a good idea to wear something on your feet in the water.

Heading out to sea from Kinnagoe Bay, Donegal (see page 220) | Loughs Agency

SNORKELLING

Being in the sea isn't all about working on your butterfly stroke. Snorkelling is a really interesting way to enjoy the water and Ireland's temperate seas are teeming with coastal marine life just beneath the surface. The Pollock Holes in Clare (see page 104) are an ideal place for a first-time snorkelling trip, but there are plenty of other safe bays where you can experience an underwater safari.

COASTEERING

Coasteering is another increasingly popular way to enjoy the shoreline. Combining swimming, cliff jumping and scrambling, it is an active and thrilling way to spend a few hours. More and more activity providers are offering coasteering as part of their lineup, and it's highly recommended for the adventurous traveller.

KAYAKING

What cycling is to walking, kayaking is to swimming; a great way to cover plenty of ground in an active, enjoyable manner. Once the realm of the experienced enthusiast, kayaking has now become a more family-friendly pastime as boats have become cheaper and peoples' interest in the outdoors increases. Of course that's not to say that anybody can just pick up a boat and start paddling to a distant offshore island. Any activity on the water must be undertaken with the utmost respect for the sea. But with common sense and some basic knowledge there are hundreds of sheltered beaches and bays on Ireland's west coast where kayaking can be enjoyed safely.

As most people don't have their own boats, there are plenty of activity providers offering rentals and guided kayaking trips up and down the west coast - many are mentioned in the main text.

Another welcome development is the Blueways, the aquatic equivalent of the Greenway walking and cycling routes. While there aren't a huge number of these yet, hopefully in time they will be more common along the Irish coast.

For the experienced sea kayaker Ireland is a world-renowned place to paddle. A full circumnavigation of the island is a feat sought after by kayakers from all over the world, and the hundreds of offshore islands make for excellent shorter trips. While most of these adventures are beyond the scope of this book it doesn't take too much imagination to plan a good kayaking excursion in the west of Ireland.

David Walsh's excellent website www.oileain. org is an invaluable resource for paddlers looking for information on Ireland's islands. Needless to say, no matter what your level of experience, always be prepared: a detailed weather forecast, knowledge of the tides and the know-how to keep yourself safe are essential requirements for any kayak trip.

Surfing at Inch, Kerry (see page 82) | RC

SURFING

The Wild Atlantic Way faces over 4,000km of open ocean, and sits in the way of the prevailing southwest wind of the North Atlantic, and the swell that it creates. These conditions make Ireland a great spot for surfing, a fact that hasn't gone unnoticed by waveriders.

From gentle beach breaks to world famous big waves, Ireland has surfing for everybody. In the past twenty years it has gone from being a fringe activity to a sport that coastal towns thrive on. There are multiple surf schools in every county of the Wild Atlantic Way, even Leitrim, which has the shortest length of coast in Ireland.

While some of the more popular surf spots - such as Inch in Kerry, Lahinch in Clare, and Bundoran in Donegal - get busy on the best days, there are hundreds of other empty breaks.

The recent advances in weather forecasting and up-to-date online information have made getting out in good surf much easier, so there is little stopping those with enough enthusiasm.

While the winter may be the best season for dedicated surfers, there are plenty of opportunities to catch waves throughout the year. And if you've never surfed before then it doesn't really matter if the waves aren't perfect - once there's enough whitewater to stand up then anybody can experience the feeling of being propelled along by a wave that has travelled hundreds or thousands of kilometres to wash up on the shores of Ireland.

SUP

As well as surfing, Ireland is becoming increasingly popular for SUP (Stand Up Paddleboarding), kite surfing and some of the more esoteric activities like kite buggying. Paddleboarding in particular is very popular and very accessible for people of all abilities.

Mackerel

Hazelnuts

Wild Raspberries

Wild Strawberries

Blackberries

Cockles

Razor Clams

Samphire

Golden Chanterelles

Bilberries

WILD FOOD

Throughout the year there is an abundance of wild food growing in Irish waters, shores, fields, hills and hedges. And you don't need to have military survival training to find some of the more common edible foods - with a little research and a bare minimum of equipment it's quite possible to get outside and grab a free lunch.

Even though it was first published in 1972, *Food for Free* by Richard Mabey is still one of the best guides for anyone interested in foraging. As some berries and many mushrooms are toxic it's vitally important to know what you're doing when looking for wild food. Don't let the risk put you off. Armed with common sense and help from a book or a knowledgeable guide, foraging can be an enjoyable way of satisfying your hunger.

FISH

The Great Famine of the 1840s resulted in the death of over one million people and the emigration of twice that number, largely due to successive failures of the potato crop, most people's only source of food. While there were plenty of socio-economic factors at play it is often wondered why people weren't better equipped to take food from the sea, which would have lessened this reliance on the potato.

However in more recent times fish and seafood have become more popular, and it doesn't take much effort to head down to the coast and catch some for yourself. The late summer months are best suited to fishing, and mackerel and pollock are the fish that are most commonly caught and eaten. Many coastal towns have shops supplying fishing gear and the knowledge of the best spots to head to. You will also find boats offering angling trips all along the coast. River and lake fishing is also possible along much of the west coast. However, licenses are required for most species and there are strict seasons. See www.fishinginireland.info for more information.

If you are going fishing, only catch what you will eat and please take all your rubbish home with you.

SHELLFISH

Though more of an acquired taste it can be easier to gather some types of shellfish than to catch fish. Common shore species like mussels, limpets and periwinkles are straightforward to identify and they provide an easy meal for the modern day hunter-gatherer. Razor clams require a bit more work but can be found on plenty of Irish beaches. Delicacies like scallops can sometimes be found in the sand at the very lowest reaches of the shore on a low tide.

Shellfish poisoning can be an issue but with care it is easily avoided. Don't collect shellfish near towns or cities where raw sewage could be discharged into the sea. Always wash what you find very well - both inside and out. Don't cook dead shellfish – check before cooking that it is still alive by gently forcing the shell open. Any animal that is still alive will quickly shut its shell again.

SEAWEED

Freely available on most stretches of the coast, seaweed is an intriguing food full of minerals. Though many people aren't that keen on the idea of eating it, seaweed is an extremely healthy and useful food, and seaweed extracts are used in many common household products and foods. Not all seaweeds are palatable but many can be eaten raw as a tasty snack.

As for shellfish, avoid picking seaweed close to towns or villages or anywhere where there might be harmful run-off from land. Most seaweeds are best harvested in early summer, and it's best not to cut them too close to the 'root' so as to give them the best chance of re-sprouting.

BERRIES

In late summer most Irish rural roads are bordered by brambles weighed down with plump, juicy berries. Blackberry picking is a rite of passage for most children in the countryside, and they are delicious on their own or as an addition to porridge or ice cream.

Wild strawberries are far less common but don't pass one by if you see them. Though small, they are incredibly tasty.

More common than wild strawberries are bilberries, or fraughans as they are known in much of Ireland. A relative of the blueberry, fraughans are smaller but far tastier. The shrub mostly grows in thick heather, making it hard to find sometimes, but a good haul in late July is a just reward for the effort.

FUNGI

Most people are very reluctant to gather wild mushrooms as there is a real danger of serious, potentially fatal poisoning if you make a mistake. However the majority of mushrooms are safe to eat, and the better tasting ones are vastly superior to anything from the shops.

Autumn is generally the best time for mushroom picking, and Ireland's mild and wet climate is ideal for many types of fungi. If you don't know what you're looking for then you'd better get help, and there are guides and workshops available that will help you get the most from your foraging trip.

The photos on facing page are by Richard Creagh, David Flanagan, Yoko Nekonomania, Chris Cant, Féron Benjamin, Conor Ryan.

Summer meadow flowers

Bog Cotton

Sea Campion

Early-purple Orchid

Ramson (Wild Garlic)

Foxglove

Lesser Black-Backed Gull

Razorbill

Red Deer

Rabbit

Gannets

WILD ATLANTIC WILDLIFE

The west coast of Ireland is the border between two worlds; the edge of Europe and the northeast Atlantic. As a consequence, it is a haven of biodiversity, a huge number of species from both land and sea are found here. From the tiniest barnacles to the largest whales, there is a wide range of wildlife all along the Wild Atlantic Way.

IN THE COUNTRYSIDE

At first glance Ireland doesn't seem a world leader in the wildlife stakes. Though there used to be more large land mammals in the past (like the wolf and wild boar), the majority were made extinct by human encroachment.

Nowadays deer are the only sizeable land mammals left. The mountains of Kerry and Donegal are home to most of the deer on the west coast, though they can also be found in lowland areas. Wild goats aren't uncommon, and like the deer, they were brought to Ireland by humans as a domestic animal. Herds of feral goats can be found on the Beara Peninsula in Cork, in parts of The Burren in Clare and many other wilder pockets further north.

The farmed landscape in much of the country may not be suited to bigger, wild mammals but plenty of the smaller ones, including foxes, badgers, stoats,

red squirrels, hares and rabbits, can still be found. In the past, when most of the population lived in the countryside, people were more familiar with these elusive creatures, but now unfortunately most sightings of Irish mammals are as roadkill. You are most likely to see a live fox or a badger at dawn or dusk in summer, when they're heading out to hunt at night. Hares are relatively common in the uplands, and if you're very lucky you may see a stoat on a quiet country lane. These charming animals can be quite ferocious, and will often catch rabbits far bigger than themselves. They will even stand and stare down an approaching human before darting away. Otters can be seen near rivers and low-lying coast, and a sighting is a welcome bonus to any walk.

HEDGE LIFE

The little-used byways of rural Ireland may be the best place to spot mammals but that's not all the wildlife they're home to. In a country with only a small amount of woodland, the hedgerows that line many of our country roads are important refuges and corridors for birds, wildflowers and thousands of invertebrate species. A walk between healthy hedges in summer will reveal countless butterflies, hoverflies, bees and bugs as well as songbirds and a huge range of

Small Copper Butterfly

Emerald Damselfly

Blue-rayed Limpets

Dahlia Anemone

Humpback Whale

Common Dolphin mother and calf

Grey Seal

36

Curlew

Puffins

wildflowers. Those with a keen eye could easily while away an hour along a 100m stretch of roadside just watching the life in the verges.

BOGLAND

The bogs of the northwest may appear empty but there's a lot more going on than first impressions suggest. There is a range of species that are well adapted to the waterlogged, acidic conditions of blanket bog. Many species of orchids are found here, as well as plants like lousewort, bog asphodel and great swathes of bog cotton. Some plants have adapted to the low nutrient habitat by becoming insectivores. Sundew and butterwort are both common insect-eating bog plants. Many birds favour open moorland too. The red grouse is common in the blanket bog of Mayo and geese and plover, among others, depend on the bogs for feeding and breeding too.

ON THE COAST

As an island, perched at the fringe of an enormous ocean, the seas around it are home to many times more species than dry land. Though most of us never see it, the wildlife in the sea is rich and varied and Ireland's position at the edge of Europe makes it a major stopping ground for migrating animals that feed in our coastal waters.

There are huge colonies of seabirds making use of the cliffs and remote islands. Many of these outposts host internationally important numbers of certain species, like gannets on The Little Skellig and storm petrels on the Blaskets. While most of us are familiar with gulls, who often come inland, the majority of ocean-going birds only come to shore to breed. Once breeding is complete most of these birds head to sea; Manx shearwaters spend the winter off the coast of South America and the summer in Ireland. For a bird that can live over 60 years that's a lot of mileage.

OPEN SEA

The water off Ireland's coast is an important habitat for whales, dolphins, sharks and seals. The Blasket Islands off Kerry and the Inishkea Islands off Mayo

hosts plenty of grey seals, an animal whose life has long been interwoven with coastal people.

Recently the whales and dolphins off the Irish coast have been attracting more attention, and it's clear that the south and west coasts in particular are important feeding grounds for some of the largest animals in the world. Fin whales (the second biggest whale) can be seen close to land every year and humpback whales have been seen around the Blaskets in increasing numbers over the past few years.

Added to this is Europe's largest group of resident bottlenose dolphins at the mouth of the Shannon and annual sightings of basking sharks (the second biggest shark in the world) all along the coast.

Most people probably aren't aware that Ireland has about 30 species of shark but don't let that stop you from getting into the water. The chances of a shark attack are practically zero.

THE SHORELINE

While the well-known megafauna are undoubtedly impressive, there are many equally interesting species to be found almost everywhere along the shorelines. Rock-pooling is a fantastic seashore activity, especially for kids. There are hermit crabs, fish, urchins, seaweeds and a range of alien-like anemones to be seen.

Snorkelling is a superb way to inspect this underwater world, and there is no shortage of suitable spots along the Wild Atlantic Way. Even the humble barnacle becomes a fascinating creature when viewed under water; if you look closely you'll see thousands of minute, feathered 'arms' reaching out to filter food from the sea.

So while you may not have travelled to the west of Ireland specifically to watch wildlife it's worth keeping an eye out - you never know what you might see.

All photos on this spread and the previous spread by Richard Creagh.

Sunset and storm, Smerwick Harbour, Kerry (see page 89) | RC

THE WILD ATLANTIC WAY

Garrylucas (see page 43) | RC

CORK

From its starting (or finishing point) in the town of Kinsale the Wild Atlantic Way travels west along the coastline of Cork. Initially the terrain is gentle with grassy green fields, but gradually it becomes wilder and more rugged.

Along the West Cork coast there are sheltered harbours, open cliffs, gourmet towns, offshore islands, seaside hills and miles of beaches.

The quiet country lanes west of Kinsale are ideal for cyclists and the beaches around Clonakilty are golden. The seas between Galley Head and Baltimore welcome some of the planet's largest animals each year. The islands of Roaringwater Bay are a world away from the mainland. Sheep's Head is a walker's paradise and Beara is rugged and remote.

West Cork is generally somewhat tamer than the rough-edged landscapes in the rest of the west of Ireland. The climate is a little more forgiving than in the counties further north, though nobody in Ireland can make any guarantees about the weather. Nonetheless, the coast of Cork is a pleasant one, with enough variety to keep all lovers of the seashore happy.

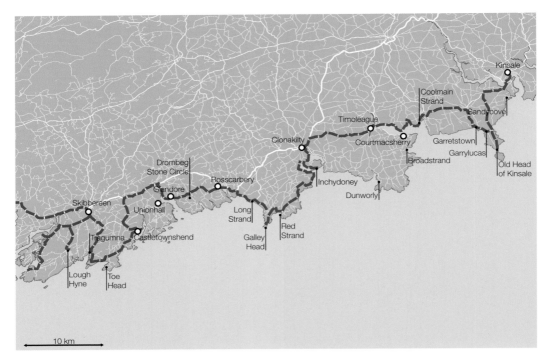

10 km

KINSALE TO SKIBBEREEN

This, the first, or last, stretch of the Wild Atlantic Way serves as a gentle introduction or wind down. The terrain is, in contrast with counties further west and north, more gentle, with abundant rolling green fields and thick hedges.

And while it may not have the drama of the Kerry mountains or the wide-open spaces of County Mayo, this is an incredibly attractive length of coastline. There are countless small bays, classically beautiful beaches and peaceful coastal walks where you're unlikely to meet another soul. Pockets of woodland reach down to the sea in many of the sheltered coves, an unusual feature in most of Ireland.

There are plenty of options for watersports enthusiasts, and both surfing and sea kayaking are popular in these parts. As is wildlife watching; this section of the West Cork coast is a haven for all sorts of migrants, from the smallest birds to the biggest whales.

KINSALE

This pretty seaside village is a very popular tourist hub. It has a number of excellent restaurants and is considered by many to be the gourmet capital of Ireland.

CHARLES FORT

A pleasant walk east of town takes you out to the historic ruins of Charles Fort, where there is a great view of Kinsale Harbour *[51.6979, -8.4988]*. From the main carpark *[51.7055, -8.5215]* follow the road east along the water's edge (signposted Scilly Walk and Charles Fort). Leave the road and follow the wooded path that emerges at Summer Cove, and shortly after that at Charles Fort.

JARLEY'S COVE

If you fancy a swim, head west from the town and cross the bridge over the Bandon River. Turn left and follow the road down to a small sheltered beach known as Jarley's Cove *[51.6964, -8.5144]*. Call in to The Dock for a pint afterwards, or take a look around the lesser-known James Fort.

SANDY COVE

About 3km south of Kinsale is an attractive little bay, known as Sandy Cove. It's sheltered from the worst of the weather by the island lying just offshore. Swimming around the island (about 1.8km) is a rite of passage for outdoor swimmers from the area, but be wary of tides and sea conditions if planning

Garrylucas Cliff Path | RC

a circumnavigation. The beach at the cove and the sandy shores on the island opposite are lovely, and make for a pleasant few seaside hours close to Kinsale. The sand is covered at high tide but there is a nice stroll along the clifftop path that starts alongside the whitewashed cottage near the carpark.

Heading west from Kinsale look our for the signs for 'Sandycove' after the bridge. Follow the coast road to the carpark [51.6771, -8.5240].

THE OLD HEAD OF KINSALE
The Old Head is one of the finest headlands along the Irish coast, sticking nearly 5km out to sea and almost cut off from the mainland in the middle. Unfortunately there is a private golf course on the southern half of the headland, so you must end your journey at the entrance to the course [51.6178, -8.5415]. Nonetheless, the views to the east and west are excellent.

GARRYLUCAS
The Blue Flag beach at Garrylucas is a pleasant one, and popular with Cork holidaymakers [51.6387, -8.5606]. There is a lifeguard on duty every day in July and August and at weekends in June and September. At the east end of the beach there is a path along the cliffs that leads to some smaller, scenic sandy bays (see the photo on page 40).

While the walk to the end isn't very long there is a spectacular sea cave worth seeking out. Only accessible at low water, it's a dark, deep and damp cavern, hidden until you're at the mouth. We'll leave you to explore and find it yourself (see the photo on page 4).

GARRETTSTOWN
Just west of Garrylucas is Garrettstown [51.6438, -8.5787] and it's possible to walk between the two beaches at low tide. Garrettstown is popular with beginner surfers in both summer and winter. If you plan on taking to the water, be wary of the wooden posts in the sand, which are submerged at high tide. G Town Surf School (www.surfgtown.com) rents boards, offers lessons and runs coasteering trips during the summer. There is a lifeguard on duty at the beach every day in July and August and at weekends in June and September. Manning's Caravan Park (www.fb.com/ManningsCaravanPark) is located between the two beaches and is open during the summer. Garrettstown House Holiday Park (www. garrettstownhouse.com) is another campsite based around an 18th century mansion, just 1km north of the beach [51.6532, -8.5909].

COOLMAIN STRAND
The fine sandy shoreline, also known as Harbour View Beach, makes for a decent walk, with plenty of

Cliff jumping, Seven Heads | RC

Courtmacsherry Woods | RC

opportunities for bird watching. There is a carpark on the western end of the beach [51.6486, -8.6794].

TIMOLEAGUE

Timoleague is a quiet town, with pubs, restaurants and a few B+Bs. Dominating the village is the 13th century Franciscan Abbey. During the winter especially, the mudflats between Timoleague and Courtmacsherry are a good place for bird watching. Thousands of shorebirds feed in the estuary when the tide is low.

There is a pleasant 5km stroll along the path of the old railway line that used to link Timoleague to Courtmacsherry.

SEVEN HEADS PENINSULA

The Wild Atlantic Way heads slightly inland from Timoleague, heading directly to Clonakilty, bypassing the Seven Heads Peninsula. Which is a pity as this is a compact area of quiet, rural countryside with a beautiful coast. It's a wonderful place to walk or cycle, and there are sheltered bays for swimming, rock-pooling, snorkelling and kayaking.

COURTMACSHERRY

Courtmacsherry is an attractive village, and justifiably popular. There are pubs, a safe beach and a family festival in August.

FUCHSIA WALK

A very pleasant trail taking in woodland, coastal paths, farmland and rural roads. Do it during mid-May to see the bluebells and wild garlic carpeting Courtmacsherry Woods.

Start in the carpark at the beach [51.6359, -8.6974]. There is a track running parallel to the shore just above the carpark. Follow this to the woods and keep on the path until you come out into the open again at Wood Point. The path contours the shore with great views over to the Old Head of Kinsale. Pass through a number of fields and a small conifer wood until you reach a pleasant, narrow lane with high hedges on each side that almost join at the top. Follow this tunnel to the road and take a left. At the next crossroads [51.6285, -8.7030] a right brings you back to the main road into Courtmacsherry and hence to the carpark. For a longer option take a left at the crossroads, down to Broadstrand and walk the beach.

BROADSTRAND

A nice beach and a sheltered place for kayaking, with a few smaller bays to explore to the north and another beach (Blind Strand) around the headland to the south, for those who want a longer paddle. From Courtmacsherry take the road south for Barryroe. After a tight bend in the woods take the second left and follow the road to a small carpark [51.6214, -8.7016].

Bluebells, Courtmacsherry | RC

WEST CORK MARKETS
Most of the bigger towns hold weekly markets, some of which are listed below.

KINSALE
Wednesday, 09:30-14:30, The Temperance Hall.

CLONAKILTY
Friday, 09:00-14:00, Recorder's Alley.

SKIBBEREEN
Saturday, 09:30-14:00 at The Fairfield.

SCHULL
Sunday, 09:30-14:00 (Easter to the end of September and Christmas), Pier Road carpark.

KILCROHANE (SHEEP'S HEAD)
Sunday, 11:00-14:00 (Easter to the end of September), Village Square.

BANTRY
Friday, 09:30-13:00, Town Square.

CASTLETOWNBERE
First Thursday of each month and every Thursday in summer, 09:00-14:30, Town Square.

SEVEN HEADS WAY
The Seven Heads Way takes a coastal walking route from Timoleague, through Courtmacsherry and around to Dunworly. Follow the way over a couple of days or make your own shorter loop incorporating a section of it. More information is available on www.sevenheadspeninsula.ie.

SEVEN HEADS BAY
On calm days this bay is a great spot for rock-pooling, swimming and to launch a kayak and explore the coast [51.5913, -8.7057]. There are caves and gullies at the southern end while the northern coast of the bay has a sandy beach when the tide is out, and more caves. The Coolim Cliffs are just a bit further north and are worth a look too. The beach below the huge cliffs is only accessible by boat.

DUNWORLY
There are two beaches in Dunworly Bay, both signposted from Barryroe. The first beach is near the castle that's blocked by a big blue house [51.5931, -8.7591]. At low tide there is plenty of exposed sand, however it's usually a little too shallow for swimming.

The second is a little further south and has plenty of parking [51.5836, -8.7514]. It's covered at high tide but low water leaves a brilliant sandy beach. There are plenty of caves and rock pools and it's a good spot for swimming, though the waves can be powerful.

CLONAKILTY
The town of Clonakilty is world famous for its black pudding but it's also home to De Barra's Bar. This legendary pub is one of the best live music venues in Ireland, and they do good food and drink.

INCHYDONEY
Inchydoney is renowned for its luxury hotel and the adjacent Blue Flag beach [51.5970, -8.8625]. It's a good surfing spot, with beginner friendly waves for the most part, though watch for rip tides. There is a surf school (www.inchydoneysurfschool.com) renting boards and offering lessons. A lifeguard is on duty every day in July and August and at weekends in June and September. There is plenty of parking just below the hotel.

CLONAKILTY TO ROSSCARBERY
The next section of the Wild Atlantic Way takes you close to the iconic lighthouse at Galley Head and has some nice beaches.

BEACHES
As you travel west from Clonakilty on the Wild Atlantic Way the coast becomes indented with small bays. For the most part these are sheltered, safe and secluded coves, ideal for anyone looking for some peace and quiet. Look out for Duneen Bay just beside the road

Surfing, Long Strand | RC

[51.5794, -8.8734]. Further along the road Dunnycove Bay and Sands Cove are signposted to the left.

The first bigger beach you arrive at is Red Strand, a great place for a swim with a lifeguard in the summer [51.5482, -8.9270]. Galley Head is the prominent lighthouse in the distance. The first light was built here in 1875. It's only possible to go as far as the main gates, where there is a good view [51.5350, -8.9517]. The lighthouse itself is available as self-catering accommodation (www.greatlighthouses.com).

LONG STRAND
Long Strand is the next point of interest to the west. It's a superb stretch of beach with high dunes behind and often-wild surf eating into the soft shoreline. Swimming is not recommended but surfers sometimes take to the waves here.

There is also a very enjoyable 5km loop walk to be had from the carpark at the western end [51.5607, -8.9764]. Start by walking east along the beach. As you reach the river at the far end turn left and follow the road back to an attractive stone cottage. Take the rougher road past this house, along a pleasant track that hugs the shore of Kilkeran Lake. On meeting the road again head straight past another stone house and take a left into the woods at the sign for Castlefreke. The track eventually ends at a barrier, where you gain the main road again, until the next large layby on the left. Re-enter the woods for a short walk back to the carpark, not before a great vista of the beach where the track leaves the woods.

OWNAHINCHA AND ROSSCARBERY
Further west are more two beaches, Ownahincha [51.5671, -9.0010] and the Blue Flag beach at Rosscarbery [51.5659, -9.0143]. Both are worth a visit, though they can get busy. It's possible to walk the clifftop path that joins them.

The estuary behind the beach at Rosscarbery is another good place for bird watching. There is a lifeguard daily in July and August and at weekends in June and September at Rosscarbery.

DROMBEG STONE CIRCLE
West of Rosscarbery is Drombeg Stone Circle [51.5659, -9.0864]. On the winter solstice the setting sun passes through the portal stones of this ancient monument before dipping below a notch in the hills beyond.

GLANDORE HARBOUR
The Wild Atlantic Way bypasses the intricate coastline west of the villages of Glandore and Union Hall, but those with a wandering mind will find plenty of interest in this area. The OSI map (sheet 89) will guide you to little bays such as Carrigillihy, Squince Harbour (a good place to embark on the short kayaking trip to

Drombeg Stone Circle | RC

the beautiful Rabbit Island) and Blind Harbour. There are a half dozen walks described at www.unionhall.ie.

RINNEEN WOODS

This small woodland hugs the shores at The Narrows, a long inlet. A local artist has built fairy houses in the trees, giving the place a mystical feel. Wear boots as the trail can be muddy. From the church outside Union Hall follow the twisting hilly road to Skibbereen as far as the large layby on the left [51.5518, -9.1704].

WHALE AND DOLPHIN WATCHING

Unbeknownst to most people, the coast of Cork has some of the best whale watching in Europe. In the right season you can see fin whales (second in size only to the blue whale), humpback whales and minke whales, sometimes all on the same day. Various dolphin species, harbour porpoise, grey seals, and basking sharks are often seen too, as are many different seabird species, and of course, the fantastic West Cork coastline.

There are a few different boat trips available in West Cork, the best of which is probably Cork Whale Watch (www.corkwhalewatch.com). Skipper Colin Barnes has been doing it for longer than anybody else in Ireland and plays an active role in the research and conservation of these charismatic megafauna, as they're know in the zoological world.

WILDLIFE TOURS

Calvin Jones of Ireland's Wildlife (www.irelandswildlife.com) offers personalised, guided tours on the wildlife of West Cork. Covering animals and plants of all shapes and sizes there is plenty to be seen and even seemingly boring, common species can be full of interest once you learn about them and their habitats.

CYCLE WEST CORK

Cycle West Cork (www.cyclewestcork.com) offer guided bike tours of West Cork, from 3 to 7 nights, with accommodation and luggage transfer provided. Itineraries can be tailored to the group, but usually take in the major towns, as well as some of the more popular sights along the coast. Or you can just arrange the basics with them and head off on your own.

SEA KAYAKING

H20 Sea Kayaking offer half and full day sea kayaking tours in the area surrounding Kinsale and beyond. They also teach paddling skills for those looking to improve on what they already know. For more information see www.h2oseakayaking.com.

Sea Kayaking, Castletownshend | RC

Humpback Whale | RC

Castlefreke Castle | RC

Shore fishing | RC

July to January is usually the best time to see big whales but trips operate throughout the year, weather permitting, and each season has its own species of interest. Trips depart from Reen Pier, near Union Hall [51.5320, -9.1656].

ATLANTIC SEA KAYAKING

West Cork is full of sheltered bays and inlets, as well as more remote islands and headlands that are best seen from a boat, or even better a kayak.

Atlantic Sea Kayaking (www.atlanticseakayaking. com) offer trips to suit all tastes and abilities. From multi-day excursions taking in the best of West Cork, to half-day taster sessions there's something for everybody. The night trips are hugely popular; at the right time of year (usually spring and autumn) the water is full of bioluminescent plankton that sparkles with every paddle stroke. It is something that everyone should experience at least once.

CASTLETOWNSHEND

Built up around the 17th century castle, Castletownshend still retains an air of little old England about it. It's an attractive village, with some small beaches (Tracarta Strand and Sandy Cove) and historic megalithic monuments (Gurranes Stone Row [51.5308, -9.1883] and Knockdrum Stone Fort [51.5266, -9.1937]) nearby.

TOE HEAD

Toe Head is the most prominent headland in the area, rising high above its surroundings. The view from the top is wide ranging and it's a good place to spot whales and dolphins when the sea is calm. Not far from the headland are two stony beaches which might not be the prettiest West Cork has to offer, but are pleasant and safe for bathing.

TRAGUMNA

A little west of Toe Head is the Blue Flag beach of Tragumna [51.5029, -9.2652]. A safe and enjoyable swimming spot, there is a lifeguard every day in July and August and at weekends in June and September.

Toe Head | RC

SKIBBEREEN

Every year at the end of July this bustling town hosts the Skibbereen Arts Festival, which includes community based projects as well as national and international films, theatre, visual art and music.

The Skibbereen Heritage Centre has two excellent permanent exhibitions - on the history of the Famine and the ecology of nearby Lough Hyne. See www. skibbheritage.com for details including opening times.

CYCLING

The town is the start and finish point for three cycling routes through the nicest parts of the surrounding countryside. The routes are 24km, 35km and 46km, offering something for all fitness levels. Roycroft's Cycles offer bike rental and maps of other routes.

LISS ARD ESTATE

A little outside of town is the 200 acre Liss Ard Estate (www.lissardestate.com). While the accommodation may be a little upmarket for most travellers the gardens have become quite famous for the landscape installation by James Turrell known as The Crater. The centre of this giant crater has a 'Vault Purchase' where visitors are encouraged to lie on their back and gaze up at the sky. The gardens are open freely to the public but The Crater is viewed by appointment only and there is a small fee.

From Skibbereen take the R569 for Castletownshend. The estate is 1km down this road on the right [51.5301, -9.2537].

RUSSAGH MILL

Shortly after the turn for Liss Ard is the hostel and adventure centre at Russagh Mill (www. russaghmillhostel.com). There are plenty of activities on offer, such as kayaking and archery, as well as dorm and private rooms [51.5366, -9.2485].

LOUGH HYNE

Lough Hyne is an unusual saltwater lake south of Skibbereen [51.5061, -9.3036]. Its wildlife has attracted academics for over 100 years and in 1981 it was designated as Ireland's first marine sanctuary. It's impressively deep and a popular spot with divers (a permit is required). There is great snorkelling on the edges of the lake, where the steep walls are plastered with marine life.

Knockomagh Hill looms over the lake to the north and a pleasant woodland path leads to its top, which gives great views over the attractive West Cork coastline. From Skibbereen, head west along the Wild Atlantic Way towards Baltimore. There is a left turn for Lough Hyne 3km from the edge of town. ∎

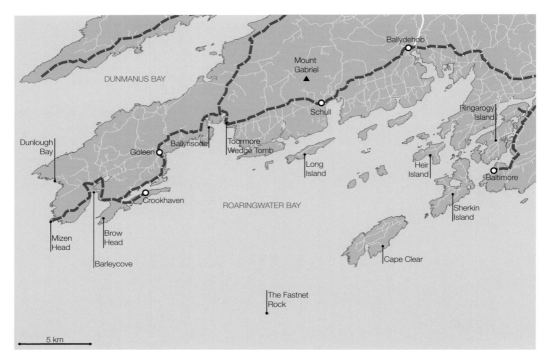

BALTIMORE TO MIZEN

If you look at a map of West Cork it's easy to imagine the peninsula that once struck southwest from Baltimore, now divided by the sea into the islands of Roaringwater Bay. These islands are havens from the rest of the world, some still inhabited and some long abandoned, but all are peaceful and ideal for those looking to get away from the busy pace of city life. The remotest of the islands, The Fastnet Rock, lies over 10km from the closest point on the mainland.

To the north is the Mizen Peninsula, the southernmost of the five fingers of land that make up the bulk of the southwest of Ireland. Indeed Mizen Head itself is the most southwesterly tip of the country. Here the landscape is wilder; more mountainous and craggier, and the coast is more exposed to the Atlantic's anger.

RINGAROGY ISLAND
Though connected to the mainland by a bridge this small island feels as remote as many of the true offshore lands around the Irish coast. There is little to do here but walk, but what walking there is to do! The roads are quiet and the hedges luxuriant in the summer months, making it a fine place for an easy evening stroll or a short cycle from Baltimore.

Coming from Skibbereen along the Wild Atlantic Way turn right at the sign [51.5063, -9.3507] for Beacon Designs.

BALTIMORE AND THE ISLANDS
In the summer Baltimore is a busy seaside hub, with ferries to Sherkin and Cape Clear coming and going amongst the many yachts, fishing charters and sailing dinghies. Every May the village hosts a world famous Fiddle Fair (www.fiddlefair.com).

The Top of the Hill Hostel is a good option for budget accommodation.

There are also plenty of water-based activities on offer, a few of which are listed below:

• Snorkelling, diving www.aquaventures.ie
• Diving www.baltimorediving.com
• Sailing www.baltimoresailingschool.com
• Whale watching www.whalewatchwestcork.com

There is a nice, short walk out to the Baltimore Beacon on the western end of town [51.4746, -9.3864]. This unusual structure was built in 1849 to act as a marker for Baltimore Harbour to passing ships. The view out to Sherkin and Cape Clear is one of the classic vistas of West Cork.

Baltimore Beacon | Denis Dineen

SHERKIN ISLAND

This beautiful island is only 15 minutes by ferry from Baltimore. Upon arrival you can't miss the impressive Abbey, built all the way back in 1460. It's possible to traverse all the roads in a day and visit the two biggest beaches, Silver Strand [51.4740, -9.4235] and Trabawn [51.4654, -9.4258], which are among the nicest in West Cork, offering safe swimming and good snorkelling in fine weather.

There isn't a shop on the island, but you can get food and drink at The Jolly Roger (the local pub) or The Islander's Rest (the hotel) while you wait for the ferry back to reality.

There is a hostel on the island, Sherkin North Shore (www.sherkinnorthshore.com), which provides accommodation in a relaxing setting [51.4778, -9.4253]. The ferry runs all year round, but is more frequent in the summer (www.sherkinisland.ie).

CAPE CLEAR

Cape Clear (or Clear Island on the map) is one of only two Gaeltacht (an area where Irish is the main language) areas in County Cork. The rugged island is well worth a few days of exploration. The Bird Observatory [51.4413, -9.5059] is world famous and provides accommodation for nature lovers. There's a hostel (www.capeclearhostel.com) [51.4347, -9.4995] at the South Harbour, and a campsite [51.4350 -9.5047] that rents yurts (www.chleire-haven.com).

The coastal walking is superb, with the high cliffs either side of the South Harbour providing great sea views. There are two impressive sea arches, one east of the harbour at Pointanbullig, the other to the west at Blananarragaun.

There are two signposted loop walks on the island which both start from the shop - Cnoicín's Loop (4km, green arrows) and the Gleann Loop (7km, red arrows).

Also worth visiting are the Cape Clear and Fastnet Rock Heritage Centre, the goat farm which produces ice cream, and the disused lighthouse that was built too high up and is often obscured by fog. There are plenty of historic monuments and three pubs, a seemingly generous number for a relatively small community.

The ferry runs daily from Baltimore and seasonally from Schull. See www.capeclearferries.com and www.schullferry.com for timetables.

THE FASTNET ROCK

The Fastnet Rock is the most southerly point of land in Ireland and sees few visitors. The lonely outcrop was known locally as the Teardrop of Ireland, as the lighthouse would see on the long boat trip to America. The current lighthouse is one of the best designed in the world.

The first attempt to build a lighthouse here was completed in the 1850s, but it wasn't considered

Sherkin Island | RC

sound enough. The current tower is built of Cornish granite and was an incredible feat of engineering. Construction began in 1899 in England. The 2,074 numbered blocks (weighing up to 3 tons each) were assembled, then disassembled and brought to Ireland. Happy that the feat could be repeated, the tower was reconstructed on the Fastnet Rock. The whole project took five years and, surprisingly, nobody died in the process.

It's possible to take a boat out to get a close look at the Fastnet, and marvel at what a feat of engineering it was to build a lighthouse in such an exposed situation. See www.fastnettour.com for more information on day trips from Baltimore and www. schullferry.com for trips from Schull.

HEIR ISLAND
Tucked into the eastern end of Roaringwater Bay is Heir Island, a small, pleasing little world. It's worth a trip over in the summer to see the hedges in full bloom and to explore the little beaches and bays. There is plenty of accommodation and even a very well regarded restaurant (www.islandcottage.com), which offers cookery classes as well as excellent meals. The ferry runs from Cunnamore [51.5041, -9.4249] which is signposted off the Wild Atlantic Way at Church Cross, between Skibbereen and Ballydehob. For a timetable see www.heirislandferries.com.

BALLYDEHOB
At the gateway to the Mizen Peninsula stands this village, notable for its twelve arch railway bridge. Three signposted walks along quiet back roads start and finish at the eastern end of town beside the river

[51.5622, -9.4580]. As most of the trails follow roads it's also possible to cycle them.

SCHULL
With the imposing bulk of Mount Gabriel looming above the town it might seem as though Schull was named after the cranial appearance of the hill behind it. The Irish name, An Scoil (The School) or Scoil Mhuire (Mary's School) gives a better hint at the source of the name; the town was built on the site of a medieval monastic school, of which no trace remains.

The town has an upmarket vibe, and there is a gourmet food market held every Sunday, and numerous sailing schools.

Outside of the harbour are three pleasant islands; Horse Island to the east, Castle Island in the middle, and Long Island to the west. On a calm day a competent kayaker could easily visit all three islands, where they will find solitude, shoreline exploration and pleasant camping.

A ferry service runs to Long Island for those without their own means of getting there. The signpost in town directs you to the pier from where the boat departs [51.5066, -9.5616]. See www.longislandferry.org for the details.

MOUNT GABRIEL
Copper was mined extensively on this hill behind Schull as far back as the Bronze Age. These days, the main industrial action on the mountain is the collection of air traffic information in the two massive radar domes on the summit.

A pleasant cycle takes a circuit around Mount Gabriel, and masochists will enjoy the tough climb to the top (the lazier among us can drive to the

Barley Cove | RC

Blananarragaun and Fastnet Rock, Cape Clear | Becky Williamson

Ballyrisode | RC

summit) where there are unrivalled views of Ireland's southwest.

Heading west from Schull take the second right opposite a blue farmhouse [51.5279, -9.5795] and follow this road around the northern slopes of the mountain. Another right past the road to the summit will take you back to Schull through Barnancleeve, a tight gap between hills that frames a great view of Roaringwater Bay.

It's possible to rent bikes in Schull. See www.westcorkbikehire.com for details.

TOORMORE

A little west of Schull is the Toormore Altar Wedge Tomb, built between 2,000 and 3,000 years ago [51.5138, -9.6437]. It is well signposted just off the road, with nice views to the distant hills of Mizen.

On the other side of Toormore Bay is Ballyrisode Beach, a gorgeous strand with woodland behind and clear water before you [51.5111, -9.6622]. The beach is signposted off the Wild Atlantic Way between Schull and Goleen. The carpark is at the second of the two beaches. The road past the beach is quite narrow, so please park considerately if the carpark is full.

CROOKHAVEN

The protected harbour at Crookhaven has been used by ships seeking shelter for a long time. White Strand is a pleasant beach at the back of the harbour, and is a good place to launch a kayak to get a sea level perspective of the area [51.4632, -9.7512].

Just a stone's throw to the south is Galley Cove [51.4616, -9.7443]. It is a pleasant walk from the Cove to Brow Head, the most southerly point of mainland Ireland, where there are great views of the West Cork

The footbridge at Mizen Head | RC

coast. At the summit is a Napoleonic watchtower from the early 19th century and the remains of a telegraphic station from the early 20th century.

BARLEYCOVE

A favourite among West Cork holidaymakers, Barleycove's popularity is easy to understand [51.4685, -9.7790]. Its gorgeous Blue Flag beach is surrounded by gentle hills on three sides, offering shelter on a nice summer's day, or funnelling the wildness of a strong southwesterly during storms. There are lifeguards and a surf school during the summer months (www.barleycovesurfcamp.com).

Barley Cove Holiday Park (www. barleycoveholidaypark.ie), a campsite for tents, camper vans and caravans, is open in the summer months [51.4645, -9.7567].

MIZEN HEAD

Mizen Head is the southwestern tip of Ireland, and well worth a trip to experience its 'edge of the world' feel. There is a visitor centre [51.4515, -9.8110] with a café, and a footbridge leads across the impressive steep-sided chasm to the lighthouse. In the summer the centre is open daily and between November and mid-March it only opens at weekends. The small entry fee is well worth it for the views of the outrageous cliffs from the footbridge and the very informative local

history exhibits. During winter storms the carpark is a good place to watch a heaving sea.

DUNLOUGH

A little north of Mizen Head is Dunlough Bay and Three Castle Head. There is room for a few cars at the small pier [51.4788, -9.8151] and it's possible to walk across the private land to see the coastline and castle at Dunlough. The cliffs are over 100m high in parts and this must have been a dizzying place to live back in the 15th century when the castle was built.

MIZEN NORTH SHORE

The northern coast of the Mizen is much quieter than the southern one. Following the signposted coast road from Barleycove [51.4804, -9.7627] will take you along a beautiful, open road with the sea to the left and the hills to your right. Though hilly, it's ideal for the cyclist. Equipped with a map, it is quite easy to concoct a loop linking the north and south shores. ▨

Mizen Head Cliffs | Seán Murray

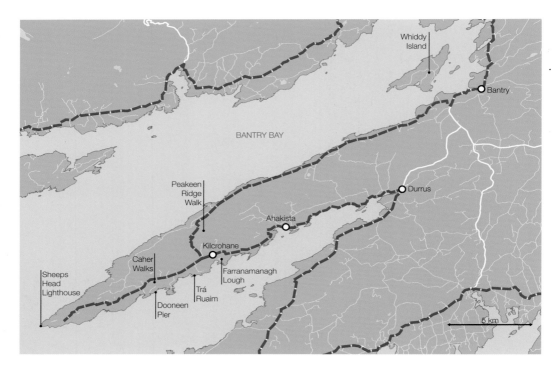

SHEEP'S HEAD

Sheep's Head is the slender finger of land that stretches out to sea between the Beara and Mizen peninsulas. Only 25km long and never much more than 3km wide, it's a quiet place, perfect for hikers.

There are a large number of signposted walks through the low hills that form the spine of the peninsula. Not every walk has been included but there should be more than enough to keep all but the most avid walkers occupied for a few days.

Its largely traffic-free roads are also ideally suited to a multi-day bike tour.

See www.thesheepsheadway.ie for details of all the walking and cycling routes on the peninsula, including The Sheep's Head Way, a multi-day 200km walking route around the peninsula.

DURRUS

The pretty village of Durrus straddles the Mizen and Sheep's Head peninsulas. It is probably best known for the soft cheese that is made locally - Durrus Farmhouse Cheese.

AHAKISTA

This tiny village lies right on the sheltered shores of Dunmanus Bay. It's a popular stop with the sailing fraternity and every August bank holiday weekend it hosts the Ahakista Regatta.

It's also the starting point for three worthwhile walks [51.6000, -9.6324].

- Barán Loop 9km (green arrows)
- Seefin Loop 13km (blue arrows)
- Glanlough Loop 20km (purple arrows)

KILCROHANE

The small village has a few shops and pubs as well as plenty of self-catering and B+B accommodation. Every Easter weekend it hosts a traditional music festival.

A pleasant 5km loop walk, marked with red arrows, starts and finishes in the village. Walk east from the village centre and follow the signposts left up a quiet road to Farranamanagh. Take a right where the trail forks to head south for the coast, crossing the main road and eventually hugging the shore of Farranamanagh Lough and the stony beach here. Follow the signposts back to Kilcrohane.

DOONEEN PIER

This sheltered harbour has a Green Coast award and is ideal for swimming. It's also a popular place to fish

Windblown tree near Ahakista | RC

for mackerel and pollock *[51.5636, -9.7305]*. Look out for the signposted left turn 2km west of Kilcrohane.

CAHER WALKS

There are two looped walks between Kilcrohane and the end of Sheep's Head. They start at the long two-storey stone building on the left hand side of the road about 4km west of Kilcrohane *[51.5647, -9.7567]*.

- Caher Loop 5km (green arrows)
- Cahergal Loop 8km (blue arrows)

SHEEP'S HEAD LIGHTHOUSE

This tiny lighthouse lies in a wild setting at the very end of the peninsula. Accessed via a series of steep steps it offers some wonderful views - to the north is Bantry Bay with the Beara beyond, and to the south is Mizen Head and Dunmanus Bay.

The road ends about 2km from the lighthouse, at a café, Bernie's Cupan Tae, that opens in summer *[51.5448, -9.8288]*. Even though the views from the café are brilliant, it's highly recommended that you go the extra mile (literally).

LIGHTHOUSE LOOP

From the carpark follow the well-worn path past Lough Akeen to the lighthouse. The 4km loop returns to the carpark along a rough track on the north side of the peninsula. If you are looking for a shorter walk

then you can just retrace your steps back to the carpark. Note no dogs are allowed.

POET'S WAY LOOP

A longer (16km) version of the Lighthouse Loop that continues further up the spectacular north coast before returning to the carpark via a track along the south coast.

SEEFIN AND PEAKEEN

From Kilcrohane a narrow road, known locally as the Goat's Path, leads over the hills to the north side of the peninsula. At its high point is a carpark with panoramic views *[51.5952, -9.711]*.

To the east is Seefin, the highest point of the peninsula at 345m. There are a number of hills named Seefin in Ireland, the name coming from the Irish for the Seat of Fionn. Fionn Mac Cumhaill was the leader of a mythical band of warriors in ancient Ireland and these lookout posts must have been of interest to him and his men.

PEAKEEN RIDGE WALK

This is a linear 6km walk west along the spine of the Sheep's Head, staring from the carpark. Decent walking shoes are recommended as this walk crosses open mountainside and can be wet underfoot. Follow the cream and red arrows along the ridge to the

Stone waymarker on the north coast | RC

townland of Letter West. Return by the same route or have a pick up arranged.

BEACHES

Unfortunately Sheep's Head doesn't have many beaches of note, which may be why it stays relatively quiet during the summer when other nearby areas are packed.

The strand at Farranamanagh Lough [51.5802, -9.6911], just outside Kilcrohane, is rocky but pleasant, and there is another beach at Trá Ruaim [51.6000, -9.7558]. Both of these beaches are probably more suited to launching a kayak than sunbathing, provided it's calm of course.

There is an impressive puffing hole on the coast close to Trá Ruaim, and there are also a few popular shore fishing spots in this area.

BANTRY BAY

Bantry is a bustling town with all the facilities you might want, with pubs, restaurants, hotels and tourist information. Bantry House (www.bantryhouse.com) is an elegant 18th century mansion turned B+B [51.6771, -9.4654]. The beautiful formal gardens that extend across seven terraces are well worth a visit.

It's also possible to go horse riding with Bantry Pony Trekking. See www.bantryponytrekking.com.

BLUEWAY
There are three kayak trails in the Bay. The trails, which start from the pier in Bantry [51.6806, -9.4618], are 2km, 6km and 9km in length. The two longer trails cross over to Whiddy Island. Download the excellent pocket guide from www.bantrybayport.com/pocket_guide.

WHIDDY ISLAND
Not far off the coast from Bantry is the unassuming Whiddy Island. It's a quiet place, with one pub, some self-catering accommodation and bike hire available on the island. The Ocean Star III, which operates daily from Bantry Pier, offers guided tours of the harbour as well as crossings to the island. See www.whiddyferry.com for a timetable and more information on the island. ⬚

Sheep's Head Lighthouse | RC

Seefin | RC

Dooneen sunset | Patricia Ronan

GUIDED WALKS
Charlie McCarthy is a registered guide and historian and operates a B+B, offering walking and accommodation packages. See www.seamountfarm.com for more. Sheep's Head walks (www.sheepsheadwalks.com) also offer guided walks of many of the loops described here.

CYCLING
The Sheep's Head Cycle Route flanks the north and south shores of the peninsula and is an excellent way to explore this quiet coastline. It is poorly signposted but the OSI maps of the area (85 and 88) show the route. A few roads link the north and south sides of the peninsula so it's easy to make shorter loops. Be warned, it's hilly! Nigel's Bike Shop in Bantry rents bicycles.

WATERSPORTS
Based in Ahakista, Carbery Sailing (www.carberysailing.com) offer full, half day and evening trips. The sheltered waters of Dunmanus Bay offer a great place for kayaking. Based in Durrus, Darren's Kayaks (www.darrenskayaks.com) offer trips and tuition. For paddleboarding hire and lessons see www.gsup.ie.

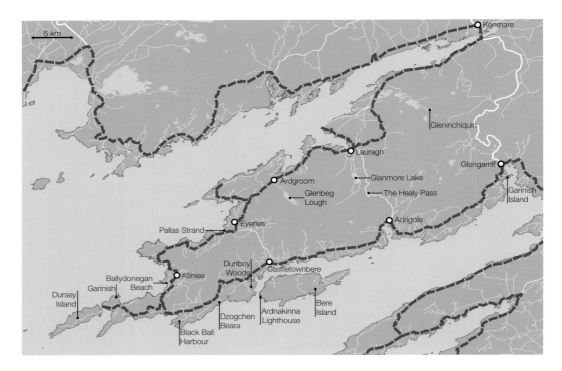

BEARA

The hilly terrain and acres of exposed rock give the Beara Peninsula as much a feeling of wildness as any place in Ireland's southwest. The open coastline and bare mountainsides are rugged and craggy, but in some sheltered pockets there is also lush green woodland, offering quiet and refuge and a more welcoming climate. Like the rest of the southwest the climate here is mild, bathing in the relative warmth of the Gulf Stream.

Though not rich in beaches there are a few worth seeking out, and way out on the western end of the peninsula you are unlikely to meet any crowds. There's a quietness here you might not expect. Bring your walking boots and your bike and enjoy the peace and quiet.

GLENGARRIFF

Coming from the Irish for rugged glen (Gleann Garbh), Glengarriff is true to its name, though the town itself is nestled at the foot of the valley and is a lot more hospitable than the wild landscape surrounding it.

GARINISH ISLAND

World famous for its gardens, this small island in Glengarriff Harbour enjoys a balmy climate and is home to some plant species that are very unusual for this part of the world.

The gardens aren't all about the plants; there are a number of unusual historic structures on the island including the Clock Tower, Grecian Temple and Italian Temple and Tea House.

Between April and October ferries run from the main pier in Glengarriff [51.7506, -9.5424] and the Blue Pool [51.74, -9.5487]. The short cruise passes Seal Island, unsurprisingly home to a colony of quite tame harbour seals. See www.garnishisland.com and www.bluepoolferry.com for ferry times.

THE BLUE POOL

Well signposted from the centre of town, the Blue Pool is a convenient swimming area. There are steps leading down into the water, making access easy. Just be wary of the ferries taking people out to Garinish.

GLENGARRIFF NATURE RESERVE

Home to some of the last remaining natural woodland in Ireland, the Glengarriff Nature Reserve (www.glengarriffnaturereserve.ie) is an important pocket for biodiversity. The warm, wet climate means the woodland here is similar to a rainforest. Lichens and mosses grow on the old oaks, which also support

Garinish Island Gardens | Shaun Dunphy

Glengarriff Nature Reserve | RC

Ardnakinna Lighthouse, Bere Island | RC

more than 200 species of insect. The rivers are some of the cleanest in the country and a last refuge for the freshwater pearl mussel, a slow growing species that can live to 130 years. Bats can be seen at dusk in the summer and if you're lucky you might see other mammals like otters, stoats and red squirrels.

There are five short signposted trails in the reserve. It's possible to combine them into a big loop that takes in the best aspects of the area. The walks all start from the main carpark [51.7536, -9.5643], which is well signposted off the N71 to Kenmare.

ADRIGOLE

As you travel west from Glengarriff towards Adrigole the craggy profile of the Sugarloaf mountain dominates the skyline, protruding over the layered rocky hillsides to your right, while Bantry Bay stretches out to sea on the left.

The Hungry Hill Lodge and Campsite (www.hungryhilllodgeandcampsite.com) in Adrigole [51.6936, -9.7250] provide tents as well as dorm and private rooms at reasonable prices.

Adrigole Harbour is handy for a quick swim and is a safe bay for kayaking [51.6827, -9.7160]. The Mare's Tail is the very impressive waterfall that cascades down the lower slopes of Hungry Hill to the west of the harbour. It's one of the highest waterfalls in Ireland and makes a very impressive sight after heavy rain. Enquire locally if you'd like to see it up close.

HUNGRY HILL

West of Adrigole is Hungry Hill, a looming presence on the Beara Peninsula. Its massive bulk can be seen from many points along the south coast but be warned - the steep, rocky ground and capricious weather mean a trip up the mountain is for experienced walkers only.

THE HEALY PASS

Even if you're planning on following the Wild Atlantic Way west it's worth making a trip up the Healy Pass. This winding mountain road, which links Adrigole and Lauragh, twists and turns its way up through the hills, culminating in a breathtaking viewpoint overlooking Kerry to the north and West Cork to the south [51.7211, -9.7565]. Once a classic stage in the Circuit of Ireland rally it's not for the nervous driver!

BERE ISLAND

Continuing west there is a long stretch of road past more of the characteristic sandstone outcrops that define this peninsula.

Eventually the views of Bere Island open up on the left. Though close to the mainland this island is a quiet place, and has an ongoing military history. Unlike most of the Irish islands there is a regular car ferry. There isn't space for many cars so if you don't arrive early it might be best to travel as a foot passenger.

Sunrise at Dzogchen Beara | RC

The island hosts three marked walking loops. The Ardnakinna Loop is a 10km round trip starting from the west pier [51.6389, -9.9003]. It follows minor roads and green tracks out to Ardnakinna Lighthouse [51.6192, -9.9175]. The trail is a little indistinct in places. Coming from the pier take the first right at a T junction and look out for various markers from here.

The Doonbeg Loop is a short (5km) but hilly loop that starts near the Gallan Standing Stone in the centre of the island [51.6306, -9.8621]. The views are far-reaching and well worth the walk.

The Rerrin Loop starts from the quay at the east end of the island [51.6344, -9.8199]. This 7km trail passes many old military structures as well as some well-marked bronze age sites.

Cycling is the best way to see as much of the island as possible in a day. There are plenty of B+Bs and self-catering options for an overnight stay too. Ferries for the island leave daily from Castletownbere (www.bereislandferries.com) and Pontoon [51.6550, -9.8552] (www.murphysferry.com). See www.bereisland.net for more general information.

CASTLETOWNBERE
This is one of the biggest fishing towns in Ireland, with a long maritime history. There are plenty of shops and cafés, and some decent pubs too. MacCarthy's is worth seeking out, as is the book written about its name.

DUNBOY WOOD
This pleasant little sheltered bay with old woodland backing a secluded beach is a little known gem with a fantastic signposted stroll.

Head west from Castletownbere along the Wild Atlantic Way. After 3km take the left turn signposted 'Puxley and O'Sullivan Bere Castles' and take a right at the fork in the road soon after. Take the next left at a fishing signpost and park at the entrance to Dunboy Woods on your left [51.6318, -9.9403].

Follow the purple arrows around the 4km trail through the forest that reaches down to the shores of Bullig Bay and back inland at Piper's Point after a great view of Bere Island.

DZOGCHEN BEARA
Situated in a stunning position overlooking the entrance to Bantry Bay this Tibetan Buddhist Retreat Centre is unique in Ireland [51.6148, -9.9799]. There are daily meditation classes and longer weekend breaks for those who want to delve deeper into their soulful side. The café on site is quite pleasant and there is a hostel too, offering affordable rooms in a quaint converted farmhouse. You might not want to leave. See www.dzogchenbeara.org for details.

CAHERMORE AREA
The southwestern corner of Beara between Castletownbere and Allihies is a quiet one. There are

Dursey Island Cable Car | Ilaria Leschiutta

Allihies | RC

small quays at Cahermore *[51.6035, -10.0446]* and Black Ball Harbour *[51.5964, -10.0410]* for those looking to get into the water. In suitable sea conditions a paddle between these two piers makes a great day on the water, taking in the impressive cliffs of White Ball Head.

GARINISH

Out near the end of the peninsula is this nice safe beach. It's a good starting point for a pleasant 12km loop walk along the Beara Way *[51.6168, -10.1356]*.

From the beach follow the trail markers up a pleasant green lane between fields until back on the road that leads to Dursey Sound. Take a left on the road and follow it back through the Firkeel Gap, following the yellow signposts for about 2km to the end of the road. Cross the stile into the fields and stay on the track, which loops back around to meet a road again at two farm gates. Follow this road to regain the main road, where you turn left towards Dursey Sound. At the cable car head up the hillside for great views over the islands off Beara and South Kerry as well as back east towards Allihies. Follow the trail markers back to the quay at Garinish.

DURSEY ISLAND

Way out at the end of the Beara Peninsula Ireland's only cable car links this quiet island *[51.6103, -10.1550]*, which is home to only a handful of

permanent residents, with the mainland. The cable car runs daily throughout the year. See www.durseyisland. ie for the details.

There are no facilities on the island so bring food and warm clothes. There is a water tap in the first old village. Camping is permitted but speak to a farmer on the island about where is best to stay.

The Beara Way does a 14km loop around Dursey, taking the main road west to the end of the island before returning along the hills. Make sure you allow plenty of time to ensure you don't get stranded on the island. It's worth keeping an eye on the sea for whales, dolphins and seabirds.

The Bull, The Cow and The Calf are three distant rocks with lighthouses in various states of repair off the western end of the island. The Skelligs can also be seen on a clear day and the views to Kerry in the north and West Cork in the south, are superb.

ALLIHIES

Allihies is the biggest of the colourful little villages along the north shore of Beara. There is a hostel (www.allihieshostel.net), B+Bs, a shop, restaurants and pubs, as well as the Allihies Mine Museum *[51.6390, -10.0460]*. Copper has been extracted from the mountainsides here for at least 3,500 years and the remains of the last working mines are visible on the hills above the village. The museum is open daily

Kilmackillogue Harbour, Lauragh | Alan Cronin

from April to October and intermittently for the rest of the year (www.acmm.ie).

ALLIHIES LOOP WALKS
There are three fantastic looped walks around Allihies, which start from the Mine Museum [51.6390, -10.0460]. They mix coastal paths with mountain tracks and give great views of the sea and landscapes in this beautifully rugged area.

- North Engine Loop 7km (green arrows)
- Kealoge Loop 10km (blue arrows)
- Ballydonegan Loop 18km (purple arrows)

BALLYDONEGAN BEACH
This is a very nice beach which is partly man-made. Sand was a by-product of the mining and the river swept it down here where it has stayed. There is a campsite at the carpark [51.6334, -10.0611].

EYERIES
The road between Allihies and Eyeries winds its way through some spectacular landscape. Eyeries is another vibrant village along this quieter coast of Beara. Two lovely coastal walks start and end in the village. From O'Sullivan's Shop the blue arrows lead the way along the 6km Creha Loop, while the red arrows track a slightly longer walk along the Coastguard Loop.

Pallas Strand is a nearby beach, a little west of the village. Look out for signs before you enter the village [51.6848, -9.9723].

ARDGROOM
Ardgroom is a good base for two things; fishing and cycling. In nearby Glenbeg Lough [51.7222, -9.8806] brown trout fishing is open between the 15th of February and the 12th of October.

CYCLE LOOP
This cycling loop isn't marked but is easy to follow and isn't too strenuous. Starting in the small village of Ardgroom head west along the R571 for just over 3km and turn onto the L4910 at a sign for the Ring of Beara. You soon pass Lough Fada, and then An Cailleach Bheara, an old stone said to once have been a woman of which many stories have been told. Continue along the coast road, passing quiet harbours with great views north to the Ring of Kerry. The round trip back to Ardgroom is about 20km.

LAURAGH
Between Ardgroom and Kerry lies the Cork/Kerry border and Lauragh is the first or last town in Kerry, depending on which way you're travelling. Lauragh is beautifully situated at the head of Kilmackillogue Harbour, not far from the peaceful surroundings of Glanmore Lake.

Gleninchiquin Waterfall | Alan Cronin

THE BEARA WAY

The Beara Way is a signposted walking trail that travels around the peninsula in a loop from Glengarriff. It's approximately 200km long (the exact distance depends on whether you visit Bere and Dursey Islands) and usually takes 8-10 days to complete.

For the fit walker there is no better way to see this part of the world. You see a lot more of the landscape than a person does from inside their car. For information see www.bearatourism.com.

THE BEARA WAY CYCLE

A 138km route covers the whole peninsula but shorter variations are also possible. A clockwise circuit from Castletownbere to Allihies and back via the north shore of the peninsula is a good long day out with plenty of hills. Allihies to Dursey Sound is a little less punishing. For bike rentals in Castletownbere see www.bikenbeara.ie.

STAR OUTDOORS

This activity centre between Lauragh and Kenmare [51.8449 , -9.6513] offers plenty of land and water based activities (www.staroutdoors.ie).

The Pedals and Boots café is well worth a visit [51.7627, -9.7800]. After eating you can rent a bike and head off on one of their suggested cycling routes. They have some walking recommendations with maps available on their website. The café is open from April to September. See www.pedalsandboots.ie for more.

CAMPSITES
Near Glanmore Lake, Creveen Lodge (www.creveenlodge.com) offers camping and cottage rentals [51.7639, -9.7598]. A little further east Beara Camping (www.bearacamping.com) is open from April to October and has tent pitches, mobile homes and cabins with meals served throughout the day. [51.8257, -9.7354].

GLENINCHIQUIN

A family owned hill farm and parkland (www.gleninchaquin.com) set at the back of an impressive, remote valley [51.8021, -9.6607]. The main feature is the massive waterfall spilling down the mountainside but there's plenty more to be seen in the area, like wonderful woodland and restored famine cottages.

There are six walking trails, from gentle strolls around the farmland to long hikes in the surrounding hills. All are well signposted and very worthwhile. There is a small charge for parking. Coming west along the R571 look out for signs for Gleninchiquin Park. ∎

Eyeries | RC

Knocknadobar (see page 79) | Denis Dineen

KERRY

Known in Ireland as The Kingdom, Kerry could indeed be a seat of royalty. It has a richly varied coastline, spread around the southwest corner of the country. Kerry has some of the finest mountains in all of Ireland, and they form the spines of each peninsula, dividing and providing a backdrop to the north and south coasts of each. There are plenty of well-known tourist traps, but even more places to escape the summer crowds.

Though we've included the entire Beara Peninsula in the Cork chapter, the northeastern corner of Beara actually flies the Kerry flag, and as is common in much of the county, the landscape here is a wild one.

Coming into Kenmare, an attractive town tucked into the head of a long sheltered bay, the famed Ring of Kerry begins. This route overlaps the Wild Atlantic Way at the coast, and along this seaboard there are plenty of stops worth taking; the quiet bays and beaches along the Kenmare River, the paradise that is Derrynane and the awesome otherworldliness of The Skelligs are just a few.

The Dingle Peninsula, with its world-class scenery and thriving music scene, is busy, but understandably so. The landscape here seems to have been designed to please the human eye, and few who travel west of Dingle Town are left unimpressed.

Humble North Kerry is a place far from the madding crowds, but with enough hidden gems to make it a worthwhile destination for anyone who wants to do more than just tick the usual boxes.

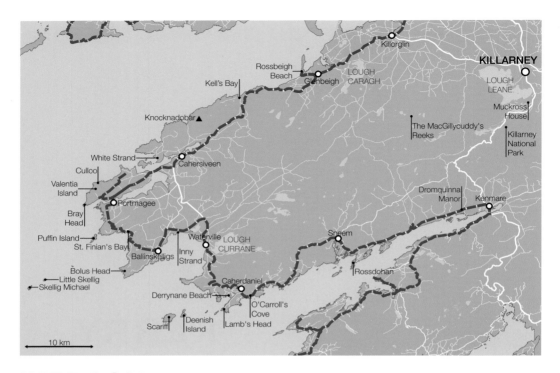

IVERAGH

Iveragh is the largest of the three main peninsulas of Kerry and as such, has a huge amount to offer the visitor. As well as some of the most famous attractions in the country, such as the Skelligs and the Ring of Kerry, there are numerous small headlands and hills worth seeking out.

The mountainous interior is never far from the coast and it makes a worthy diversion as well as an impressive backdrop. There you will find a lifetime of empty peaks to climb and mountain lakes to swim in.

THE RING OF KERRY

The Ring of Kerry is a 180km driving route around the Iveragh Peninsula that starts and finishes in Killarney. The Wild Atlantic Way follows most of the route with the exception of the inland sections. There is so much to see it's better to take your time, spending at least one night along the way, rather than rushing around it in a day.

The many tour buses that travel along its narrow roads do so in an anti-clockwise direction. To avoid getting stuck behind them it's preferable to travel clockwise around the ring (which is south to north along the Wild Atlantic Way). Be warned the route can get congested in the summer and many sections follow small, winding roads. If you aren't a confident driver you may find it a little nerve-wracking.

RING OF KERRY CYCLE ROUTE

There is an variation of the Ring of Kerry for cyclists. It's over 215km long and around two-thirds of it avoids the busy main road. The route isn't signposted but it is marked on the relevant OSI maps (sheets 78 and 83).

KENMARE

This attractive small town is the first one on the Iveragh Peninsula when coming from the south. It's a good base for exploring the Beara Peninsula (see page 60) and the mountains of Iveragh.

COASTEERING IRELAND

Coasteering - scrambling around the rocky coast and jumping into pools, gullies and sea caves - gives a totally new way to experience the shore. It's the perfect activity for a rainy day as getting soaked is going to be the least of your worries. See www.fb.com/coasteeringIRE for details.

Dromquinna Glamping | Dromquinna Manor

The Milky Way above the Skelligs | Michele Cati

White Strand, near Sneem | RC

DROMQUINNA GLAMPING

Luxury camping for those reluctant to stay anywhere but a hotel [51.8743, -9.6445]. The coast nearby is good for kayaking, with sheltered water and plenty of small wooded islands to explore out in the bay. The campsite is well signposted when driving west from Kenmare along the Wild Atlantic Way (www. dromquinnamanor.com).

ROSSDOHAN

Though not signposted, a short walking or cycling loop around this little known peninsula is worthwhile and should help you forget about the busy Ring of Kerry road.

Park at the church at Tahilla [51.8304, -9.8225]. Heading west, take a left after the church, down a quiet country road and follow this to Rossdohan Island, passing small lakes and attractive cottages on the other side of the rich hedgerows. Either return the same way or turn left at the crossroads 800m after the pier and enjoy the peaceful boreen that leads back to the busier N70. Turn right to return to the start. An 11km round trip.

SNEEM

The pleasant village of Sneem is a popular stop on the Ring of Kerry. Two signposted walks start from the North Square.

- The 13km Fermoyle Loop follows a mix of minor roads and open ground, passing plenty of sites of historical interest (white arrows).
- The 10km Lomanagh Loop takes a slightly shorter route across gentle hillsides and through forestry plantations (red arrows).

If you're looking to explore more of this area bikes can be hired from M. Burns Cycle Hire in the village.

For the past few years Sneem has hosted a storytelling festival which attracts storytellers from all over the globe. It's usually held in November, offering something for the winter tourist.

WHITE STRAND

West of Sneem there are a number of small sandy beaches, at least two of which are known as White Strand. Some are right beside the main road, while others lie at the end of one of the many minor roads that lead south to the sea. Grab a map (OSI sheet 84) and explore. Though some are popular local spots, there are plenty of quiet, sheltered coves to be found on all but the busiest of days.

KERRY DARK SKY RESERVE

Due to the lack of light pollution, the western part of the Iveragh Peninsula has been designated as an International Dark Sky Reserve. While the landscape is certainly impressive during the day, the show doesn't

Abbey Island, Derrynane | RC

stop once the sun goes down, at least not if you're lucky enough to get clear skies.

The winter is the best time to stargaze as the nights are long and it gets dark early. Grab some warm clothes and a flask and head out into the night. In high summer the sun is never too far from the horizon so it doesn't get as dark, though it's still worth looking up if you find yourself outside in the small hours.

O'CARROLL'S COVE
Just off the road before Derrynane is O'Carroll's Cove, with its beach bar and caravan park [51.7603, -10.0806]. A lovely sandy beach, it can get busy in the summer.

DERRYNANE
With lush woodland, gently sloping hills and a collection of beautiful beaches Derrynane isn't too far from paradise (at least on a sunny day). If you are happy to walk, lounge on the beach, snorkel in the sea or fish from the rocks you'll never be short of things to do.

Derrynane is situated around the small village of Caherdaniel. Lamb's Head [51.7440, -10.1356] is a quiet cul de sac, favoured by shore fishermen and walkers. The Blue Flag beach extends around the east and northern shores of the bay, and there are lifeguards in the summer. In the woodland bordering the bay is the historic Derrynane House and gardens.

A local artist has developed an interactive smartphone app which guides you along a nature trail around the beach, providing information, pictures and videos of Derrynane's rich biodiversity. See www.vincenthylandartist.com for more information.

The beach at the old quay [51.7604, -10.1434] is very safe for swimming and Derrynane Sea Sports (www.derrynaneseasports.com) offer equipment rental for a variety of water-based activities.

WALKING
The following walk (12km) takes in the best of the area and can be finished with a drink in Caherdaniel.

Heading west out of the village, pass an Ogham Stone and take a left off the road at the signs for Nature Trail and Carpark. Leave the carpark through a short wooded section and come out on a flat, grassy area behind the beach. Having reached the beach walk west along the strand, admiring the surrounding views. As you come to a wooden house on a small headland follow the track up to the road or you can keep going along the beach if the tide is low enough. Abbey Island is a worthy detour from here, for those with the time [51.7574, -10.1446].

Just up the road from the small stone quay is a yellow signpost pointing past a small shed. The path twists along heathery slopes with great views over the harbour and a pleasant little bay, ideal for a quick swim. From this little beach follow the well-worn

Derrynane Woods | RC

Seaweed | Paul Tomlin

grooves in the rock to find the path along the coast again, eventually arriving at a more modern pier. Follow the winding road up the hill and take a right at signs for The Kerry Way at a sharp bend. Continue straight at the next Kerry Way sign, passing over a stile shortly after it. The next sign guides you up and left from the track along a very pleasant upland section. You soon reach a road where you turn right and almost immediately left again. There are two tracks in the woods; take the upper one, eventually leaving the shaded forest to follow signs for the Kerry Way back to Caherdaniel.

DERRYNANE HOUSE

For those looking for a shorter stroll, Derrynane House and the surrounding woodland are worth a visit [51.7630, -10.1305]. The house was the ancestral home of Daniel O'Connell, a man known for his political defence of local customs at a time when the natives were being persecuted for their beliefs. There is a small entrance fee for the museum.

ATLANTIC IRISH SEAWEED

In times gone by seaweed was a valued resource along the Irish coast. Its use as a nutritious food is known worldwide, but seaweed extracts are also used in many everyday products, from beer and ice cream to toothpaste.

Saint Finian's Bay | RC

At one point seaweed was one of the biggest exports from Ireland, but these days it's an undervalued resource which has the potential to provide opportunities in many dwindling rural areas.

Atlantic Irish Seaweed (www.atlanticirishseaweed.com) is a new company based in Caherdaniel, offering foraging trips to budding hunter-gatherers. These excursions are highly informative and hands-on, and the fruits of your labour will be cooked up afterwards for a delicious, self-sourced meal.

BOAT TOURS
There are boat tours available around Derrynane and Kenmare Bay with www.ribtrips.ie. Starting at Wave Crest Caravan Park [51.7587, -10.0911] they offer wildlife tours, moonlit trips and exploratory cruises around the surrounding coastline.

HORSE RIDING
Eagle Rock Equestrian offer horse riding excursions in this fantastic setting, catering for beginners and experts alike [51.7638, -10.1021]. See www.eaglerockcentre.com for details.

WATERVILLE
The road from Caherdaniel to Waterville is cut into the mountains, culminating in the pass at Coomakista. Further north is Waterville, which has a beach, shops and restaurants. There is also plenty of accommodation, including B+Bs and a hostel/café, Peter's Place [51.8239, -10.1718].

FISHING
Behind the town lies Lough Currane, which is well known for its sea trout and salmon fishing. If you fancy your chances, Neil O'Shea, a fourth generation ghillie, is the man to talk to (www.oshealoughcurrane.com). Note that fishing permits are required by law. They can be purchased online at www.salmonlicences.ie.

WALKING
There is a 24km walk starting and ending in Waterville. A long day out, it would make a decent challenge for the adventurous runner.

Starting at the The Lobster Bar [51.8271, -10.1720], follow the Kerry Way north, soon leaving the village to follow the track up a pleasant ridge. After 5km along the ridge take the signposted right turn down towards Lough Currane. Follow the markers up over a shoulder of mountain and back down to a forestry track. When you meet the road turn right to return to Waterville.

INNY STRAND
This fine stretch of sandy beach is a 10km drive north of Waterville [51.8456, -10.2317]. It's good for swimming and walking, with an easy 6km loop walk taking in part of the beach and the land behind

Kerry Cliffs | Alan Cronin

Gannet | RC

it. Coming from Waterville, the beach is on the left, marked by a sign for the Emlagh Loop Walk.

BALLINSKELLIGS BEACH

This is a very nice Blue Flag beach, good for swimming, and popular with walkers *[51.8209, -10.2734]*. There are lifeguards on duty daily in July and August and on weekends for most of June and September.

The unmissable McCarthy Mór tower house dates back to the 16th century, and is believed to have been built to protect the coast from pirates and to perhaps charge a tariff on passing ships.

Skelligs Watersports offer a variety of watersports camps and rental in the summer months. See www. skelligsurf.com for more information.

BOLUS HEAD

Bolus Head is a hilly promontory guarding the south arm of Saint Finian's Bay. There is an excellent signposted 9km loop walk here, with high cliff scenery and beautiful views. The Skelligs are a near constant presence in the corner of your eye, drawing your gaze westwards again and again. Follow the purple arrows.

Coming from Ballinskelligs, take a left off the R566 at the sign for the Bolus Head trailhead. Park at the U.S. Navy Liberator Monument *[51.8141, -10.3371]*, dedicated to the eleven lost airmen who crashed into the Atlantic here in 1944.

Walking near Bolus Head | RC

Steps to the Monastery, Skellig Michael | Alan Cronin

The Monastery on Skellig Michael | Valerie Hinojosa

An Atlantic Puffin | RC

SAINT FINIAN'S BAY

This is a nice beach with good views to the Skelligs and good surf when conditions align [51.8463, -10.3353]. Beside the road, not far from the beach is Skelligs Chocolate (www.skelligschocolate.com), a chocolate factory and café [51.8458, -10.3299].

PORTMAGEE

The Wild Atlantic Way continues north from Saint Finian's over Coonanaspig, a high road with incredible views to the north [51.8562, -10.3670].

Before Portmagee there are signs on the left for the unimaginatively named Kerry Cliffs, described as the most spectacular in the county [51.8696, -10.3797]. This is a bold statement in a county with such an impressive coastline, but nonetheless, it's worth paying the small fee to park the car and make the short walk west for what is indeed a magnificent view.

Portmagee, a cute fishing village with pubs and restaurants, is the embarkation point for most of the boats to The Skelligs. There is a bridge from here to Valentia Island (see page 76).

THE SKELLIGS

There are few places in the world quite like the Skelligs, and words do little to convey the feeling of the place. These two rocky islands, Skellig Michael and Little Skellig, lie 10km off the coast of Portmagee, their sharp summits pointing to the sky.

Skellig Michael is a UNESCO world heritage site, owing to the monastic site established there between the 6th and 8th centuries. The monastery stands testament to the dedication of the monks, who must have had a tough existence out on the fringe of society with little in the way of food and shelter.

The stone dwellings on the island were all made using a technique known as corbelling, a system that has kept the cells watertight since they were first constructed. The monks levelled flatter areas near the monastery for use as gardens and built sophisticated water catchment systems as there is no fresh water supply on the island. Over 100 stone crosses have been recorded, and the last family to live in the lighthouse were still using the oratory as their church during the 19th century.

The ridges that make up these summits could rival similar scenery from any mountain range in the world, only these precipitous cliffs rise out of the ocean, taking the brunt of the bad weather that this area often sees. The cliff scenery and exposure are second to none in Ireland.

Recently the islands became even more famous thanks to their appearance in two Star Wars films.

The Little Skellig is the second biggest gannet colony in the world, home to over 25,000 pairs. It's an incredible sight during the summer breeding season.

Skellig Michael is home to a large population of seabirds, including kittiwakes, storm petrels, Manx shearwaters and everybody's favourite, Atlantic

Ancient remains and Little Skellig | RC

Valentia Lighthouse | RC

Autumn colour on Valentia | RC

Culloo, Valentia | RC

puffins. The puffins are quite tame and extremely photogenic.

Be warned; the steep nature of the island has been known to cause vertigo and there have been accidents in the past. The steps to the monastery are unguarded and uneven, and are slippery when wet. All that said, unless you are particularly afraid of heights this is an experience not to be missed.

A limited number of boat tours are permitted to the island between May and October, see www. skelligexperience.com for a list of boatmen. They sail from Portmagee and Ballinskelligs. Bear in mind that landing on Skellig Michael is very much weather-dependent. Book well in advance and pray for a calm sea.

VALENTIA ISLAND

In the northwest corner of the Ring of Kerry sits Valentia, a large hilly island with two contrasting shores. On the south side is the relatively calm and low-lying coast bordering the Portmagee Channel. The north side is a totally different place, with high cliffs along much of the coast and an open, exposed aspect.

The island was the site of one end of the first transatlantic telegraph cables in the mid nineteenth century. The cable, which landed at Newfoundland, was replaced regularly until the sixties. The Valentia Island Heritage Centre houses an exhibition about the

Sunset at the Fogher Cliffs | RC

telegraph cable as well as plenty of other fascinating exhibits *[51.9254, -10.2943]*. See www.valentiaisland.ie for the opening hours.

It is possible to drive onto the island from just outside Portmagee *[51.8863, -10.3630]*. Between March and September a car ferry links Knight's Town, on the eastern end of the island with Reenard Point, near Cahersiveen *[51.9291, -10.2777]*.

The island's proximity to the mainland dulls its overall sense of remoteness but there is still plenty to be seen here. A cycle around the island's main road would be a good hilly challenge.

BRAY HEAD LOOP WALK
Coming from Portmagee, take a left after crossing the bridge and follow the signs for the Bray Head loop walk. This 5km walk takes you out to the island's western end, past the old signal tower and up past high cliffs. There is a small charge for parking *[51.8920, -10.3965]*.

CULLOO
Following the northern road east there is a sign to the left for Saint Brendan's Well. Follow the rough road to the signs for Culloo Rock and park here if your car makes it that far *[51.9087, -10.3970]*. There is a short but worthwhile walk to be done from here. Walk further on along the road to the holy well and two old crosses. Having crossed the stile to see the second

cross it is possible to take a reasonably dry track straight out to the shore. It's a lonely, pleasant stretch of coast here, ideal for a picnic on a sunny day in May when the sea thrift is blooming in profusion. Walk east to Culloo Rock (a popular, but exposed shore fishing spot) and follow the track beside the stream back to the car to complete the circuit.

GEOKAUN MOUNTAIN
Well signposted at the eastern end of the island is Geokaun Mountain *[51.9158, -10.3501]*. As with many places along The Ring of Kerry, there is a small charge for parking, and for this place in particular, the few euro is well spent. There are three stopping points along the road to the summit. The first is at a short walkway to the huge Fogher Cliffs, which fall away to the sea from the north side of the mountain.

The second stop is at the beginning of a mile-long pathway around the hill, which shouldn't be missed. It's not exactly adventurous but well worth it for a quick fix of scenic inspiration. The views are extensive, with the Dingle Peninsula to the north, the stately rise of Knocknadobar to the east, the rounded hills of South Kerry inland, and the distant Skelligs to the west. The top of the mountain has picnic benches and dotted all along the track are information boards about the natural and cultural heritage of the area.

Walking trail on Seefin | Denis Dineen

SLATE GROTTO
On the lower slopes of Geokaun Mountain is a slate quarry that operated for much of the 19th century. It's open again these days, though on a much smaller scale. The place became a site of pilgrimage after 1954, which explains the religious statues in the top of the main cave. The place has a strange air of industry in a very rural setting, with a bit of religious devotion thrown in for good measure [51.9249, -10.3427].

TETRAPOD TRACKWAY
Another popular feature at this end of Valentia is the tetrapod trackway, the world's oldest in-situ record of a vertebrate walking on land [51.9295, -10.3458]. The tracks, which date back 385 million years, belonged to one of the first vertebrates to come from the sea and colonise the land.

The story these fossilized footprints tells us is far more inspiring than the sight itself, which, after reading the information board, is a little underwhelming. Still, it's worth a quick visit.

CAHERSIVEEN
At the foot of Beentee mountain is the busy market town of Cahersiveen.

CYCLING
Casey's Cycles (www.bikehirekerry.com) do rentals, and cycling is an ideal mode of transport for exploring the surrounding area. The same company provides maps of four cycling routes in the area, from 29km to 53km. Each of these routes takes you on a different journey through the surrounding countryside, along quiet back roads and stunning seaside paths.

BEENTEE LOOP
There is an information board at the Fairgreen carpark (turn right after the petrol station if coming from the south) where a number of walking routes start and finish [51.9467, -10.2203]. The Beentee Loop is an excellent walk for those looking for a good view. The 9km round trip takes you to the summit of Bentee (376m), from where you can take in Cahersiveen and Valentia, the MacGillycuddy's Reeks and the Dingle Peninsula.

LAHARN BOG LOOP
This walk is a longer (14km) loop around the base of the mountain that avoids the steep climbs of the previous route.

WHITE STRAND
Just north of Cahersiveen is an area known as 'Across the Water' by locals. This area has some sites of historical interest and a gorgeous Blue Flag beach.

Take a left after the church in Cahersiveen, and cross the bridge. Heading left, there are signs for Leacanabuaile and Cahergal stone forts [51.9555,

Rossbeigh | Denis Dineen

-10.2615], as well as Ballycarbery Castle [51.9495, -10.2595], all worth a visit if you have an interest in history.

Continuing past the carpark at Cahergal, you come to a T-junction at a stony bay. White Strand is at the end of the left turn [51.9451, -10.2759].

Not too far offshore is Beginish Island, whose quieter beaches are an enticing sight. Those with kayaks and some experience should have little trouble getting out there on a calm day. It's well worth the short paddle.

KNOCKNADOBAR

Knocknadobar (Hill of the Wells) is the prominent peak north of Cahersiveen. The walk to the top is a great way to spend a few hours on a nice day. The mountain is a site of pilgrimage and crosses have been erected most of the way up to the summit to guide the devout.

After crossing the bridge from Cahersiveen go right. Take the second left and park at the end of the road near the quaint pier at Coonanna [51.9893, -10.2125].

Walk back along the road for 10-15 minutes to the start of the Stations of the Cross path. Follow the crosses (not always easy to find) or one of the many paths up the southwest ridge to the summit at 690m. The views on a clear day are extensive (see the photo on page 66). Return by the same way for a 15km round trip.

Because of the mountainous nature of the walk you should have a map (OSI sheet 83) and compass (and know how to use them), as well as spare clothing, rain gear and plenty of food and water.

KELL'S BAY

This very pleasant bay is tucked between the mountains and the open water of Dingle Bay to the north [52.0246, -10.1041]. The Blue Flag beach is beautiful, and there is a campsite just behind it (www.kellsbeachcamping.com).

ROSSBEIGH BEACH

Rossbeigh is a nice Blue Flag beach backed by impressive sand dunes. It's safe for swimming, surfing is possible when conditions are right, and the strand is long enough for a decent walk [52.0552, -9.9760]. Burke's Horse Riding offer treks on the beach as well as trips around the area. See www.beachtrek.ie for details.

GLENBEIGH

The village of Glenbeigh has a few pubs and restaurants as well as a hostel (www.thesleepycamel.com) and campsite (www.campingkerry.com).

There is a nice 12km loop around Seefin that starts from the church in Glenbeigh [52.0560, -9.9400]. Follow the quiet road west from the church as far as a picnic bench opposite two bungalows. Turn left

Looking down the Hag's Glen from Carrauntoohil | Denis Dineen

here and follow the yellow walker signposts up to Windy Gap. After taking in the view descend to the left along a track overlooking Lough Caragh. This track eventually meets a quiet road and then the main road, which takes you back into Glenbeigh.

KILLORGLIN

This town is the last or first port of call on the Iveragh Peninsula as you travel along the Wild Atlantic Way. It is famous for the Puck Fair, which is held during August every year. The three-day event is the oldest traditional fair in Ireland and has been running for over four hundred years. A wild goat is taken from the hills and the Queen of Puck traditionally crowns the goat King Puck, as he is paraded around town.

INLAND

It would be shame to miss out on the mountains and lakes that comprise the interior of Iveragh.

KILLARNEY

Killarney is probably the busiest tourist town in Ireland, with tens of thousands visiting every year. The town has plenty of pubs, cafés, restaurants, hotels and hostels and is an excellent, if a little busy, base for exploring the Iveragh Peninsula.

KILLARNEY NATIONAL PARK

This, the oldest national park in Ireland, is a beautiful area of wild mountains, ancient native woodland and sprawling lakes. In and around the park's boundaries you will find popular attractions such as Torc Waterfall and Mountain, Muckross House and Gardens, and the Lakes of Killarney.

There are various walking and cycling routes in the national park which take you through some of the oldest natural woodland in the country, which is home to our oldest population of red deer, and a huge range of other wildlife. It's also possible to take a boat trip on the lakes. See www.killarneynationalpark.ie for more.

THE MACGILLYCUDDY'S REEKS

The Reeks, as they're known locally, are the highest mountain range in Ireland, with 10 of the 12 highest points in the country including the highest of them all, Carrauntoohil. While small by international standards, the Reeks are rugged and rocky and prone to unpredictable weather. They should only be approached by experienced walkers with good navigation skills. If you're unsure of your ability Kerry Climbing (www.kerryclimbing.ie) offer a guiding service, including not just Carrauntoohil, but the many other less well known mountains in the area. ⬚

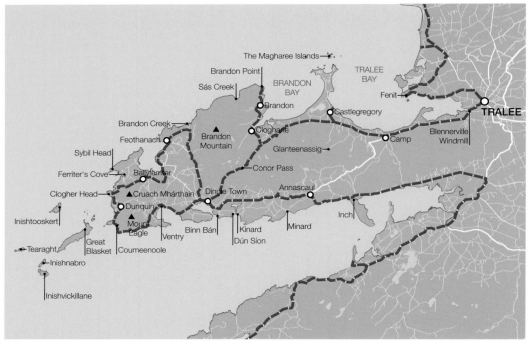

THE DINGLE PENINSULA

Many people would argue that the Dingle Peninsula (Corca Dhuibhne in its native language) is the most beautiful corner of Ireland. This Irish-speaking region certainly has a lot going for it with wonderful beaches, mountains, rolling green fields, a ragged coastline, lonely islands and a treasure of heritage. All of Ireland's clichés can be found here, but it's easy to love it.

INCH STRAND

The first port of call for most people coming from the south is the fine strand at Inch *[52.1422, -9.9813]*. This is a surfer friendly beach, popular with seasoned locals and visitors alike (see the photo on page 30). The Offshore Surf School (www.offshoresurfschool.ie) and Kingdom Waves (www.kingdomwaves.com) offer rentals and lessons.

If surfing isn't your thing, then a walk might be, and there's enough beach here to keep you on your feet for hours. On sunny days when the carparks get full people park on the sand. Watch out for people, especially children, if you're driving on the beach, and remember the tide. Every year somebody parks on the sand and heads out for a walk, only to come back and find the flood tide washing out their engine bay.

SOUTH COAST BEACHES

Between Inch and Dingle Town are a few more quiet beaches that are worth seeking out.

• Minard is a pleasant beach near a 16th century castle *[52.1268, -10.1092]*.
• Kinard occasional has surf. Look out for the iconic sea stack known as An Searrach offshore *[52.1213, -10.2064]*.
• Dún Síon is a lovely beach *[52.1257, -10.2168]*. There are strong currents so swimming in the sea is dangerous, but it's possible to swim in the river.
• Binn Bán is a small cove on the outer edge of Dingle Harbour *[52.1212, -10.2495]*.

DINGLE TOWN

The animated town of Dingle is usually thronged with tourists in summer time. This is a place that knows how to attract visitors, and even during the winter there are festivals and events. There are plenty of great places to eat and drink but don't miss out on Reel Dingle Fish, their fish and chips are as good (and fresh) as it gets. Murphy's Ice Cream is worth trying too.

If there's an icon of Dingle it's Fungi, a bottlenose dolphin that arrived at the harbour in 1984 and has been around since. There are a number of tour boats

Walking near Dingle Harbour | RC

Riding in Smerwick Harbour | Dingle Horseriding

Kayaking along the cliffs west of Dingle Town | RC

offering trips to see this solitary animal. What they'll do when he finally kicks the bucket is anybody's guess. Check in the tourist office [52.1391, -10.2745] for information on boat trips.

There are plenty of accommodation options in Dingle, from hotels and self-catering to B+Bs and hostels (see the list below). During the summer it's advisable to book in advance.

• The Grapevine Hostel (www.grapevinedingle.com) and The Hideout Hostel (www.thehideouthostel.com) are both located in the centre of town.
• The Rainbow Hostel is less than 2km outside town [52.1478, -10.2888]. It's a quieter hostel with camping available www.rainbowhosteldingle.com.

HARBOUR WALK
This walk follows the coast east from the town. Follow the narrow road opposite Moran's petrol station to the shoreline of Dingle Harbour. If you carry on along the coast you eventually reach the lighthouse and the pleasant beach at Binn Bán. After the beach a path climbs to Ceann na Binne [52.1172, -10.2480], a lofty place to take in the views over Dingle (4km each way).

SEA KAYAKING
The rugged coastline west of Dingle Town is best appreciated from the water. Not far outside the mouth of the bay the cliffs rise to impressive heights and there are plenty of atmospheric sea caves to explore (on a calm day!). The marina in the town is a good, sheltered place to launch your boat.

Various different kayaking trips can be booked with Irish Adventures (www.irishadventures.net) in Dingle Town, who cater for all ages and abilities. Don't be surprised if you meet Fungi.

HORSE RIDING
There's something romantic about travelling through a wild place on horseback, and the following operators will help you do just that. See www.dinglehorseriding.com and www.burnhamhorseridingdingle.com for trips from Dingle, and www.longsriding.com for treks from Ventry.

SLEA HEAD DRIVE
This winding coastal drive takes in many of Dingle's most compelling sights. The road west of Ventry has been carved into the seaward side of Mount Eagle and each turn reveals new views over the Blasket Islands and the sea beyond.

Once around Slea Head itself the views of Coumeenoole open up and with the steep green fields, black cliffs, golden sand and emerald ocean, it's surely one of the best views in the country. And that's only a small section of the 57km route.

Most people drive the route but it is far better enjoyed on a bike. There are a number of places to rent bikes in Dingle Town, including Paddy's Bike

Dingle Bay | Matt Gillman

Shop (www.paddysbikeshop.com), and The Mountain Man Outdoor Shop (www.themountainmanshop.com).

It's possible to make the cycle shorter or longer, depending on fitness and time. The shortest variation leaves the main road at Dunquin and crosses Mám Clasach [52.1417, -10.4255] (the narrow road that passes between Mount Eagle and Cruach Mhárthain) to drop down to Ventry. It's a gruelling climb but the views are spectacular and the descent back down to Ventry is fun.

Another option is to do the route at a more leisurely pace, over two days. This allows plenty of time for savouring and exploring the landscape along the way.

VENTRY

As you travel west from Dingle towards Slea Head you will soon reach Ventry, Ceann Trá in Irish. This picturesque bay is perfect for a day on the beach. It is more sheltered than most of the other beaches nearby and is safe for swimming and good for snorkelling. Park beside the caravan park [52.1326, -10.3639], or at Páidí Ó Sé's pub, a bar owned by the legendary local footballer [52.1277, -10.3805].

CRUACH MHÁRTHAIN

Not far inland from Ventry is a prominent hill known as Cruach Mhárthain [52.1496, -10.4309]. It's a fairly straightforward walk to the summit and there are spectacular views over West Kerry.

As you arrive at Páidí Ó Sé's from Dingle turn right at the crossroads. Follow the road to the top of the pass and park near the signal tower [52.1417, -10.4255]. Cruach Mhárthain is the small conical peak north of the road. Follow the fence behind the tower to the summit. Descend by the same route. It's a 2km round trip.

COUMEENOOLE

Just around the corner from Slea Head is undoubtedly one of the finest beaches in the country [52.1099, -10.4653]. At high tide the sea comes all the way up to the cliffs, but at low water the beautiful golden sand stretches across the bay (see the photo on page 26).

The water can be very rough here so be careful if swimming. Don't assume that the sea will be calm just because the sun is shining and the wind has dropped.

It's worth following the well-worn path (see the photo on page 20) from the carpark to the end of Dunmore Head [52.1111, -10.4750]. There you will find one of the most famous views in Ireland. Come at the end of the day to see the sun set over the Blasket Islands.

Coumeenoole | RC

The view from Cruach Mhárthain | RC

Dunmore Head | RC

Camping on the Great Blasket | RC

THE BLASKET ISLANDS

Way out at the end of the Dingle Peninsula, right on the very western edge of Europe, lie the Blasket Islands. Made up of six larger islands and numerous smaller rocky outcrops, this is the finest archipelago in Ireland.

It was the home to a hardy community of islanders until the last inhabitants left The Great Blasket in 1954. These days nobody lives on any of the islands year round, but The Great Blasket is a popular destination for day-trippers, with ferries operating from Dingle, Ventry and Dunquin.

A trip out to The Great Blasket is well worth doing, especially if you stay overnight. The island is over 6km long and hilly, making it an excellent place to go walking. Once you leave the ruins of the village the atmosphere becomes lonely, with great views west to the other islands.

The island's high ground offers an excellent vantage point to observe the abundant marine wildlife. Keep an eye on the sea to the south and you may see basking sharks, whales and dolphins.

Hundreds of grey seals haul out on the beach below the village (An Trá Bán) and they make a fine sight. Don't disturb them - they're totally wild animals and a bite from one of them would be quite serious.

Camping is permitted on the island and there is a water tap in the village. While the island may be busy with tourists during the day, peace descends with the evening. During the night you might hear the low howling of the seals and the eerie calls of Manx shearwaters, seabirds that come ashore to their burrows at night to avoid predators.

If there is a clear sky take a look outside your tent in the middle of the night. The lack of light pollution this far west makes for a brilliant display of stars. The only alternative to camping is the hostel that opens for the summer season (www.greatblasketisland.net).

Numerous boats offer trips to the island. From Dingle see www.dinglebaycharters.com and www.greatblasketisland.net. For a shorter trip from the iconic pier at Dunquin [52.1253, -10.4598] see www.blasketisland.com.

BOAT TOURS

A boat tour with Blasket Islands Eco Marine Tours (www.marinetours.ie) will allow you to get a closer look at some of the more distant islands. Highlights include the incredible architecture of Cathedral Rocks on Inishnabro and the puffins around Inishvickillane.

If you're lucky you might get to see some of the wildlife including grey seals, dolphins, whales, basking sharks and a variety of birds. Gulls, gannets, auks and tubenoses all use the waters around the Blaskets to fish, and in large numbers can provide as good a show as the bigger species. Don't forget your binoculars. Trips last from 2.5 to 4 hours. Booking is essential and naturally all trips are subject to the sea

Cathedral Rocks, Inishnabro | RC

Blasket Tour Boat | RC

An Trá Bán, The Great Blasket | RC

The authors | RC

Wave watching at Clogher Head | RC

conditions on the day. Trips depart from Ventry Pier *[52.1317, -10.3600]*.

DUNQUIN

Dunquin, Dún Chaoin in Irish, is the most westerly village in mainland Europe. It's an open and exposed townland, with commanding views of the Blaskets. This is the edge of the world.

The Blasket Centre *[52.1332, -10.4612]* is popular with tourists, offering an insight into island life back when the Blaskets were inhabited.

There is an An Óige hostel (www.anoige.ie) and one pub, Krugers, in the village.

SIÚLÓID NA CILLE

The Blasket Centre is the starting point for a great 5km coastal and mountain walk. It takes you past the old school built for the film Ryan's Daughter and across open countryside where the wind will chill you or the sun will shine down, or both in the same day.

CLOGHER

A short journey north from Dunquin the main road bends right at Clogher Head *[52.1501, -10.4663]*. There is a layby here with room for half a dozen cars and it's worth pulling in to have a proper look. The view from here (on a clear day at least!) is one of the best around. Take a stroll out to the end point of the headland and take in the view (see the photo on page 14).

Just to the north is the nice beach at Clogher Strand *[52.1568, -10.4595]*. The soft grass behind the sand is a nice place for a tent. There are dangerous currents here so swimming is best avoided. A good 3km walking trail that starts and ends in the carpark, Cosán Cuas na nEighe, follow the blue arrows.

FERRITER'S COVE

Just before you arrive in Ballyferriter from the west there's a sign for a golf course. This road leads to the beach at Ferriter's Cove, another pleasant bay with the tall cliffs of Sybil Head looming on the right *[52.1743, -10.4395]*.

BALLYFERRITER

Ballyferriter, Baile an Fheirtéaraigh in Irish, is real West Kerry; you're more likely to hear Irish being spoken here than English, and students of the Irish language flock here to improve their native tongue. There is a shop, hotel, a few pubs and a museum (www.westkerrymuseum.com) in the village.

There is an information board at the museum that describes four walking trails in the area, from 7 to 12km in length. While they're not signposted, take a photo of the map and you will easily figure them out *[52.1664, -10.4061]*.

Sunset at Smerwick Habour | RC

Gallarus Oratory | Shaun Dunphy

Whale watching, Clogher | RC

SMERWICK HARBOUR

The southern shores of Smerwick Harbour form an almost continuous beach. This is a good place for a swim in the summer, and for long walks in any weather. Coming from Dunquin, follow the signs for Smerwick [52.1795, -10.4054] or Wine Strand [52.1806, -10.3867] to take you to a beach of your choice.

GALLARUS ORATORY

This early Christian church dates back over 1,000 years [52.1737, -10.3535]. Its beautiful, gently curving stone walls are reminiscent of an upturned boat. It's located near An Mhuiríoch and is well signposted on the Slea Head Drive. There is a small charge for admission and parking at the visitor centre, which is closed in winter though access to the church remains open.

Close by is Campail Teach an Aragail, a camping and caravan park open from April to September [52.1730, -10.3559]. See www.dingleactivities.com/camping for more.

AN MHUIRÍOCH

The beach at An Mhuiríoch is accessed at the far end of the football pitch [52.1834, -10.3638] and is a nice spot for a stroll and a swim.

Peddler's Lake | Pauric Ward

Standing Stone, Brandon | RC

The east side of the Brandon Mountain Range | RC

BALLYDAVID

The road that leads northwest along the coast from An Mhuiríoch will take you to Ballydavid, or Baile na nGall, another Irish language stronghold. Tigh TP and Tig Beaglaoic are good pubs overlooking the small beach at the pier [52.1905, -10.3759].

SIÚLÓID NA FAILLE

A 6km signposted (red arrows) loop starts from the pier. It follows the coastal path towards Fheothanach and returns along a quiet country road. It's a good way to build up an appetite for the pub.

BRANDON CREEK

Just over 4km north along the Wild Atlantic Way from Fheothanach is the small, steep-sided cove known as Brandon Creek. In 535 AD Saint Brendan set sail from here and reportedly discovered the North American continent, long before the Vikings or Columbus.

In 1976 Tim Severin and a small crew set sail from the creek in a boat made of wood and leather to prove that the voyage was possible. They followed the route that Saint Brendan described and reached Newfoundland just over a year later.

The creek is a deep natural harbour, good for a swim [52.2378, -10.3097].

BRANDON MOUNTAIN

Steeped in history and beautifully situated, Brandon Mountain is a must-do for any hillwalker in Ireland. There are few more spectacular summit views for those lucky enough to reach the top on a clear day. Ireland's longest beach, Brandon Bay, and the iconic coastline of West Kerry are but two of many inspiring sights.

Anyone planning to venture up the mountain should carry a map (OSI sheet 70) and compass as it is frequently shrouded in thick mist. They should also pack rain gear, plenty of food and warm clothing.

There are two approaches, from the west and east, and both are very different in character.

FROM THE WEST

The western route is the easiest way to the top, offering a gentle slope for most of the ascent.

Head west from Dingle, taking the R549 north at the Milltown Roundabout (signposted ' An Fheothanach/Cuas'). After 7.5km take the right fork at the sign for Mount Brandon. Take the next right (signposted again) to the car park [52.2148, 10.2923].

The route follows a clear, well marked path to the top. There are fourteen crosses along the way, with white marker posts between these. The path zigzags up some steeper ground near the summit, and care is required on a few short rocky steps. Descend by the same route. The round trip is 7km with 780m of ascent.

Overlooking Sás Creek | RC

FROM THE EAST

The climb from the east side takes you through some steep and dramatic mountain scenery, and is a little more challenging than the previous route.

From the village of Cloghane head north. There is a sign for Mount Brandon not far outside the village. Follow this to the carpark at the end of the road *[52.2393, -10.2057]*. From here follow the well-worn track along the Faha Ridge, taking the lower of two paths after about half an hour. After passing through the jumble of small lakes and outcrops on the floor of the glaciated valley, the path becomes much steeper as it weaves its way up the intimidating back wall. Take your time along this section, it's tricky but not nearly as intimidating as it looks from the distance.

When you reach the ridge, follow it to the left for the short distance to the summit, which is marked by a wooden cross. Savour the view if you're lucky enough to get one. Descend by the same route. The route is 10km with 950m of ascent, making for a long day for anybody not used to hiking.

CONOR PASS

The Conor Pass is one of the highest and most scenic roads in Ireland, but it's unsuitable for nervous drivers or big camper vans. It's the most direct route over to the north side of the peninsula from Dingle Town.

At the highest point of the pass there is a carpark with great views in all directions. Just over 1.5km down the pass towards Cloghane is another carpark beside a small waterfall *[52.1868, -10.1903]*. It's worth stopping here and following the stream uphill for a short distance to Peddler's Lake *[52.1863, -10.1888]*. The picturesque lake sits in a very impressive mountain corrie and is a great place for a wild swim.

CLOGHANE AND BRANDON

The two small villages of Cloghane and Brandon are signposted soon after dropping down from the top of the Conor Pass. Both are the antithesis to Dingle Town; a toned down version of a west of Ireland seaside settlement, with enough facilities for most tourists, and a quietness that will appeal to many. The Mount Brandon Hostel is open all year round (www.mountbrandonhostel.com).

There are some pleasant beaches nearby including: Cappagh Strand *[52.2494, -10.1614]*, Brandon Pier *[52.2648, -10.1628]* and An Trá Bháin *[52.2768, -10.1574]*.

SÁS CREEK

At the northern tip of the Dingle Peninsula the mountains run down directly to the sea. Here you will find Sás (pronounced Sauce) Creek, a beautiful steep-sided bay.

No roads cross this remote stretch of coast and Sás Creek can only be reached on foot (or by boat!). A hilly 14km walk, Siúlóid a' Sás, will take you there and

Brandon Bay | RC

back in a loop. The walk is signposted (red markers) but it can be hard to follow where it crosses open ground. As the area is prone to mist and changeable weather walkers should be equipped with a map (OSI sheet 70) and compass.

Starting in Brandon village *[52.2682, -10.1616]* follow the red markers along the small roads west of the village. As you gain height you enter open hillside and the road becomes a track. Look out for the signposted turn right, which leads to the edge of the Creek. If the visibility is bad or you aren't confident in your navigation then you should retrace your steps.

If you decide to continue then follow the signs along the edge of the steep slopes, down across the hillside, and through a small valley. A final slog to a stony track leads to Brandon Point *[52.2878, -10.1606]*. From here the road will bring you back to the village.

BRANDON BAY
The eastern and southern curves of Brandon Bay are fringed by Ireland's longest beach. The 12km stretch of sand can be accessed along the Wild Atlantic Way between Fermoyle and Castlegregory at four points (from west to east):

- Fermoyle Strand *[52.2431, -10.1252]*
- Kilcummin Strand *[52.2445, -10.1016]*
- Gowlane Strand *[52.2481, -10.0855]*
- Stradbally Strand *[52.2547, -10.0696]*

The beach is exposed and windswept, offering little shelter, but great tracts of privacy.

CASTLEGREGORY
A popular summer spot, especially for watersports enthusiasts. There are vast sandy beaches either side of the narrow spit, which extends north from the mainland for over 7km.

Jamie Knox's watersports centre offers surfing, windsurfing and paddleboarding lessons and rentals (www.jamieknox.com). Waterworld also offer surf rentals and lessons, as well as diving courses off the Magharee Islands and Brandon (www.waterworld.ie).

There is a pleasant walk around the north end of the peninsula. Starting from the grassy carpark at Magherabeg *[52.2793, -10.0262]* it's just a matter of following either coastline north to Scraggane Bay and returning south along the opposite side.

THE MAGHAREE ISLANDS
The Magharee Islands, also known as The Seven Hogs, are the collection of seven small islands north of Scraggane Bay. They will be of interest to the experienced sea kayaker.

GLANTEENASSIG
This spectacular mountain valley, with its conifer forest, steep cliffs and waterfalls, could be somewhere in the Swiss Alps *[52.2117, -10.0194]*.

Glanteenassig | RC

There are three signposted walking trails. Unfortunately they are very short (0.3km, 1.1km and 2km), but they provide easy access to some very dramatic mountain scenery.

Head 5km west of Camp along the Wild Atlantic Way and look out for the signposted left turn. Another 4km will bring you to the entrance of the forest park.

TRALEE BAY

The stretch of coastline between Castlegregory and the mouth of Tralee Bay is mostly made up of long stretches of sand. The Wild Atlantic Way runs parallel to the coast and pretty much every road north of it will take you to a sandy beach.

Near the mouth of the bay is Derrymore Island. A nature reserve, it supports many rare salt marsh plants as well as wigeon and brent geese who graze on the eastern side of the spit.

THE DINGLE WAY

The Dingle Way is a multi-day walk that starts and finishes in Tralee, and follows the coast around the western end of the peninsula. The 162km trail takes about a week and features a mix of mountain tracks, coastal paths and quiet roads.

There is plenty of accommodation along the route so it's straightforward to plan each day's walk. There are also lots of wonderful places to camp.

TRALEE

The large town of Tralee has all the modern conveniences you will need after a few days in the countryside.

BLENNERVILLE WINDMILL

Just west of Tralee is Blennerville windmill. The tall white building was used during the 19th century to grind corn and is the tallest of its kind in Europe [52.2566, -9.7371]. There is a visitor centre and café as well as guided tours of the five-storey windmill.

TRALEE BAY WETLANDS CENTRE

Tralee Bay Wetlands Centre has something for everybody, from bird hides, guided nature tours and a wildlife exhibit, to a watersports centre, a café and a viewing tower with great views over the bay [52.2619, -9.7113]. See www.traleebaywetlands.org for more.

FENIT

North of Tralee is the lighthouse at Fenit. A local landmark with the mountains of Corca Dhuibhne serving as a backdrop, it's a favourite with photographers. The beach is very family friendly, with a playground, toilets, lifeguards in the summer and plenty of parking [52.2758, -9.8651]. ⬚

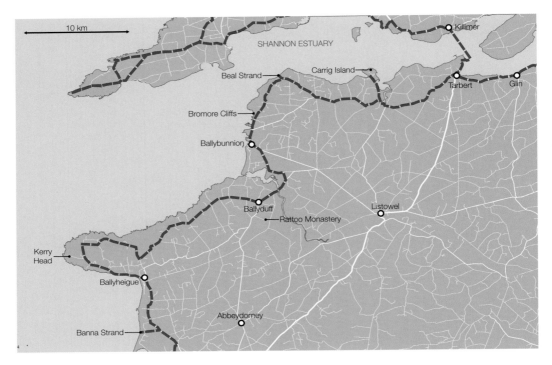

NORTH KERRY AND LIMERICK

While not as well known as the Iveragh or Dingle Peninsulas, North Kerry has much to offer, including spectacular seascapes, some of the finest beaches in Ireland and many ancient sites, churches and field monuments.

The Wild Atlantic Way makes a brief diversion east along the southern bank of the River Shannon to the sea port of Foynes in County Limerick.

The car ferry across the Shannon Estuary, which links North Kerry and Loop Head in Clare, is a convenient and novel shortcut between the two counties. The short boat crossing saves a 130km drive around the Estuary via Limerick City.

BANNA STRAND
This a nice long sandy beach, popular with families, great for walks and a beginner-friendly surfing venue *[52.3384, -9.8346]*. The Shore Break Surf School (www.shorebreaksurfschool.com) offers rentals and lessons. There are lifeguards on duty in the summer months.

BALLYHEIGUE
Ballyheigue is a pleasant town that enjoys expansive views of the mountains of the Dingle Peninsula. The beach is a great place to swim or wander the dunes.

Further south the long stretch of sand is interrupted by The Black Rock, a tiny island that is ideal for a picnic at low tide. Just make sure that the tides don't cut you off. There is a lifeguard during the summer months and a playground in the carpark *[52.3879, -9.8344]*.

KERRY HEAD
A popular spot for shore fishing with a good, remote coastal walk. From the end of the headland there are great views to the south of Tralee Bay and northwards to Loop Head. A section of the North Kerry Way loops around the roads at the end of the headland but a better alternative is to walk to the cliffs on the tip of the headland.

Coming from Ballyheigue, drive north along the Wild Atlantic Way and take the second left (about 5km from Ballyheigue). Ask permission to park in the farmyard *[52.4101, -9.9362]* and follow the rough track to the coast. Be very wary near the cliffs as they are exposed to very big swells and have been the site of drownings in the past.

Kerry Head and Ballyheigue are linked by an 18km signposted cycle route called The Kerry Head Cycleway.

Banna Strand | RC

Wild Water Adventures (www.facebook.com/wildwaterKerry) offer coasteering and wild swimming trips along the coast near Kerry Head.

RATTOO MONASTERY
A few miles south of Ballyduff is the 6th century monastic settlement at Rattoo, which consists of a cemetery, an old church, an abbey and a 28m high round tower [52.4425, -9.6504]. It's signposted about 1km south of Ballyduff on the R551 to Tralee.

BALLYBUNNION
Kerry's traditional seaside town is often bustling in the summer time. On the edge of the town is a fine beach that stretches away to the south. In the other direction there is a path along the tops of the cliffs, which are full of caves and gullies where seabirds nest and great flocks of starlings roost in the autumn evenings.

The beach at Ballybunnion occasionally has good surf. Ballybunion Surf School (www.ballybunionsurf.com) runs kids camps in the summer time.

Collins's Seaweed Baths was established in 1932 and is still going strong [52.5137, -9.6749]. The baths are situated on Ladies Strand and come highly recommended.

For a guided historical walking or cycling tour of the area contact EcoTrek Ballybunnion (www.ecotrekballybunion.com).

KAYAKING
One of the best ways to appreciate the coastline is to see it from water level. The coast north of Ballybunnion has many caves that have to be seen to be believed. Some are connected by tunnels and there is even a skylight in one. Other must-see sights for the sea kayaker include the Nun's Beach below the convent and the impressive sea arch at The Virgin Rock.

Bottlenose dolphins are common in the area. If you meet them on the water treat them with respect, they're big animals.

You should only take to the water when the conditions are calm and the forecast is good. The sea here can get quite rough and big swells are particularly treacherous around the cliffs.

BROMORE CLIFFS
About 3km north of Ballybunnion are the Bromore Cliffs. The cliffs' soft rock has been carved by the sea into impressive caves and sea stacks. There are fantastic colours in the cliffs, abundant wildlife and a few waterfalls spilling into the ocean below.

The landowner has a wealth of knowledge on the history and folklore of the area, and if you don't meet him while out walking you can still learn plenty about the area from the information boards. There is a small charge for the carpark [52.5361, -9.6663].

Ballybunnion sea cave | RC

Rattoo Monastery | RC

Ballybunnion Beach | RC

BEAL STRAND

With a name derived from the Irish word for mouth (béal), this gorgeous stretch of sand overlooks the mouth of Ireland's longest river. It's not nearly as popular as some of Kerry's other beaches, but the long empty strand is the perfect place for a walk.

There are strong currents not too far from shore, so swimmers should stay close to the beach. Keep an eye on the water off the strand in the summer months when bottlenose dolphins hunt salmon on a rising tide. Park at the western end *[52.5739, -9.6312]*.

CARRIG ISLAND

Carrig Island is a historic place. The gun battery on the western point was strategically placed; opposite a similar one on Scattery Island. The narrow channel between them was well guarded and would almost certainly have prevented Napoleon's ships from sailing any further up the Shannon. In the end the French invasion never came. Going further back in time however, there were other attacks. Carrigafoyle Castle was built in the late 15th century, and was destroyed in 1580, less than a century later by the English.

Visitors can take a self-guided tour of the castle, and it's worth walking around the island itself, taking in the views of the lower Shannon Estuary. Follow the signs from the village of Ballylongford to the carpark *[52.5695, -9.4948]*.

SHANNON FERRY

The Wild Atlantic Way skips across the mouth of the Shannon River between Tarbert in Kerry and Killimer in Clare, saving a long drive around the Estuary. The roll-on roll-off car ferry takes twenty minutes to cross and leaves hourly throughout the day. Check sailing times on www.shannonferries.com.

GLIN

The small village of Glin has a rich heritage, and its centrepiece is the 13th century castle. The town square is of Georgian design and was built in the 18th century. Three signposted walks start at Saint Paul's Heritage Centre *[52.5709, -9.2848]*.

- The Path 4.5km (green arrows)
- Knockaranna 8.5km (blue arrows)
- Knight's Walk 4km (red arrows)

See www.glin.info for details.

FOYNES

The town of Foynes on the southern shore of the Shannon Estuary has a rich maritime and aviation history. In the 1930s it was the point of departure for flying boats crossing the Atlantic. The Flying Boat Museum (in the old terminal building) exhibits a full size replica of the Boeing B-314 Flying Boat and is well worth a visit *[52.6116, -9.1093]*. ■

Peeking over the edge of the Cliffs of Moher | RC

CLARE

Clare has some of Ireland's best known coastal scenery, as well as some of its least known treasures. The Cliffs of Moher need little introduction, but there are beautiful stretches of coastline all along this county; from the sea-washed, sandstone cliffs of Loop Head to the terraced coastal hills of the Burren.

Music and surfing feature heavily in the modern culture here, with professionals from both disciplines travelling to Clare specifically for both sea and sound waves. There are wildlife sanctuaries too; the Burren, so distinct as to almost be a county in itself, is a wildflower garden known to botanists all over the world. The Cliffs of Moher and Loop Head are important seabird colonies, and the mouth of the Shannon is home to Europe's largest group of resident bottlenose dolphins.

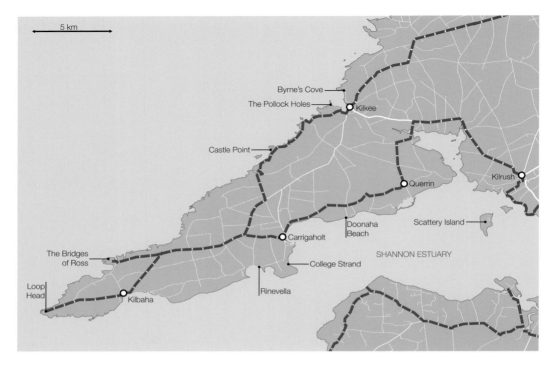

LOOP HEAD

This southwestern promontory of County Clare is often overlooked but it has no shortage of attractions, particularly for those interested in wildlife and exploring the jagged coastline. The Loop Head area has managed to provide for tourists while maintaining an unspoiled feel. It's a quiet place, but it's every bit as impressive as the more famous parts of the Wild Atlantic Way.

While the karst landscape of the Burren in the north of Clare may attract all the plaudits, Loop Head also has some very interesting and impressive cliffs where the contortions and turmoil of the earth's movements can be clearly seen.

The many miles of cliffs are home to a diverse population of birds, however they aren't the only wildlife to be found here. The Shannon Estuary is home to around 200 bottlenose dolphins (the largest resident population in Europe), as well as plenty of other marine wildlife such as seals and sunfish.

One of the best times to visit is late May, when the coastal wildflowers are in full bloom and the bird colonies at Loop Head are at their busiest.

See www.loophead.ie for plenty of useful information.

KILRUSH

After crossing the Shannon the first town you will meet along the Wild Atlantic Way is Kilrush. It has plenty of shops, pubs, a very nice bakery and a hostel (www.katieshostel.com). The Shannon Dolphin & Wildlife Foundation has a visitor centre [52.6356, -9.4959] near the marina where you can learn about Irish marine life (www.shannondolphins.ie). There are dolphin watching tours from Kilrush but the trip from Carrigaholt is better.

SCATTERY ISLAND

About 1.5km off the coast of Kilrush is Scattery Island, a compact area of low-lying land with a long and varied history. The island has a strong association with Saint Senán, who was local to the area, and many saints who followed after him. There are the remains of six churches on the island, as well as a lighthouse, a gun battery, the old village and Ireland's second tallest round tower. The island was sieged many times down through the ages and was finally abandoned in the seventies.

Throughout the summer there are free guided tours of the island. This is a place well worth a day's exploration but unfortunately it's not that easy to get to. There are no regular ferry sailings, and when they

Dolphin watching | RC

Pure Camping, Querrin | Pure Camping

do run they don't leave much time to explore the island before returning to the mainland. Hopefully this situation will change soon and give more people a chance to visit this heritage-rich site. Griffin's Boat Hire in Kilrush Marina [52.6351, -9.4947] operates the ferry.

QUERRIN

A small village on the shore of the Shannon Estuary with good beach walking, horse riding and a very worthwhile campsite.

HORSE RIDING

Carmen's Riding School offers horse riding camps for children during the summer months and full and half day treks for those looking to see the area on horseback. Different abilities are catered for, from beginners to more experienced riders (carmen877@eircom.net).

PURE CAMPING

This is a campsite like you've never visited before [52.6313, -9.5982]. It has all the usual stuff; like space for tents and camper vans, toilets, showers and laundry services. And then there are the things you're not likely to find in most other campsites. Like a sauna. Or yoga classes. There's a pizza oven. And a communal 12m dome tent for chilling out in if your own tent is a bit small.

If you don't have any camping equipment you can stay in one of the luxury on-site bell tents, with bed linen provided if you need it and a mini wood stove if you're worried about the cold. There's a ten acre native woodland on the site and plenty of walking to be done in the surrounding area. A place worth seeking out (www.purecamping.ie).

CARRIGAHOLT

This picturesque fishing village has a nice beach, and a few good pubs, The Long Dock serves excellent food.

DOLPHINWATCH

The Shannon enters the sea between Loop Head and North Kerry, ending its 360km journey south of Carrigaholt. From here the M.V. Draíocht sails out to the mouth of the river to see the wildlife, scenery and history of the area.

The highlight of most people's trip is in the name; the area is home to approximately 200 wild bottlenose dolphins. But there's a lot more to these tours than just the dolphins. There are plenty of other wild animals, local heritage and beautiful scenery along the Clare and Kerry seaboards. The skipper has over 30 years experience of the area and the trip is fully guided, making for a highly informative few hours at sea.

Rinevella Bay | RC

There's a real emphasis on responsible tourism and the encounters strike a good balance between respect for the wildlife and satisfying the customer.

Of course wild animals being wild, sightings cannot be guaranteed, but there are few other boat tours around the world that can compete with this one's encounter record. Advance booking recommended. For more see www.dolphinwatch.ie.

THE BRIDGES OF ROSS

Close to the small townland of Ross is a very interesting section of coastline. The Bridges of Ross [52.5913, -9.8731] are well signposted from the main road to Loop Head.

Only one of the sea arches remains intact (there were three not so long ago) and it's an impressive sight. There are also plenty of other natural features to marvel nearby. In the bay below the carpark is an interesting cleft in the coast, which leads to a tunnel under the cliffs. The passage opens up at a small stony beach where the ground has caved in. The tide doesn't reach the roof of the tunnel so it's possible to swim through, once the sea is calm of course.

Further west, close to the bridge, are a few sea caves that can be accessed from the land at low tide. Be extremely careful when scrambling around the cliffs here; it's all too easy to get down to places that are difficult to climb back out of. But with care it's

possible to get to some otherworldly caverns that are submerged at high tide.

The water beneath the bridge is a good place for snorkelling, but a calm sea is needed as the easiest way to get in and out is where the inlet opens out to the Atlantic. It's possible to jump from the bridge on a high spring tide, but isn't necessarily recommended!

Heading east from the carpark brings you to some more fascinating places, with sea arches, caves, cliffs and blow-holes, enough to make the mind boggle.

This stretch of coastline is also a Mecca for birdwatchers, particularly in August.

KILBAHA

The little village of Kilbaha has a small beach and a children's playground, as well as two pubs that serve food. Just over a kilometre west of the village is a gallery and café that specialises in local crafts (www.kilbahagallery.com).

LOOP HEAD

A circuit walk around the cliffs surrounding Loop Head lighthouse [52.5610, -9.9300]. is a must. There are great views over to County Kerry, a pleasant ledge for picnics known as The Hanging Garden, and the famous sea stack, Diarmuid and Gráinne's rock. Keep an eye on the water for bottlenose dolphins, minke whales and seals. Guided tours of the lighthouse grounds are available between April and October.

Castle Point Cave | RC

WAVE WATCHING

Wave watching is one of Ireland's most under appreciated pastimes. Our western seaboard is wonderfully exposed to an enormous stretch of ocean and the prevailing winds carry the weather towards us in a never-ending tide. When the sea is wild it is these western extremities that take the brunt of the storm and sitting to watch the drama unfold as sea meets land is entertainment that most people never tap into.

The very end of Loop Head is a superb place to witness the awesome power of the sea. The shallow shelves below the high cliffs force the cavernous emerald waves to smash into the cliffs with immense force. The skies that accompany the rough weather are often worth watching in their own right.

The dangers of hanging around a high cliff on a windy day hardly need mentioning but with due care and common sense there is no reason why you can't enjoy this spectacle when the conditions are right. Wrap up warm, bring a packed lunch and prepare to be amazed at the weight of water.

NORTH SHORE WALKS

The north coast of the Loop Head Peninsula is one of high, steep cliffs and wide open views. These two walks give a good flavour of this quiet but remarkable coast.

LOOP HEAD TO FODRY

This walk starts at Loop Head lighthouse [52.5610, -9.9300]. From the car park beside the lighthouse follow the northern coastline eastwards. You will soon pass a striking sea arch near the bird colonies. There are more islands and arches further east until the cliffs gradually decrease in height and you reach the rocky beach at Fodry [52.5798, -9.8810]. Either retrace your steps or have a pick up arranged. It's 4.5km each way.

TULLIG TO GOLEEN

Heading west from Carrigaholt take the second right after the church in the village of Cross. A rough track leads to a quarry on the left. Park considerately here [52.6105, -9.8026].

Follow the coastline east, with views over the offshore islands, imposing precipices and remarkable caves and gullies. The cliffs increase in height towards Knocknagarhoon before a gentle descent leads to another quarry at Goleen Bay [52.6410, -9.7350]. Walk back along the coast or have a car shuttle organized. It's 8km each way.

CASTLE POINT

The sign at Castle Point [52.6559, -9.7204] welcomes you to Kilkee Cliffs, a seemingly made up name. The old name for this headland was Dunlicky (Fort of the

The Pollock Holes | RC

Flagstones) and the remains of the fort can just about be made out past the car park.

It's a popular spot for mackerel fishing though unfortunately there is often a terrible mess left behind. If you fish here please take your rubbish home.

There is a very impressive sea cave in the cliffs below the car park, but it's quite tricky to get into and is flooded at high tide. It would be a very dangerous place to get stuck. Those who can get in and out won't be unimpressed.

KILKEE

Kilkee is a popular seaside holiday village, with a long tradition of tourism. Holidaymakers have been coming here since the early 19th century, and continue to flock to the town in the summer months. The beach is the best in the area [52.6834, -9.6474].

The newly opened Cois Fharraige Hostel (www.coisfharraigehostel.com) offers affordable accommodation in Kilkee [52.6787, -9.6487].

CLIFF WALKS

Starting and ending at the beach in Kilkee are two signposted loop walks that are well worth the effort. There is a 5km circuit (blue arrows) and a longer 8km variation (red arrows), both of which take in the impressive coastal scenery on the southern side of Moore Bay.

The cliffs at the east end of town can be easily reached by a short walk from the beach. There are no signposted trails but it is a beautiful area worthy of exploration nonetheless. Byrne's Cove [52.6921, -9.6543] is a popular swimming spot, though it can be wild.

COASTEERING/KAYAKING

There are plenty of opportunities for kayaking, swimming, snorkelling and coasteering in the bay. So get out and explore the bay yourself or if you would like instruction and equipment contact Nevsail Watersports (www.nevsailwatersports.com).

There used to be diving boards at the west end (drive out towards the Diamond Rocks café and look for the small gap in the wall), but at the time of writing they are missing. Hopefully they will be reinstated soon.

THE POLLOCK HOLES

If you aren't an experienced snorkeller and want a safe place to give it a go with plenty to look at then head for the Pollock Holes [52.6832, -9.6659]. The huge rock pools retain seawater after the tide has retreated. With starfish, sea anemones, urchins and various fish and crustaceans, this is a shoreline safari that couldn't be more accessible. It's the perfect place to start exploring the underwater world.

Moore Bay, Kilkee | RC

Coasteering | RC

Get stuck in and investigate the edges, take a peek behind the seaweed and marvel at the colours. Just remember to treat the wildlife with respect.

The best pools are closest to the sea, at the furthest corner from the carpark. The pools remain uncovered about two hours either side of low tide. If there is a large swell the outer pools will be affected by waves and are best avoided. Keep an eye on the sea conditions and leave as soon as the sea starts spilling back in. The lie of the land here allows the incoming tide to approach from the sides so be careful not to get cut off.

BEACHES

While the Loop Head Peninsula isn't famous for its beaches there are a few that are worth checking out.

- Doonaha *[52.6163, -9.6504]* is a pleasant sandy beach, good for swimming.
- College Strand *[52.5883, -9.7046]* is a quiet beach of sand and stone at low tide. Fishing and swimming on the northern end (southern end has oyster cages).
- At Rinevella *[52.5868, -9.7323]* there is a sand and shingle beach which is good for swimming. ∎

Looking east from Loop Head | RC

Sea Kayaking near Rinevella | RC

GUIDED WALKS
There are a number of local walking guides whose knowledge of the Loop Head area can add an extra dimension to a day's hiking. Carmel Madigan (www.carmelmadigangallery.com) offers walks that focus on the biodiversity of the region. The Long Way Round Walking Company (www.thelongwayround.ie) organises walks on a range of subjects from bird watching to local heritage. Ina Krieger (www.loophead.ie) leads walks for German speakers.

KAYAKING
The sea kayaking around the Loop Head Peninsula is among the best in Ireland, though it's not a place for the inexperienced. The northern coast of the peninsula is very exposed, with few safe landings, and the southern side - where the Shannon meets the sea - is prone to strong tides.

That said, there are options for good weather days that don't require a lifetime's worth of experience. On calm days the coast around and outside of Moore Bay (Kilkee) is worthy of exploration, see page 104. Kilbaha is another safe place to launch when the weather allows. Just west of the bay you can see the Reading Room, a small tower built on the cliff edge by a landlord's agent in the 19th century.

Rinevella is another good area to embark from. Just east of here the lighthouse and caves at Kilcredaun are best seen from sea level. Be aware of the strong tides in this area. The sea is squeezed in and out at this narrow gap between Clare and Kerry, creating fast currents. Carrigaholt is generally quite a sheltered place to kayak. There are great views of the 15th century tower house from the water and the small caves to the south are interesting.

CYCLING
Loop Head is best explored by bike. Unlike some of the more popular tourist areas along the coast there are no tour buses filling the roads and the peninsula is compact and flat enough that most areas can be seen in a long day trip. However it could be worth slowing down and allowing yourself more time to explore the stunning coastline in this quiet corner of West Clare.

Starting and ending in Kilkee the 65km Loop Head Cycleway brings you along the coast of the peninsula, off the busiest roads and within striking distance of some of the famous sights like Carrigaholt Castle, Loop Head Lighthouse and the Bridges of Ross. Bikes can be hired at Williams Hardware in Kilkee.

DOONBEG TO LAHINCH

The stretch of the Atlantic coast between Loop Head and Lahinch is renowned for its traditional music and expansive beaches. There's probably nowhere else in Ireland that attracts more surfers than Lahinch and likely no better town than Milltown Malbay for aspiring musicians. What could beat a visit to a pub with good tunes after a few hours of thrashing around in the sea or walking a long Atlantic strand?

BALTARD

The cliffs at Baltard are very tall, very steep and very impressive. They aren't signposted, but are worthy of an evening's exploration. Coming from Kilkee, pass through the village of Bealaha and take the left turn signposted 'White Strand B&B'. Go straight through the crossroads and turn left shortly after. Park at the end of the rough road *[52.7331, -9.6075]*. Take care at the cliffs and respect the signs regarding trespassing.

DOONBEG

A small village with an iconic ruined castle where the Doonbeg river meets the Atlantic. It is the trailhead for two signposted trails, the 8km Doonbeg Loop (green arrows) and the 17km Tullaher Loop (purple arrows). Just outside the village is a campsite (www.

strandcampingdoonbeg.com) with all the usual facilities in a pleasant location.

WHITE STRAND

The small Blue Flag beach lies to the northwest of the village. There is a lifeguard on duty on weekends in June and September and daily during July and August.

Coming into Doonbeg from the west look out for a left turn signposted 'White Strand B&B', take the turn and continue for 3km, turn right at the junction and follow the road down to the beach *[52.7477, -9.5508]*.

DOUGHMORE BAY

A classic west coast strand, open to the Atlantic and backed by sand dunes. A great place for a long evening walk. It is signposted to the left as you travel north from Doonbeg. The carpark *[52.7456, -9.5041]* is beside the golf course (see the photo on page 12).

QUILTY

The little village of Quilty is flanked to the north and west by beaches, all of which are best when the tide is out.

Spanish Point | RC

Surfing in Lahinch | RC

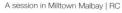

A session in Milltown Malbay | RC

In 1588 one of the Spanish Armada's ships sank near Lurga Point, while retreating from battle. The few survivors of the wreck who managed to get ashore were all hanged. Thankfully a walk on the beach in this day and age is less likely to get you in such trouble.

Southwest of Quilty is the Green Coast beach at Seafield. There are actually two beaches either side of the headland. The beach inside the quay *[52.8088, -9.4904]* is sheltered, while the other is west-facing and takes the brunt of the elements.

Further south is Carrowmore (signposted 'Carrowmore Point' off the main road) another open beach *[52.7745,-9.4827]*.

SPANISH POINT

Spanish Point is a popular Blue Flag beach *[52.8431, -9.4328]*, best at low tide when the sand is exposed. The White Water Surf Company (www. whitewatersurfco.com) offers rentals and lessons.

MILLTOWN MALBAY

Just inland from Spanish Point is the village of Milltown Malbay, renowned as one of the hubs of traditional Irish music in the country. Every July it is packed with the best musicians during the Willie Clancy week (www.scoilsamhraidhwillieclancy.com). Students of Irish music from all over the world come for workshops and to take part in sessions in the many excellent pubs. The sight and sound of up to

twenty musicians of all generations sawing fiddles and squeezing accordions to the same tunes is fairly special. Even when the festival isn't on there are few other towns in Ireland with better music.

TRAVAUN

This pleasant little bay *[52.8687, -9.4279]* offers safe swimming, kayak rental (www.clarekayakhire.com and www.clarewatersports.com) and has a campsite behind the beach for tents and mobile homes. It has a Blue Flag and is patrolled by lifeguards during the summer. As you travel north from Milltown it's signposted to the left as White Strand.

LAHINCH

During the summer Lahinch is a bustling town with cafés, pubs, shops and a hostel (www.lahinchhostel. ie). Known to local watersports enthusiasts as Surf City, the Blue Flag beach *[52.9348, -9.3488]* is ideal for board riders of all abilities. Walkers will be happy too, with 2km of golden sand to stretch the legs on. It's possible to swim at the beach, but there are rip tides and the water is often packed with surfers. There is a lifeguard during the summer.

There are at least six surf schools in Lahinch so there's no problem finding somewhere to hire gear or get lessons. Soul Kite (www.soulkite.ie) offers kite surfing, kite buggying and paddleboarding if you are looking for something a little different. ∎

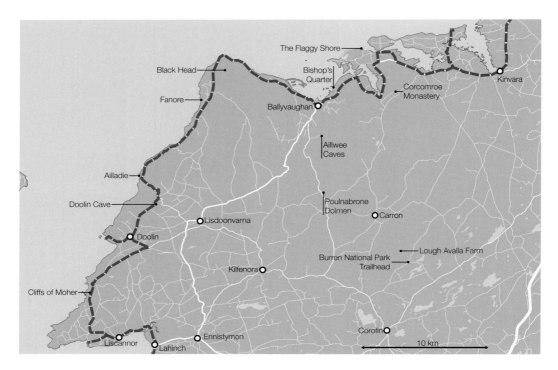

THE BURREN

The Burren is an area of exposed limestone covering the north of Clare. The unusual and fascinating landscape, known as Karst, was formed around 340 million years ago, when this part of the earth's crust was the bed of a shallow tropical sea.

The terraced hills of the Burren are composed of limestone pavements with intersecting cracks known as 'grikes', which leave isolated slabs of rock called 'clints'. The barren landscape was once described in rather morbid terms as *"a country where there is not enough water to drown a man, wood enough to hang one, nor earth enough to bury him"*.

A flying visit to the Burren cannot do it justice. There is a lifetime of learning and discovery to be had in this surprising, rocky land.

While obviously of great interest to geologists, the Burren landscape is also world famous for its botany. There is a curious mix of Arctic-Alpine and Mediterranean species, which rarely appear side by side. The summer meadows are a blanket of colour and even areas of extensive limestone pavement can be dotted with thousands of wildflowers growing from the cracks in the stone.

The archaeology of the Burren is also of great interest and there are monuments of all types from every age of the past 6,000 years. One of Ireland's most famous ancient structures, the Poulnabrone Dolmen, lies in the heart of the Burren but there is evidence of man's engagement with this landscape in every valley and on each hillside.

Though the Cliffs of Moher aren't of the same geological formation as the Burren, they are interesting enough and close enough to have been grouped together as the Burren and Cliffs of Moher Geopark. This international designation aims to promote sustainable tourism and livelihoods for those living in the region. See www.burrengeopark.ie for more information.

CLIFFS OF MOHER

The world famous Cliffs of Moher are Ireland's most popular natural attraction. Stretching for 8km and reaching up to 214m high, there are amazing views in all directions (see the photo on 98).

The visitor centre is located almost midway along these spectacular cliffs, set into the hillside *[52.9719, -9.4262]*. Nearby is the 19th century O'Brien's Tower and a stretch of protected cliff side path with viewing areas. Entry costs €6 per person and it can be very busy. Please be careful near the edge and obey the warning signs.

Looking towards O'Brien's Castle, Cliffs of Moher | Jennifer Boyer

Doolin sea cliffs | RC

The best way to experience this awesome stretch of coastline is on the Doolin to Liscannor coastal walk (see page 114).

AILEEN'S
A specific combination of wind and swell can combine to create a huge wave near the foot of the cliffs. As it's hidden from view and lost in the scale of its surroundings it was only discovered relatively recently by big wave surfers. The wave, known as Aileen's, can get up to ten metres high and attracts surfers from across the world.

Near the northern end of the cliffs there is a steep path that leads down to sea level. The steep descent is well worn by surfers who use it to access Aileen's. Seeing the cliffs from below is a humbling perspective, one that's only suitable for those comfortable with the adventurous descent.

DOOLIN
Though it can get busy during the summer, Doolin is an excellent base for exploring the Cliffs of Moher, the Burren and the Aran Islands. There is plenty of accommodation, including at least half a dozen hostels, and the pubs in the village are renowned for traditional music. A terrific place to wave watch when the winter storms pound the coast.

The pier at Doolin [53.0153, -9.4045] is used by ferry companies to take people to the Aran Islands and the Cliffs of Moher from March to October. Book well in advance during the summer, as things can get quite hectic at the pier. See www.doolinferry.com, www.doolinferries.com and www.doolin2aranferries.com for timetables.

CYCLING
The village is the hub for the four signposted routes of the North Clare Cycle network. With both coastal and inland routes, there is plenty to see, including Atlantic views, ancient portal tombs and picturesque villages.

• Loop 1 the shortest tour (18km), goes from Doolin south towards the Cliffs of Moher.
• Loop 2 (39km) passes through the villages of Liscannor, Lahinch and Ennistymon. A shorter 26km variation is also possible.
• Loop 3 (43km) heads inland towards Kilfenora passing by the Poulnabrone Dolmen.
• Loop 4 (47km) travels north from Doolin along the coast road with spectacular views of the Aran Islands. A shorter 21km variation is also possible.

Bikes are available to rent from Doolin (www.doolinrentabike.ie).

DOOLIN CAVE
A few kilometres north of the village is Doolin Cave, home to the largest known stalactite in the Northern

A surfer on Aileen's | RC

Dog Rose | RC

Scurvy Grass | RC

Blackthorn | RC

Bloody Crane's Bill | RC

A green road in the Caher Valley | RC

Hemisphere *[53.0411, -9.3449]*. The tour of the cave is well worth a go, especially on a wet day. There is a café and nature trail on the premises, and even a sunny day discount! Open daily from March to October.

DOOLIN TO LISCANNOR COASTAL WALK
This walk is arguably the best way to experience the Cliffs of Moher. At 18km it isn't short, but there aren't many more easily accessible, spectacular coastal hikes anywhere in Ireland.

The walks starts on the main road through Doolin and is marked with blue arrows. Walking southwest out of the village you soon leave the road and hug the coastline above increasingly tall cliffs. In wild weather the many small waterfalls that empty into the sea are blown back onto land. Before long the route meets the northern end of the massive Cliffs of Moher.

Continuing south, the cliffs rise and projecting stone slabs at the edges make for perfect natural viewing platforms. The famous O'Brien's Castle is soon reached and you can either stop at the visitor centre or rush through the crowds depending on your inclination. Most people miss out on the scenery south of here but there is no shortage of interest with sea arches, caves and huge bird colonies in the summer months. Gradually losing height, you eventually arrive at Hag's Head before turning east towards the small village of Liscannor.

THE DOLMEN CYCLEWAY
Starting and finishing in Lisdoonvarna this signposted 45km loop takes in many of the interesting inland sights including the steep hairpins of Corkscrew Hill.

FANORE
The main beach along the Burren coastline has beautiful rich sand and hilly dunes behind it *[53.1173, -9.2872]*. It has a Blue Flag and there are lifeguards on duty during the summer. The Aloha Surf School (www. surfschool.tv) offers surf and kayak lessons during the summer months.

WALKING TRAILS
The Black Head Loop is a tough 26km loop (purple arrows) but it's a great way to experience the bizarre landscape of the Burren up close. There are great views over the ocean from Black Head, as well as inland to the green valleys and flat topped rocky peaks. The shorter loop, back through the Caher valley, is about 14.5km (red arrows). Both loops start and finish in the carpark at Fanore beach *[53.1173, -9.2872]*.

BALLYVAUGHAN
This small harbour village lies on the sheltered southern shore of Galway Bay.

Typical Burren landscape at Oughtdarra | RC

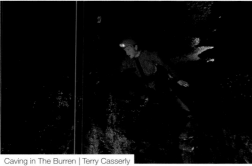
Caving in The Burren | Terry Casserly

Fertile rock | RC

BALLYVAUGHAN WOOD LOOP
This 8km loop follows quiet roadways and green lanes through the countryside behind the seaside village of Ballyvaughan. There are splendid views of the distinctive folded limestone layers of the surrounding hills. It's not that well signposted so keep your eyes peeled for the purple arrows.

BURREN FOOD & WINE
A few kilometres south of Ballyvaughan at the foot of Corkscrew Hill is this seasonal café [53.0903, -9.1733]. Situated in a renovated stone stablehouse they serve homemade, local, seasonal lunches and afternoon teas. They also offer cycling tours. Check www.burrenwine.ie before visiting to confirm it will be open.

BISHOP'S QUARTER
A pleasant stretch of strand about 2km north of Ballyvaughan [53.1295, -9.1287]. Look out for the signposted left turn.

THE FLAGGY SHORE
At first glance the Flaggy Shore might seem an unspectacular length of coastline, but the interest here is in the finer details. This region is like a natural outdoor geology classroom. There are fossils in the rocks, left over from when this area was the bed of a tropical sea. There are signs of more recent

Poulnabrone Dolmen | Nicolas Raymond

(in geological terms at least) activity too - there are granite boulders that were dragged here from Connemara by glaciers, and the marks from that slow grinding process can still be seen on the ground. The area is best accessed from the small beach between New Quay and Finavarra Point [53.1570, -9.0864].

CORCOMROE MONASTERY

Close to Ballyvaughan is the ruin of the 13th century Corcomroe Monastery. It is noted for its unusual ornamentation and carvings. There is a legend that the king who ordered the construction executed the five masons once it was completed, to ensure no similar structure could be built for any rivals. It is signposted off the Wild Atlantic Way at Bell Harbour [53.1265, -9.0543].

KINVARA

Just across the Clare/Galway border is the attractive seaside village of Kinvara. There are shops and pubs and a few other places nearby that are well worth a visit. A little north of the village is the Blue Flag beach at Traught, which is safe for swimming and has lifeguards in the summer [53.1721, -8.9851].

The famous landmark on the northern end of the village is the 16th century Dunguaire Castle [53.1421, -8.9260]. It is open to visitors from April to October and hosts medieval banquets in the evenings - see www.shannonheritage.com for information.

A short journey from the village is the Burren Nature Sanctuary, an interpretive centre for the Burren's unique landscape and flora [53.1292, -8.9301]. It is great for young families and also has a café (www. bns.ie).

AILLWEE CAVES

During the guided tour through the caverns [53.0904, -9.1464] you will cross over bridged chasms, under weird formations, and alongside the thunderous waterfall (www.aillweecave.ie). There is also a Bird of Prey centre which offers flying displays of birds including eagles, falcons, hawks, and owls. From Ballyvaughan head south along the N67, after 1.5km turn left onto the R480. You will see a signposted turn left after another 1.5km.

AN RATH FAIRY FORT

Close to the turn for the caves is Ballyallaban Ring Fort [53.0900, -9.1585]. This fort consists of an earth wall and deep trench. It is in good repair and is in a very pretty setting surrounded by beech trees.

POULNABRONE DOLMEN

This ancient portal tomb is one of the most famous landmarks of Ireland, and attracts a few hundred thousand visitors each year [53.0487, -9.1401]. When the tomb, which was built almost 6,000 years ago,

The trail at Lough Avalla | Conor Lawless

was excavated in 1986 the bodies of 16 adults and 6 children were found buried inside.

It is located just off the R480 between Killnaboy and Ballyvaughan. From Ballyvaughan head south along the N67, after 1.5km turn left onto the R480. After 7.5km you will see a parking area on the left. The dolmen is just a short walk from the carpark.

CARRON TRAILS

The small village of Carron is the trailhead for two nice walks [53.0352, -9.0767]. The longer one, the 9km Carron Loop (purple arrows), follows minor roads, animal tracks and grassy lanes, taking in the Clab Valley, Saint Fachtnan's Holy Well and part of Termon Hill. It traverses fields of stone slab and passes a 'turlough' (an area which floods in winter but is dry in summer).

A shorter route, the 5km Templecronan Loop (green arrows), visits Termon Cross and Teampall Chrónáin to the north of the village. Both walks start opposite Cassidy's Pub [53.0353, -9.0768].

Just down the road is Clare's Rock Hostel (www.claresrock.com).

LOUGH AVALLA FARM LOOP

This walk is a must do for anybody looking to stretch their legs in the Burren's magical landscape. It passes through both woodland and farmland and offers great views of Mullaghmore, the National Park's signature hill.

The walk is very well signposted and local hazelwood was used to make the beautiful gates and stiles along the way. It starts and finishes at Mullaghmore Crossroads as for the National Park trails [52.9966, -9.0376]. Walk up to the crossroads and turn left to start the walk following the purple markers.

After your walk you should call into the Lough Avalla Tea Room, a delightful café run by the family who owns the farm. The homemade cakes and hot drinks will be well deserved after the walk (www.fb.com/loughavallatearoom). On the east side of the lake is a jetty. Follow the wide track beside it for a short distance to reach the café [53.0045, -9.0457].

BURREN NATIONAL PARK

Though the Wild Atlantic Way hugs the coast, it's worth deviating inland to the Burren National Park. The roads are narrow and winding but it's a captivating place to explore.

The trailhead for the Park's seven signposted trails around Mullaghmore is on the southeastern side of the Burren. From Corofin head north along the R476. Turn right in Killnaboy (signposted 'Kilnaboy Church & School') and follow the road for 5km. Just before the crossroads is a lay-by on the right [52.9966, -9.0376]. Park in the lay-by, not on the crag road, to avoid

Mullaghmore in winter | RC

Rock climbing at Ailladie | RC

damage to the vegetation. The following walks start from the crossroads:

- Nature Trail (green arrows) 1.5km
- Knockaunroe Turlough (orange markers) 1.3km
- Mullaghmore Return (green markers) 6.5km
- Mullaghmore Loop (blue markers) 7.5km
- Mullaghmore Traverse (red markers) 6km

You can download a trail map from www. burrennationalpark.ie. There are guided walks during the summer months, see the website for details.

NATIONAL PARK INFORMATION POINT
This information point is on the ground floor of the Clare Heritage Centre on Church Street in Corofin [52.9448, -9.0626]. It is open to the public from April until the end of September, providing information on the flora and fauna of the National Park. From May to August a free shuttle bus takes people to various points in the park.

COROFIN CAMPING AND HOSTEL
If you're looking to camp close to the Burren's interior look no further than this campsite and hostel [52.9454, -9.0653]. It's centrally located, making it a great base from which to explore this part of Clare. Open from April to September. See www. corofincamping.com for details. ∎

Mountain biking near Black Head | RC

WALKING

There is such a wealth of interest in the Burren that a knowledgeable walking guide can significantly enhance your experience. The following offer guided walks in the area - www.heartofburrenwalks. com, www.burrenguidedwalks.com.

ROCK CLIMBING

The sea cliffs and inland crags of the Burren are very popular with rock climbers. Ailladie, on the coast road north of Doolin, is one of the best climbing areas in Ireland. See www.burrenoec.com or www.lahinchadventures.com if you are interested in giving it a go.

CAVING

The Burren landscape is a hollow one. As limestone is a relatively soft rock it is constantly being eroded by rivers and rain at a much faster rate than other types of stone. Most of this water finds its way underground where it gouges out incredible subterranean caves and caverns.

There are a few famous caves in the Burren that are established tourist attractions (Aillwee and Doolin) but if you want a real caving experience you can book a few hours with Backwest Adventures

(www.fb.com/backwestadventures). Their trips are an excellent introduction to a pastime that is usually reserved for a select few experts. The outings are tailored to your personal ability so there is a challenge available for everybody.

SEA KAYAKING

Sea kayaking is a great way to get a different perspective of the coast. North Clare Sea Kayaking (www.northclareseakayaking.com) offer guided tours of this world famous stretch of the Wild Atlantic Way. There are plenty of options to make the most of the given weather, from the sheltered bays around Ballyvaughan to the tall cliffs further south. If you're lucky you might even see dolphins, seals and seabirds.

MOUNTAIN BIKING

Mountain biking is an interesting alternative to walking, and as well as being great fun it allows you to cover a lot of ground. Many of the trails in the area are ideal for bikes.

Burren Way Mountain Bike Tours offer a variety of guided tours along the Burren's scenic green roads and lanes. See www.burrenwaymountainbiketours. com for details.

Rossadillisk | Anne Phillips

GALWAY

The vast majority of the coastline of County Galway lies within Connemara, which due to a lack of an official definition, has boundaries that are a little unclear. Everyone agrees on the northern border, Killary Harbour, and the Atlantic defines it in the south and west. The uncertainty relates to the eastern edge - some say it stretches to the edge of Galway City while others draw a line from Killary Harbour to Kilkieran Bay. Either way, Connemara is one of the most popular tourist areas in Ireland.

Compared to the most rugged parts of Ireland's Atlantic coast Galway's coastline is reasonably low-lying, and as a result the area between land and sea is easily accessed. This coupled with the extremely jagged, indented nature of the coastline means that it is home to a massive number of tiny bays, rocky coves and sandy beaches.

Galway City, the only city that the Wild Atlantic Way passes through, is a vibrant, youthful place. With a bustling nightlife and plenty of the pubs and restaurants it's the ideal place to spend some time before heading back into the wild.

It's worth noting that from a geological point of view The Aran Islands have much more in common with the rocky landscape of the Burren in Country Clare, but they are part of County Galway. They are the strongholds of island life in Ireland, still relatively well populated after most other offshore communities have dwindled. Their combination of sea-locked isolation and lunar landscape is enough to keep attracting tourists for many years to come.

The predominantly flat terrain near the coast, particularly south of Clifden, is ideal for cycling and there is a network of many hundreds of kilometres of small, very quiet roads, known as boreens, to explore.

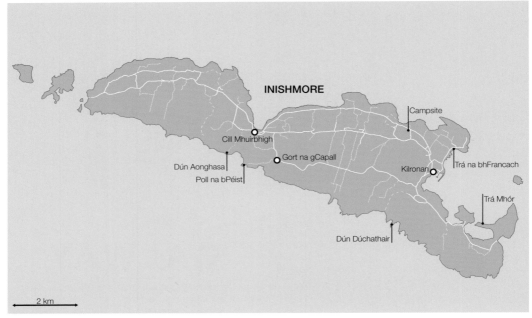

INISHMORE

Campsite

Cill Mhuirbhigh

Gort na gCapall

Dún Aonghasa

Poll na bPéist

Kilronan

Trá na bhFrancach

Trá Mhór

Dún Dúchathair

2 km

ARAN ISLANDS

The three Aran Islands (Oileáin Árann) are Inishmore (Árainn), Inishmaan (Inis Meáin) and Inisheer (Inis Oírr). While each of the islands has its own distinct character, they all share a rugged karst landscape and an intense sense of culture and place. A visit is a chance to experience the distilled essence of Ireland's west coast.

During the summer the islands, particularly Inishmore, can get busy, but it's always possible to escape the crowds. The rest of the year is much quieter and the islands are an amazing place to be during a winter storm. The only way to properly experience them is to stay overnight. Even on the two smaller islands there is too much to see in a day and you will miss out on that essential Irish cultural experience - a night in the pub.

Like many of the other islands off Ireland's west coast, the Irish language is still predominant on the Aran Islands. You will hear plenty of Irish spoken in the shops and pubs.

The islands are very exposed to the prevailing wind and there is little shelter so it can feel raw, but the clouds often pass over the islands before releasing their payload on the mainland so they are relatively dry.

With very little in the way of trees or vegetation they are a barren and sometimes bleak, but very beautiful place. One of the most distinctive visual features of the islands are the stone walls. Approximately 1600km

of hand-built dry-stone walls divide the arable land into thousands of tiny plots.

There are three ways to reach the islands. Either fly (see page 131 for more information) or take the ferry (www.aranislandferries.com) from Rossaveel (see page 131) in County Galway. The other option, between March and October, is the shorter ferry crossing from Doolin in County Clare (see page 112).

INISHMORE

The largest and most popular of the Aran Islands. Inishmore is basically a huge slab of limestone that rises gradually from north to south, terminating at the huge cliffs (up to 100m in height) that run without interruption along the full length of the south coast. During the summer months it is a lively place where the busy pubs serve late into the night.

Cartographer Tim Robinson's map of the island is a must-have for anyone who wants to spend time exploring the island. The beautiful hand-drawn black and white map depicts every nook and cranny and is full of place-names and points of archaeological and historical interest (www.foldinglandscapes.com).

There are a number of B+Bs, hotels, and a hostel (www.kilronanhostel.com) in the main village, Kilronan. There is also a small supermarket, an ATM, a few restaurants, a café and plenty of pubs. A short distance west of the village is another hostel, Mainistir

Dún Aonghasa | Christopher Brown

House (www.aranislandshostel.com) and a basic campsite [53.1312, -9.6796].

CYCLING

The most popular mode of transport on the island is cycling. There isn't much traffic and barring a few short steep hills, the roads are pretty flat so it's a great way to get around. As you arrive off the ferry you will be met by representatives from the various bike hire companies. Their prices are all similar but it's worth haggling.

It is possible to take in most of the island's sights in one long 26km loop. From Kilronan follow the Cill Mhuirbhigh walking trail, passing through Gort na gCapall before diverting to visit Dún Aonghasa. Then head west along the main road to the end of the island before following the quiet coast road back to Cill Mhuirbhigh beach. From the beach return to Kilronan along the second half of the Cill Mhuirbhigh loop.

WALKING TRAILS

There are three signposted trails that start and finish in Kilronan. As they all follow small roads and lanes they are also suitable for bikes.

The 16km Cill Mhuirbhigh (purple arrows) loop follows wonderfully quiet roads and lanes through Gort na gCapall before turning east at the Blue Flag beach at Cill Mhuirbhigh and returning along the northern coast. This is a great way to get to Poll na bPéist or Dún Aonghasa as it avoids the (relatively) busy main road.

The two other routes, An Chorrúch 12km (blue arrows) and Dún Eochla 10km (green arrows) are shorter variations of the Cill Mhuirbhigh loop. They share the same start and finish but cut across the island earlier.

BEACHES

There is a beautiful Blue Flag beach at Cill Mhuirbhigh [53.1307, -9.7498] just off the main road between Kilronan and Dún Aonghasa. The cove is very sheltered and it's one of the few beaches on the island without dangerous currents. There is a lifeguard on duty at weekends in June and September, and every day in July and August.

Just east of the airport is Trá Mhór, a long, secluded sandy beach [53.1040, -9.6409]. Behind the beach is a massive lagoon that is covered by the tide daily. If you decide to swim remember that there is no lifeguard and watch out for jellyfish and strong currents. Follow the road east past the airport to the end of the island and then head north to reach the beach.

Trá na bhFrancach is a small roadside beach just north of Kilronan [53.1259, -9.6599].

Poll na bPéist | Nicole Johnson

DÚN AONGHASA

The spectacular Iron Age cliff top fort [53.1249, -9.7661] is the most popular sight on the island and day visitors usually make a beeline straight for it. The fort is enclosed by three massive dry-stone walls and a 'cheval de frise' (tall slivers of limestone set vertically into the ground to deter attackers). Perched precariously at the edge of a long line of 100m tall cliffs, its setting is impressive to say the least.

Mystery surrounds the fort's origins. It's not clear who built it or why. Its elevated position suggests that it may have been built for ceremonial rather than military or tactical purposes. One possibility is that it was used by druids for seasonal rites involving bonfires.

To get there either take a mini-bus from Kilronan or cycle. There is a small admission charge and be warned that the path from the visitor centre and café to the fort is quite steep and rocky, but short enough.

It's a sheer drop from the cliff edge to the Atlantic and there is no guardrail so be very careful, especially when it's windy. It can get very busy on summer days so try and visit early in the morning or late in the evening when the day trippers have left.

POLL NA BPÉIST

At the foot of the cliffs east of Dún Aonghasa the sea has cut a perfectly rectangular section of rock from the flat limestone terrace to leave an ideal swimming pool shaped hole [53.1216, -9.7547]. Its name translates as the Serpent's Hole and it's often referred to as the Wormhole.

This remarkable piece of natural architecture has twice hosted a cliff diving competition in which the divers plunged 27m into the deep water of the Poll.

Once a little visited sight, the diving competition raised its profile and it's now quite popular. You must be extremely careful as people have been washed into the water by rogue waves that, even on seemingly calm days, can sweep up the angled terraces without warning.

It's a tricky walk over rough and often slippery ground and the route is a little indistinct but it's well worth the effort. Either follow the Cill Mhuirbhigh loop, or take the main road west (turn left just before Cill Mhuirbhigh beach) to the village of Gort na gCapall. At the junction beside the shrine [53.1231, -9.7409] take the road south and look for a narrow path on the right that runs between the stone walls. Follow this path, which is marked intermittently with red arrows, down to the coast and walk west along the shore until the Poll appears.

DÚN DÚCHATHAIR

The Black Fort [53.1043, -9.6871] is more remote and much quieter than the world famous Dún Aonghasa, but no less spectacular. A high terraced wall cuts across the narrow headland which is surrounded by

Dún Aonghasa | Marcus Murphy

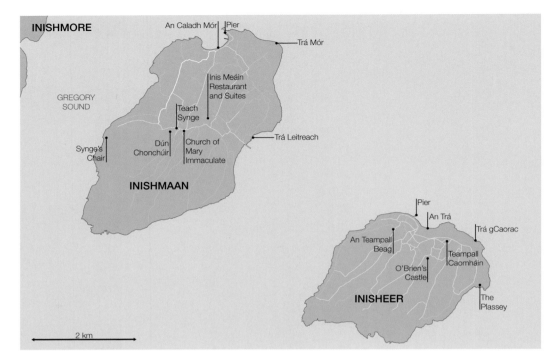

INISHMORE

An Caladh Mór — Pier
— Trá Mór
Inis Meáin Restaurant and Suites
GREGORY SOUND
Teach Synge
— Trá Leitreach
Synge's Chair
Dún Chonchúir
Church of Mary Immaculate

INISHMAAN

Pier
An Trá
— Trá gCaorac
An Teampall Beag
Teampall Caomháin
O'Brien's Castle
INISHEER
The Plassey

2 km

water and tall cliffs on three sides. When the fort was built in the Iron Age it may have been much larger but erosion of the cliff edge has left only a portion of the wall intact.

Follow the main road east out of Kilronan and past the beach. You'll see a road that climbs steeply up the hillside to the right (the turn is just past the small lake on the right). Turn right and follow this road, which fades to a rough track, up the hill. At the end of the track head directly to the coast and walk left along the top of the cliffs to the fort. Enter the fort through a small opening on the left hand side of the wall (it's close to the cliff edge so be very careful).

INISHMAAN

Inis Meáin, the middle island, is by far the quietest and least developed of the three islands. Depending on your outlook this can be either a good or a bad thing. And even though there is only one shop, one pub and limited accommodation, it is a great place to get away from it all.

The island is home to a small, close-knit Irish-speaking community. The best way to explore it is by walking. It's possible to circumnavigate the island on foot in a day.

The northern half of the island is low-lying and fertile, with a few sandy beaches. As the land rises to the south in a series of terraces, the ground becomes rockier and limestone pavements dominate,

culminating in the dramatic cliffs and storm beaches of the southern coastline.

INIS MEÁIN RESTAURANT AND SUITES
A beautiful stone-clad building which blends so well with its surrounding that it's almost invisible [53.0866, -9.5844]. The restaurant sources as many ingredients as possible from the island and the water surrounding it. Each of the five large luxurious suites have expansive windows and panoramic views across the island (www.inismeain.com).

TEACH SYNGE
Irish playwright J.M. Synge spent each summer from 1898 to 1902 on the island and drew a lot of inspiration from the island's culture. The beautiful thatched cottage [53.0845, -9.5923] where the playwright stayed during his time on the island, has been restored as closely as possible to the way it was then. The small museum, which has books, photographs and letters on display, is open during the summer months.

SYNGE'S CHAIR
Perched on top of the cliffs on the west coast is a low semi-circular stone wall that offers a sheltered spot to look across Gregory's Sound towards Inishmore and watch the waves [53.0820, -9.6136]. A favourite spot

Teach Synge | Chris Brooks

Harry Clarke stained glass window | Dave Mention

The west coast of Inishmaan | RC

of the playwright, it's a short walk from the end of the road on the western side of the island.

DÚN CHONCHÚIR
This large oval ring fort [53.0834, -9.5947] dates back to the first century AD. The fort is impressive and well worth a visit. It's one of the highest points on the island and has panoramic views in all directions.

WALKING TRAILS
There are three signposted trails on the island, all of which start from the pier. The 10km Cill Cheannannach loop (blue arrows) follows the northern coast around the island before returning along the main east-west road, taking in the tiny 8th century church of Cill Cheannannach, Synge's Chair, Dún Chonchúir and Dún Fearbhai.

The Dún Fearbhai loop (purple arrows) extends the previous route adding an extra 3km section that crosses the high ground in the southwestern corner of the island.

The best option if you are short on time is the 8km Dún Chonchúir (green arrows) loop. It sticks to the west of the island but passes close by Dún Chonchúir and Synge's Chair.

CHURCH OF MARY IMMACULATE
The island's church [53.0839, -9.5909] was built in 1939 using stone from the ruins of the much older church opposite it. If you are passing it's well worth popping in to see the beautiful Harry Clarke stained glass windows.

BEACHES
There are three beaches on the northern half of the island.

- An Caladh Mór is the sheltered rocky strand beside the pier [53.1007, -9.5774].
- North of the runway is the 1.5km long Trá Mór. The wide open sandy expanse is a great place for a walk on a stormy day [53.0992, -9.5638].
- Trá Leitreach is beside the old pier on the eastern coast and is quite sheltered from the prevailing wind [53.0829, -9.5693].

INISHEER
The smallest of the three islands, it's a mere 3km by 3km. It's only a short crossing from Doolin, hence Inisheer is a good choice for those short on time. However there is plenty to see, including lots of archaeological features with many examples of its Bronze Age, Pagan, Celtic, Early Christian, and Norman-Irish history.

There are a number of B+Bs, a hostel (www.bruhostelaran.com), a hotel and a campsite. For the latest information on events and accommodation on the island visit www.discoverinisoirr.com.

The Plassey | Carolyn Jordan

Áras Éanna, the island's Arts and Heritage Centre is housed in the renovated weaving factory *[53.0646, -9.5310]*. The centre, which contains a theatre/cinema, two galleries and a café, hosts weaving, basket making and quilting workshops (www.araseanna.ie).

THE PLASSEY
In 1960 the cargo vessel M.V. Plassey was caught in a bad storm and ran aground on the rocks off the island's coast. A group of islanders rescued the entire crew using a breeches buoy (a crude rescue device similar to a zip-line). You can see photos from the rescue on the walls of Tigh Ned's pub. The iconic wreck now lies above the high tide mark at the eastern end of the island *[53.0557, -9.5037]*.

TEAMPALL CAOMHÁIN
The ruins of Teampall Caomháin (Saint Kevin's Church) lie sunk deeply into the sandy hill opposite the runway *[53.0639, -9.5140]*. Caomháin is the patron saint of the island and the church dates back to the 10th century. It is cleared of wind-blown sand annually by the locals.

AN TEAMPALL BEAG
A tiny ruined church *[53.0659, -9.5292]*, known as Cill Ghobnait (Saint Gobnait's Church) or Teampall Beag (small church). It dates from the 10th century and is dedicated to Saint Gobnait. Nearby are the remains of three outdoor altars, two bullaun stones (Neolithic stone bowls), and a clochán (a dry-stone hut).

O'BRIEN'S CASTLE
There are great views from this 15th century church which occupies the island's highest point *[53.0608, -9.5198]*. There is also an 18th century signal tower.

WALKING
There are two signposted trails on the island. The first, Ceathrú an Locha (green arrows), loops around the eastern end of the island passing An Loch Mór and the Plassey wreck. The second, the 13km Ceathrú an Phoillín (purple arrows), is an extension of the first, adding an extra circuit around the west coast.

Another option is to walk the coastline of the island, a 10km circuit. Much of the southern shoreline is trackless, remote and quite rough, but enjoys beautiful views over to the Cliffs of Moher. If you are tight on time you can hire a bike at the pier.

BEACHES
There are two Green Coast beaches on the island. Beside the pier is An Trá, a wonderful, sheltered beach with white sand and clear turquoise water *[53.0659, -9.5198]*. The other is the smaller, quieter, Trá gCaorach, just east of the runway *[53.0636, -9.5058]*. ⬚

Inisheer beach and O'Brien's Castle | Terry Ballard

Curraghs on the Main Beach | Denis Dineen

An Teampall Beag | Allie Couture

The iconic stone walls | Richard O'Beirne

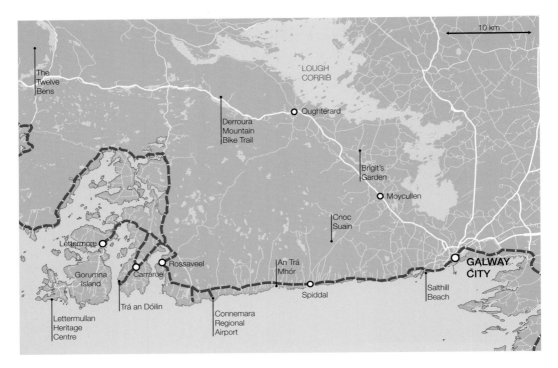

SOUTH GALWAY

This section incorporates Galway City and South Connemara. Connemara is the largest Gaeltacht (Irish-speaking area) in Ireland and the Irish language, music and culture play a big part in everyday life. You will hear locals and visitors speaking Irish as they go about their daily business. During the summer many Irish schoolchildren spend a few weeks learning their native tongue in the Irish colleges.

The Gaeltacht area can be divided into two distinctive parts. The stretch of coast west of Galway City that passes through the villages of Barna, Spiddal, Inveran and Rossaveel is known as Cois Fharraige (which means 'seaside'). And the collection of small islands and bays further west is called Ceantar na nOileán (which means 'islands district').

There is a strong boating tradition in Connemara and the traditional sail boats, known as Galway Hookers, are famous across the world. Hookers, with their tarred black hulls and their iconic red sails, were originally designed as fishing craft, but they were mostly used as cargo boats, carrying turf and seaweed between Galway and Clare. Nowadays, many of them compete in keenly contested regattas during the summer.

SALTHILL BEACH

The seaside resort on the edge of Galway City has a nice, but busy Blue Flag beach *[53.2566, -9.0923]*. At the western end of the promenade is Blackrock Baths *[53.2566, -9.0923]*, a great spot for a swim with diving boards, steps into the water and changing facilities.

Nearby Rusheen Bay is a great place for windsurfing and kayaking *[53.2585, -9.1196]*. The bay is semi-enclosed making it ideal for beginners. There is a school there which rents equipment www. rusheenbay.com.

CNOC SUAIN

This 17th century homestead in the bog north of the village of Spiddal runs short sessions on Irish culture, nature and heritage *[53.2893, -9.2645]*. The beautifully restored stone cottages are available for rent (www. cnocsuain.com). Find them 6km north of Spiddal along the Moycullen road (L1320).

AN TRÁ MHÓR

A long sheltered Blue Flag beach with clear water and great views across Galway Bay to the Burren *[53.2426, -9.3582]*. The sand slopes gradually into the water so it's a great place to swim. There is a lifeguard at weekends in June and September and daily during

Cnoc Suain | Todd Parker

July and August. Look out for the signposted left turn 3.5km west of Spiddal.

ROSSAVEEL
While there isn't much to see in Rossaveel itself, it is an important transport hub for the Aran Islands (see page 122). The ferry leaves from the busy fishing port [53.2659, -9.5600] and makes regular sailings to all three islands. Consult www.aranislandferries.com for timetables and fares.

Aer Arann (www.aerarannislands.ie) flies from Connemara Regional Airport [53.2316, -9.4695] near Inveran to all three islands. On a clear day the eight minute flight offers a spectacular view of the islands and isn't significantly more expensive than the ferry. As well as flying direct to the islands they also offer scenic flights that take in the Burren, the Cliffs of Moher, and Dún Aonghasa on Inishmore.

CARRAROE
The village of An Cheathrú Rua (Carraroe) lies in the heart of the Connemara Gaeltacht. Every year on the first weekend in August it hosts the maritime festival, Féile an Dóilín. Celebrating the region's rich maritime history, the festival revolves around the ancient and beautiful Galway Hooker boat, with races, parades, lectures on maritime history and boat-making exhibitions.

TRÁ AN DÓILIN
This Blue Flag beach, also known as Coral Beach, is noted for its sand that consists of very fine coral [53.2477, -9.6289]. It's usually quieter than the beaches closer to Galway City. There are plenty of small rock pools to explore and some good snorkelling. The water is patrolled by lifeguards at weekends in June and September and daily during July and August.

CARRAROE WALK
An 8km loop on small roads with one short stretch of rocky coastline. Park in the village and follow the main road southwest, after 3km you will arrive at Trá an Dóilin. Continue north along the coast over rough ground. Shortly after passing a small promontory you will meet a small sandy beach and carpark. Follow the narrow road back to the village, passing the football pitches.

CEANTAR NA NOILEÁN
The archipelago of islands at the western end of Galway Bay is one of the quietest parts of Connemara and is characterised by drystone walls and a patchwork of small rocky fields.

The five largest islands are linked by bridges and causeways. The Wild Atlantic Way only goes as far as the bridge that leads from Lettermore and Gorumna

A Galway Hooker | Dónal Ó Cearbhaill

Islands but it's well worth continuing further on to discover more of this hidden gem.

There are numerous small sandy beaches on the islands, particularly on the western shore of Gorumna and the southern shore of Lettermore.

LETTERMULLAN HERITAGE CENTRE
The private collection of local historian John Bhaba Jeaic Ó'Confhaola is displayed in a small cottage on Lettermullan Island [53.2329, -9.7372]. The collection, which includes old books, tools, instruments and photographs, gives a great insight into life as it once was. See www.ionadoidhreachta.com for more details.

WALKING
The islands are covered in a network of narrow roads and boreens, many of which lead down to hidden bays and beaches. Perfect for leisurely cycling and walking, Ceantar na nOileán Teo have details of six walking routes on their website www.cnnoilean.ie.

SEA KAYAKING
The maze of tiny deserted islands, sheltered bays and sandy beaches is ideal for exploration by sea kayak. Shearwater Sea Kayaking (www.shearwaterseakayaking.ie) offer kayaking instruction and guided tours, ranging from short evening paddles to multi-day camping trips.

INLAND
While the Wild Atlantic Way sticks close to the coast, the main road from Galway City to Clifden, the N59, runs much further inland, along the foot of the Twelve Bens and Maumturk Mountains. There are a few interesting places that are well worth checking out if you are travelling that way.

LOUGH CORRIB
Lough Corrib, the second largest lake on the island of Ireland, divides the mountains and bogs of Connemara from the fertile grasslands of Mayo.

Internationally renowned for its salmon and brown trout fishing, anglers travel from across the world to fish the lake. Nonaim Lodge (www.fishingcorrib.com) near Oughterard offers accommodation and guided fishing trips if you want to try your luck.

The lake is connected to the Atlantic by the Corrib River which flows through the centre of Galway City. Give it a Go (www.giveitago.ie) run kayaking trips up the River Corrib from the heart of the city.

THE TWELVE BENS
The Twelve Bens mountain range, which dominates the skyline of southern Connemara, is home to the Glencoaghan Horseshoe, one of the great Irish mountain walks. The route takes in six of the range's twelve summits, and while it's not that long (about

Swimming at Salthill | Christopher Tierney

The Twelve Bens | Tom Fahy

Brigit's Garden | DF

16km) it's a very tough walk with plenty of height gain and steep ground.

As the Bens are regularly shrouded in cloud, which can descend without warning, the ability to navigate with a map (Harvey Connemara 1:30,000 is best) and compass is essential. For full details of the walk see www.mountainviews.ie/walk/107/.

BRIGIT'S GARDEN
Enchanting gardens set on eleven acres of native woodland and wildflower meadows. As well as the gardens there is a nature trail, an ancient ring fort, thatched roundhouse, crannóg, a calendar sundial, playground, café and gift shop [53.3855, -9.2131]. It's not far off the N59 between Moycullen and Oughterard, look out for the signs (www.brigitsgarden.ie).

DERROURA MOUNTAIN BIKE TRAIL
Just over 7km west along the N59 from the town of Oughterard is Derroura Mountain Bike Trail [53.4409, -9.45050]. This purpose-built 16km trail has steep climbs and tricky descents, as well as great views over the Maam Valley and Lough Corrib. See www.irishtrails.ie for a map of the route. Moycullen Bike Works (www.mbikeworks.com) offer an excellent range of mountain bikes for hire [53.3457, -9.1730]. ⬚

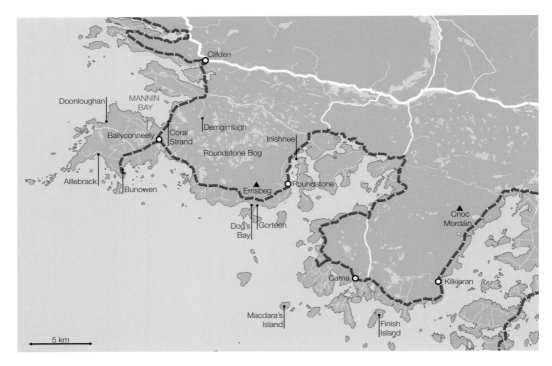

Map labels:
Clifden · MANNIN BAY · Doonloughan · Ballyconneely · Coral Strand · Derrigimlagh · Inishnee · Roundstone Bog · Aillebrack · Bunowen · Errisbeg · Roundstone · Cnoc Mordáin · Dog's Bay · Gorteen · Carna · Kilkieran · Macdara's Island · Finish Island

5 km

MID CONNEMARA

As the Wild Atlantic Way follows the rocky low-lying coastline north it leaves the shelter of Galway Bay and is exposed to the full force of the Atlantic. This extremely indented coast is a maze of bays, small islands and coves.

The villages of Carna, Roundstone and Ballyconneely and their surrounds are very popular with holidaymakers. The better-known beaches in the area can get busy on sunny summer days, but as always in Ireland there are many other beaches that you can have all to yourself.

CNOC MORDÁIN

The rocky summit of Cnoc Mordáin (353m) offers great views up and down the coast and inland to the Twelve Bens. The mountain's long, distinctive ridges of granite, known as roche moutonnée, were formed by the movement of a glacier in the last ice age.

Just over 4km north (towards Galway City) along the Wild Atlantic Way from Kilkieran village is a left turn [53.3542, -9.7048] marked by a sign for 'Hillside House B&B'. Drive up this narrow road, park at the gate and continue up the track on foot. When, after 1.5km, a forest appears on the left, leave the track and head north up the broad ridge. Cross a subsidiary peak [53.3675, -9.7290], descend in a northeasterly

direction into a saddle and then steeply up to the summit [53.3775,-9.7077]. To return to the car retrace your steps. It's a 10km round trip.

FINISH ISLAND

At low tide it's possible to walk across the sand to the small, uninhabited island of Finish [53.2996, -9.8029]. A few kilometres west of Kilkieran, turn south off the Wild Atlantic Way and follow a narrow road down to a small pier [53.3035, -9.7896]. Cross the sand (check the tide and don't get stranded) and follow the rough track to the far end of the island (7km round trip).

MACDARA'S ISLAND

Every year on the 16th of July hundreds of local people travel on boats to Macdara's Island where mass is celebrated at the oratory in honour of Macdara, the area's patron saint of fishermen and sailors. It may be possible to hitch a ride over to the island and take part in this ancient tradition.

The tiny, one room oratory, which was restored in 1975, is considered one of the finest early Christian oratories in Ireland.

Macdara's Oratory | Ronan Browne

INISHNEE WALK

The small, quiet island of Inishnee is connected to the mainland by a bridge 2km north of Roundstone. A pleasant 6km signposted walk follows the island's narrow roads and laneways (see the photo on page 16) in a loop starting from the bridge *[53.4144, -9.9082]*.

ROUNDSTONE

The small fishing village of Roundstone is a popular stop-off for tourists and has plenty of good pubs and restaurants as well as a spectacular view across Cashel Bay to the Twelve Bens.

ERRISBEG

The rounded, lumpy profile of Errisbeg rises up behind Roundstone village. Even though modest in height, at only 300m, there are amazing views in every direction from its summit. The hill is covered in rocky outcrops, the ground can be boggy and there isn't a well-defined path so the walk is only suitable for well equipped, experienced hikers.

The easiest route (3km round trip) starts from the high point of the Ballyconneely to Roundstone road *[53.3913, -9.9786]*. Park at the bend of the road (note dogs aren't allowed) and go through the gate. Then it's just a matter of weaving up through the outcrops and gullies. It's hard going and there is no obvious path, but persevere because the view from the top is very rewarding.

It's also possible to climb Errisbeg from Roundstone (5km). Park in the village and walk up the lane beside O'Dowd's pub. At the end of the lane go through a gate and follow a very faint, intermittent path to the top. You will pass many subsidiary tops marked with stone cairns but the true summit has a concrete triangulation point *[53.3952, -9.9595]*.

DOG'S BAY AND GORTEEN

Just west of Roundstone village are two of Ireland's finest beaches, Dog's Bay *[53.3809, -9.9633]* and Gorteen *[53.3809, -9.9542]*. They lie back to back, joined to the mainland by a thin neck of grassy dunes. Both beaches are sheltered from currents and are popular for swimming, windsurfing and kitesurfing. The narrow roads that lead down to them can get very busy in the summer.

The east-facing Gorteen is the larger and more sheltered of the two beaches. It has a lifeguard on duty at weekends in July and August.

The grassy headland past the beaches is a wonderful place to wander around, exploring the rocky inlets and hidden coves. Both bays have fantastic seagrass meadows just out from the beaches which make for interesting snorkelling.

Gurteen Bay Caravan Park has camping and caravans for hire a stone's throw from the beach.

Dog's Bay and Gorteen beaches | DF

Roundstone Bog | RC

ROUNDSTONE BOG

North of the coast road between Clifden and Roundstone is a vast expanse of blanket bog, streams and lakes, known as Roundstone Bog. It's remote and lonely, but very beautiful, with fascinating views of the ever changing light on the Twelve Bens. Completely devoid of trees and with over a hundred lakes there is as much water as land.

The ninety square kilometre expanse is crossed by just one narrow road, the appropriately named Bog Road, which serves as an interesting and very bumpy shortcut between Clifden and Roundstone.

The bog, while appearing barren and lifeless is in fact home to a wide range of wildlife. You can see carnivorous plants, lizards, sedges, purple moor grass, bog myrtle, wildflowers and rocky outcrops covered with lichens and heather.

THE BOG WALK

Crossing the bog from Ballyconneely to Roundstone is an excellent, but tough walk. It is only suitable for experienced hikers equipped with a map and compass and the ability to navigate across complicated ground in thick mist or fog.

Starting from Ballyconneely village follow the Roundstone road south. After just under 1km turn left and follow the minor road to its end in the heart of the bog [53.4267, -10.0057]. From there it's a matter of striking out across the heather, weaving around

Trá Mhór, Aillebrack | Olivier Issaly

Playing on Bunowen beach | DF

the numerous lakes and ponds, heading for the left-hand shoulder of Errisbeg, the serrated peak to the east. Crossing over the saddle of Errisbeg leads to a laneway [53.3965, -9.9349] that will bring you down into the village of Roundstone. If you find a fairly direct route through the maze of lakes it's about 15km.

BALLYCONNEELY

The low lying coast of the Ballyconneely Peninsula is adorned with beautiful sandy beaches. Much of the land near the coast is a complex and highly specialised habitat known as machair, which is characterised by fertile, sandy ground. Machair is found in only a few places along the northern Atlantic coast of Ireland and in a few areas in Scotland. During the summer the short grass teems with exquisite wildflowers.

BEACHES

The area is packed with sandy beaches and even on the busiest days it should be possible to find your own private beach.

The southern side of Mannin Bay (see page 139) has a series of small sandy coves that are accessed from the narrow road just north of Ballyconneely village.

On the north side of the peninsula is Doonloughan [53.4478, -10.1348]. It's one of the few surf spots in Connemara and in the summer you can rent boards

Connemara ponies | Sigita Playdon

Maerl on Coral Strand | DF

Round-leaved Sundew, Roundstone Bog | DF

or get surf lessons. Unfortunately the strong currents and big waves mean that the beach isn't ideal for swimming. The grassy area near the beach is popular with campers.

Aillebrack, beside Connemara Golf Links, has a number of sandy beaches. The largest one, Trá Mhór [53.4191,-10.1436] has a Green Coast award and is the most popular, but the smaller, quieter beaches further south are just as nice. The tidal flats near the southern tip of the peninsula are a great place to forage for shellfish at low tide. If you know what you are doing you can find clams, cockles, mussels, razor fish, sea urchin, prawns and scallops.

The small beach at Bunowen [53.4075,-10.1209] is very popular with families and has great views of the Twelve Bens. As it faces east it's reasonably sheltered from the prevailing wind. The Connemara Smokehouse (www.smokehouse.ie) at the end of Bunowen Pier is well worth a visit [53.4046, -10.1170].

PONY TREKKING

There has always been a strong interest in horses in Connemara. It's the home of Ireland's only native horse breed, the Connemara Pony, which is world renowned for its hardiness and gentle temperament. Legend has it that the Spanish horses that escaped from the galleons of the Armada when they ran

The Alcock and Brown landing site | Andreas Riemenschneider

aground in 1588 bred with the local feral Irish horses. The breed is very popular in Ireland and every August the Connemara Pony Show takes place in Clifden.

The Point Pony Trekking and Horse Riding Centre [53.4192, -10.1606] beside Connemara Golf Links offers a range of treks on ponies and horses over sandy beaches and grassy commonage (www. thepointponytrekkingcentre.com).

MANNIN BAY

Just north of the small village of Ballyconneely is Mannin Bay. From a distance the beach beside the road, known as Coral Strand [53.4419, -10.0640], doesn't look particularly interesting at first, but it's worth stopping for a closer look. The sand, known as maerl, is predominantly composed of delicate shells of coralline red algae, but you may also see pieces of sponge, clam, snail, sea urchin and quartz.

SNORKEL TRAIL
The trail follows a series of rocky pools for 400m north of the carpark. Look out for red algae, wrasse, sea urchins and red kelp. Coral Strand is quite sheltered so the water can be a degree or so warmer than other more exposed beaches.

KAYAK TRAILS
The first of the two kayak trails heads north around the tiny island of Ardillaun before returning along the coastline (4.5km). It's possible to extend this paddle by visiting the bay east of the island (7km).

The second trail follows the shore westwards passing many small beaches and rocky coves. Experienced paddlers could continue on around Knock Point and visit Truska Beach (14km).

DERRIGIMLAGH

The small townland of Derrigimlagh in the northwest corner of Roundstone Bog has loomed large in the history of the early 20th century. On Sunday June 15th 1919, the first transatlantic flight ended abruptly in its soft ground. Captain John Alcock and Arthur Whitten Brown had flown their twin-engined Vickers Vimy from Newfoundland, Canada, in just over sixteen hours, before crash landing in the bog within yards of the Marconi Wireless Telegraph Station.

The Telegraph Station was set up by Guglielmo Marconi, the Italian pioneer of wireless telegraphy, in 1905. The first transatlantic wireless message was sent from it to Nova Scotia in 1907.

The 5km trail that loops around the site features a number of interesting installations including radio sets that play recordings from the time of the Marconi station, a tuning fork that experiments with different sound frequencies, and a wind reed that creates sounds based on the wind. A white concrete marker [53.4465, -10.0223] lies close to the landing spot of Alcock and Brown. ∎

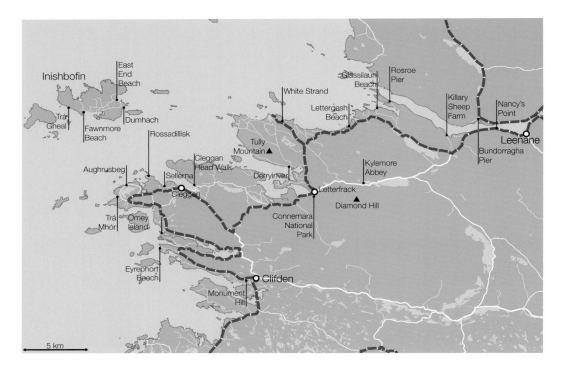

NORTH CONNEMARA

The area north of Clifden is probably the most popular part of Connemara with visitors. It's easy to understand why, as it has a great concentration of offshore islands, sandy beaches and mountains.

CLIFDEN

The unofficial capital of Connemara, Clifden is a bustling town full of pubs, cafés and restaurants. There is also a wide range of accommodation from fancy hotels to utilitarian hostels. As such it's a great base for exploring this part of the Atlantic coast.

SKY ROAD

The Sky Road is justifiably famous for its incredible views over the islands, mountains and coastlines of Connemara. While most visitors drive the loop it's a great cycle and you might enjoy the view even more after working hard to earn it. See the facing page for a suggested route.

On your way back to Clifden it's worth stopping off and making the short climb to the top of Monument Hill *[53.4870, -10.0324]* where there is a stone memorial to the town's founder, John D'Arcy, and a great view over the town towards the Twelve Bens.

Eyrephort Beach *[53.5119, -10.1366]* is a short detour off the Sky Road. It's a nice quiet beach, but be warned if driving as the road down to it is very narrow.

AUGHRUS PENINSULA

North of Clifden the Wild Atlantic Way leaves the N59 to loop around the Aughrus Peninsula. This undeveloped area has dozens of beautiful sandy beaches connected by a network of quiet roads.

The small fishing village of Cleggan on the northern side of the peninsula is the departure point for Inishbofin (see page 143).

Just opposite Omey Island (see page 141) is Clifden Eco Beach Camping (www.actonsbeachsidecamping.com), a beautiful campsite with a wild, natural feel *[53.5237, -10.1346]*. Many of its pitches lie among the dunes and long grass within a stone's throw of a the shore.

DILLISK

This seasonal restaurant based in a converted boat shed in Aughrusbeg serves a tasting menu of fresh, local and foraged food *[53.5580, -10.1639]*. It runs three nights a week from late June to early September, and you need to book well in advance. For more information see www.dillisk.com.

Clifden Eco Beach Camping | Kris Acton

BEACHES
There is no shortage of great beaches on Aughrus.

• Sellerna is a small beach with plenty of parking *[53.5572, -10.1315]*. It is signposted from Cleggan village, follow the signs for 'Trá'. Just east of the beach is a small megalithic dolmen that is worth a quick look.

• Rossadillisk is a sprawling, flat beach with a large tidal range and lots of rock pools and tiny islands to explore *[53.5649, -10.1505]*. Parking is limited and the access road is narrow. See the photo on page 120. The smaller eastern beach, Trá Bhríde, is more sheltered when a westerly wind is blowing *[53.5630, -10.1453]*.

• Aughrusbeg is actually a series of interconnected small beaches, one of which is known as Anchor Beach due to the massive anchor that lies lodged in the sand *[53.5584, -10.1771]*. It came from the Verity, a three-masted 1,000 ton barque from Nova Scotia, which was wrecked in a storm in 1890.

• Trá Mhór is a peaceful beach, hidden down a narrow lane *[53.5502, -10.1882]*. It must be accessed on foot or by bike as there is no parking at the end of the lane.

OMEY ISLAND
The small island of Omey is connected to the mainland by a vast area of sand, and twice a day,

CLIFDEN CYCLE HUB
The four cycle routes that make up the cycle hub all start and finish in the centre of Clifden. They are signposted at most junctions but not all. Download maps from www.irishtrails.ie. Bikes are available for hire in Clifden from Mannion's Cycles (www.clifdenbikes.com) and you can also hire an electric bike from All Things Connemara (www.bikeelectric.ie) if you are worried about your fitness. All the routes are best done in a clockwise direction.

1 SKY ROAD LOOP
A popular drive, some sections of the 16km route are very narrow and can be busy. There is a slightly shorter variation to the signposted routes that offers better views and quieter roads. See www.goo.gl/V4hGX6 for a map.

2 ERRISLANNAN LOOP
The Errislannan Peninsula is much quieter than its famous neighbour to the north, but the views on this 14km loop are just as good. The Alcock and Brown monument marks the highest point of the route and it's a good place to stop and soak up the view.

3 CLEGGAN LOOP
A 33km circuit that follows the coast road around the Aughrus Peninsula. It also passes through Cleggan village. It's well worth making the short detour to visit Omey Island (see page 141). Plan to reach the island at low tide. Be very careful on the busy section of the N59 out of Clifden.

4 BALLYCONNEELY AND ROUNDSTONE LOOP
This 40km route passes plenty of interesting sights including the Alcock and Brown landing site at Derrigimlagh (see page 139), Coral Strand (see page 139), Errisbeg (see page 135) and the beaches of Dog's Bay and Gorteen (see page 135).
Be careful on the road south from Clifden as there are some tight bends. The road between Ballyconneely and Roundstone can be busy. There is one steep climb over the shoulder of Errisbeg, but the rest of the route is reasonably flat.

The Omey Races | Andreas Riemenschneider

Sea thrift on Omey | DF

for a few hours around low tide, it's possible to walk, cycle or drive across the sand to the island. Check the tide in Sweeney's shop and pub in Claddaghduff village before crossing. It's easy to get seduced by the tranquillity of the island so keep an eye on the time or else you may end up spending longer there than you had planned.

The island is an incredibly beautiful and peaceful place that is full of wildflowers during the summer. The commonage on the western end is a wonderful place to wander and enjoy the views across the water to Cruagh, Friar and High Islands.

Every August the tidal sands host the Omey Horse Races, complete with bookmakers and crowds of spectators.

OMEY ISLAND WALK
This wonderful 5.5km loop follows the coast around the island. Park in the carpark [53.5388, -10.1445] on the mainland overlooking the beach and follow the signposts across the sand to the island. Take the narrow road that leads clockwise around the island to the sandy beach, Trá Rabhach. At the far end of the beach look out for a holy well known as Tobar Feichín [53.5302, -10.1682]. Now either follow the sunken path through the sand dunes or wander across the grass sticking closer to the coast. Either way you will pass the ruins of Teampall Feichín [53.5358, -10.1678]. Past the church descend to the shore

Teampall Feichín | DF

The Green Road, Inishbofin | Xavier von Erlach

and follow it clockwise, passing the graveyard before retracing your steps across the sand to the mainland.

It's also possible to explore the island and the surrounding beaches on horseback. See www.clegganridingcentre.com for details.

INISHBOFIN

Like many of the west coast's islands, Inishbofin has two distinct personalities. Its sheltered, lush southern and eastern coasts are where you will find the village and the best beaches; while the western and northern coasts are wild and remote, with steep cliffs and barren, heather-clad slopes.

The island is home to a wealth of wildlife. It's an important breeding ground for many birds including the common tern, Arctic tern, fulmar, guillemot, common gull, greater and lesser black backed gull, Manx shearwater, chough and corncrake.

The island has been inhabited for at least 6,000 years and has a rich history, the remains of much of which can still be seen.

The ferry crossing to the island from Cleggan takes about 30 minutes (www.inishbofinislanddiscovery.com), during which you have a good chance of seeing bottlenose dolphins.

Camping is available in the grounds of Inishbofin hostel (www.inishbofin-hostel.ie). Wild camping takes place on the unfenced commonage on the island. Ask locally for advice about suitable places to camp, and leave no trace of your stay.

As well as exploring the island on foot you can pony trek (www.inishbofinequestriancentre.com), charter a boat (www.inishbofinribcharter.com), scuba dive (www.islandswest.ie), go deep-sea fishing (bofinfish72@yahoo.co.uk) or hire bikes at the pier.

See www.inishbofin.com for lots of useful information and details of accommodation etc.

WALKING TRAILS
The island has three signposted trails which all start from the pier.

• The 8km Cloonamore Loop explores the eastern end of the island. A shorter all-road variation is also possible.
• The 8km Westquarter Loop is probably the most interesting of the three walks. It takes in the cliffs, blow holes and sea stacks at the western end of the island (a great place to watch the sun set over the Atlantic).
• The Middlequarter Loop is the shortest walk at 5km. It visits the highest point of the island, where there are great views across to the mainland.

Another option is to combine sections of each of the walks to make a complete circuit of the coast of the island. It will be about 15km depending on the exact route you take.

Trá Gheal, Inishbofin | RC

SNORKEL TRAIL
There is good snorkelling at Fawnmore Beach *[53.6139, -10.2291]* opposite the Doonmore Hotel. Enter the water near the carpark and make your way southwest for 300m. The rocky ground is full of sea life including anemones, limpets, mussels, barnacles, and starfish. If you are lucky you may see spider and hermit crabs.

CROMWELL'S BARRACKS KAYAK TRAIL
The harbour is very sheltered and remains calm in all but the worst weather, however it can be busy, so watch out for other boats. The trail starts from the stony beach east of the new pier *[53.6134, -10.2104]*. Follow the coast clockwise into the inner bay. Continue along the shore past a pebble beach where it's possible to land and explore the star shaped Cromwellian Fort *[53.6104, -10.2164]*. At the large white navigation beacon loop back to the starting point, avoiding the route taken by the ferry.

BEACHES
There are two Green Coast beaches, Dumhach *[53.6162, -10.1813]* and East End Beach *[53.6216, -10.1889]*. Both are wide, sandy beaches on the eastern end of the island.

The other beach of note, Trá Gheal, is on the western end of the island *[53.6160, -10.2472]*. It's a picture perfect cove with white sand, turquoise water and views across to the now deserted island of Inishshark. Take care on the steep descent from the Green Road to the beach. It's inadvisable to swim from the beach as there are dangerous currents.

CLEGGAN HEAD WALK
Back on the mainland there is an interesting 4km walk to the tip of Cleggan Head which lies on the northern side of Cleggan Bay opposite the village. The route passes through a working sheep farm and access is permitted, but under no circumstances are dogs allowed on this walk, even on a lead. The farm has six cottages for rent, see www.clegganfarmcottages.com for details.

Drive east from Cleggan village following signs for 'Cleggan Head Farm'. Turn left into the farm and park in the small parking area on the right after 600m *[53.5610, -10.0980]*. Continue past the farm buildings on foot. Just after the walled garden there is a small neolithic wedge tomb down by the sea.

Follow the track along the southern slopes of the hill (close all gates behind you) to the small, secluded bay *[53.5733, -10.1174]*. From the higher ground it's possible to enjoy views north, to the islands of Inishturk, Clare and Achill and the distinctive profile of Croagh Patrick. Return by retracing your steps.

If you want to explore the caves and coves of Cleggan Head from the water Real Adventures (www.realadventures.ie) offer guided kayaking trips.

The Twelve Bens from Diamond Hill | Julien Mattei

LETTERFRACK

The small village of Letterfrack was developed by a Quaker family as part of the post-Famine relief efforts. The large building beside the green was home to Saint Joseph's Industrial School. It now houses the National Centre for Excellence in Furniture Design and Technology.

Letterfrack Bay Water Tours (www. letterfrackwatertours.com) operate Ireland's only glass-bottomed boat, which offers a unique underwater perspective of the sheltered waters of Ballynakill Harbour. On a good day you will see a large variety of sea and cliff birds, grey seals, otters, and possibly even dolphins and porpoises.

The Old Monastery Hostel (www. oldmonasteryhostel.com) in the village has a unique atmosphere, charming and slightly rough around the edges. It serves an excellent breakfast and allows camping on the grounds.

The Ecology Centre (www.theecologycentre. ie) offers hands-on activities such as foraging, bog walks and eco-tours that will help you appreciate and understand the landscape and nature of Connemara.

CONNEMARA NATIONAL PARK

Just south of Letterfrack village is the 5,000 acre Connemara National Park. The visitor centre is worth a visit, and is the starting point for four signposted trails [53.5502, -9.9454]. The three shorter walks are interesting, but the pick of the bunch is the 7km Upper Diamond Walk which will take you to the 455m summit of Diamond Hill. The path is steep but well-maintained and the hard slog is more than justified by the amazing 360 degree view from the top. Just follow the red markers.

KYLEMORE ABBEY

The picturesque Kylemore Abbey (www. kylemoreabbeytourism.ie) lies a little inland from the Wild Atlantic Way along the N59 between Killary and Letterfrack [53.5594, -9.8915]. As well as the castle and the impressive gardens it offers guided walks along the estate's trails. The walk to the Sacred Heart statue on the hillside high above the Abbey offers stunning views over the estate and into the Twelve Bens.

RENVYLE

The small peninsula of Renvyle is very popular with Irish holiday-makers, particularly Renvyle House (www. renvyle.com), the long established hotel which lies close to a number of beaches at the northern tip of the headland.

The most popular beach in the area is White Strand [53.6070, -9.9891]. It's quite open so there isn't much shelter when it's windy. Access the beach by taking the turn right after the campsite (www. renvylebeachcaravanpark.com).

Glassilaun beach | RC

TULLY MOUNTAIN

While modest in height at only 365m, Tully Mountain offers an excellent vantage point with views up and down the coast and into the mountains. There isn't a distinct path to follow so it's a matter of finding your own way up. It's a 5km round trip.

Park at the pier at Derryinver *[53.5722, -9.9811]* and follow the road west for 400m. Walk a short way up the gravel track on the right, go through the gate and then follow the fence left and through another gate (close the gates behind you). You are now on open hillside and it's just a matter of following the broad ridge to the top which is marked by a cairn *[53.5836, -10.0048]*. Return by retracing your steps. The ground can be boggy so wear appropriate footwear.

LETTERGESH BEACH

Public access to this 1.5km long beach is via the small carpark signposted from the Wild Atlantic Way *[53.6021, -9.9083]*. At low tide it's possible to walk north along the sand, wading across the Culfin River, to the nicer, northern part of the beach. Just to the north, Connemara Caravan and Camping Park has direct access to this beach.

GLASSILAUN BEACH

The horseshoe shaped sandy beach *[53.6148, -9.8749]* just south of the mouth of Killary Harbour is one of the best beaches in Connemara (and therefore the world).

The rocks at either end of the beach are excellent for snorkelling, consult the map in the carpark for details. If it's windy use the more sheltered side of the beach. At low tide you can walk out to the tiny island at the western end of the beach where there is an old lobster holding pool. The water in it is usually a few degrees warmer than the sea.

From the Wild Atlantic Way follow signs for 'Scuba Dive West' down narrow roads to the small carpark.

KILLARY HARBOUR

The dramatic, glacier carved inlet of Killary Harbour marks the border between the counties of Galway and Mayo. And while geographers may object to it being described as a fjord it's certainly the closest thing to one in Ireland. The Wild Atlantic Way skirts the southern shore, passing through the small village of Leenane before crossing into Mayo at the point where the Erriff River meets the sea (just downstream from Aasleagh Falls, see page 150).

Connemara Campsite (www.connemaracampsite. com) is beautifully positioned overlooking the Harbour on the grounds of Killary Adventure Centre (www. killaryadventure.com), which offers a wide range of outdoor activities.

There are two kayaking Blueway trails in Killary, see the facing page for details. Alternatively enjoy

Killary Harbour | RC

the Harbour from the comfort of the catamaran Connemara Lady, which departs regularly from Nancy's Point (www.killaryfjord.com).

FAMINE WALK
This beautiful 15km walk follows a track, known as the Green Road, along the southern side of the Harbour. The track, which was built as part of the famine relief program during the 19th century, is rough but fairly level and the views are great.

The route starts at Rosroe Pier *[53.6199, -9.8593]*. Park at the pier and walk 200m back up the road. Turn left at the small white cottage and follow the track. After about 5km the track becomes a road and you pass Killary Sheep Farm (www.killarysheepfarm.com) where visitors can watch working sheepdogs, sheep shearing, turf cutting demonstrations and, in spring, bottle feed a lamb *[53.5941, -9.7909]*. The road leads uphill to the busy N59 where you turn right and take the next right. This quieter road leads past Lough Fee. Keep right at the next two junctions and the road will lead you back to your car at Rosroe.

If you are short on time you could just walk the length of the Green Road and retrace your steps.

KILLARY KAYAK BLUEWAYS
While the prevailing wind in the Harbour is from the west, these trails shouldn't be used during moderate to high winds from the east. Remember the piers are working harbours, so please park considerately.

NANCY'S POINT TRAIL
This trail travels around the western end of the Harbour. It can be done as an 11km point to point, but probably makes more sense as a 25km loop. From Nancy's Point *[53.5998, -9.7302]* follow the southern shore west to Rosroe Pier before crossing to the other side of the fjord and returning via the more remote northern shore.

If there is a boat at the slipway please use the stone beach just to the east. During busy periods or if using a trailer, park at the off road area to the west of the entrance to the slipway.

BUNDORRAGHA TRAIL
This 12km loop starts from Bundorragha Pier *[53.6061, -9.7524]* on the north side of the harbour (you could also start from Nancy's Point). It is best undertaken at mid or high tide. The trail follows the rocky northern coastline east (watch out for strong currents near where the Erriff River meets the sea) before returning along the southern side of the Harbour. ■

Achill Head | RC

MAYO

The huge county of Mayo, which has the second longest coastline in Ireland, is home to a number of world renowned sights such as the holy mountain of Croagh Patrick and the beautiful Achill Island, but it also has many less well known, but no less interesting, attractions. Mayo is the third largest county in Ireland but also the second least densely populated, so it's the ideal place for those seeking a bit of space and quiet.

The stretch of the Wild Atlantic Way that runs from the town of Westport to Achill Island is exceptionally well equipped with over a dozen signposted walking trails and the very popular Great Western Greenway cycling trail.

The spectacular scenery of Achill Island has always attracted artists, but nowadays it's also a Mecca for walkers and surfers.

The region of Erris could definitely be considered a hidden gem. It's only in recent years that it has started to be marketed as a destination and it's still very much unspoiled.

North Mayo is home to some huge cliffs and very impressive coastline. The cliffs at Benwee Head are taller than the Cliffs of Moher and steeper than Slieve League, yet they are virtually unknown.

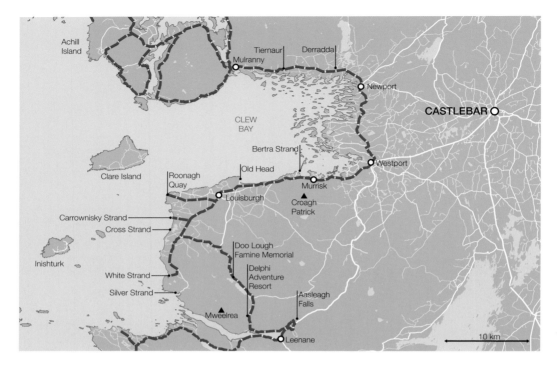

KILLARY AND CLEW BAY

The southern half of Mayo has a huge amount to offer including remote beaches, offshore islands, the iconic Croagh Patrick and the Great Western Greenway.

Just north of Killary Harbour a convoluted, but very worthwhile, spur of the Wild Atlantic Way visits two beautiful beaches.

Offshore, the neighbouring islands of Inishturk and Clare Island offer contrasting experiences. Those looking for solitude and peace should make for Inishturk, while those in search of adventure and craic will find it on Clare Island.

The Clew Bay skyline is dominated by the conical profile of Ireland's holy mountain, Croagh Patrick. To climb the mountain on Reek Sunday alongside thousands of pilgrims is a surreal and uniquely Irish experience.

The thriving town of Westport is linked to Achill Island by the walking and cycling route known as the Great Western Greenway, a real success story and hopefully the first of many around the county. This area is also well served with twelve signposted walking trails.

AASLEAGH FALLS

Just north of Leenane, the Erriff River tumbles over a picturesque waterfall shortly before it reaches the sea at the head of Killary Harbour. The waterfall, while not particularly tall, is beautifully situated and is an ideal place for a quick stop off to stretch the legs or a leisurely picnic beside the river.

There is plenty of parking just north of the bridge [53.6180, -9.6726] where a short path on the northern bank of the river leads to the falls.

The Erriff is one of the best salmon fishing rivers in Ireland and if you are very lucky you may see salmon attempting to make their way up the waterfall after heavy rain.

MWEELREA

The massive bulk of Mweelrea dominates the northern shore of Killary Harbour. Rising to 814m straight from sea level it's the highest point in Mayo and the province of Connacht. If you are lucky enough to reach the summit on a clear day you will enjoy magnificent views over the Atlantic, Ben Gorm, the Twelve Bens, the Maumturks and the Sheeffry Hills.

Mweelrea is a serious mountain, with many narrow ridges and steep cliffs, and it's frequently

Paddleboarding, Carrownisky | RC

Aasleagh Falls | Sean O'Moore

shrouded in heavy mist. It should only be attempted by experienced hikers who are capable of navigating complex ground in low visibility. If you are unsure about your ability Walk Connemara (www.walkconnemara.com) offer guided hikes up the mountain.

DELPHI ADVENTURE RESORT
Set on a 300 acre site on the eastern slopes of Mweelrea, the resort combines a luxury hotel and spa, budget dorm accommodation and an adventure centre [53.6220, -9.7543].

Catering for families, couples and groups, the centre offers a huge range of activities including kayaking, canoeing, stand up paddleboarding, surfing, coasteering, raft building, high ropes, bog challenge, mountain biking, climbing, abseiling, archery, and bushcraft. See www.delphiadventureresort.com for more information.

DOO LOUGH FAMINE MEMORIAL
Just north of Doo Lough, where the Wild Atlantic Way follows the valley between Mweelrea and the Sheeffry Hills, is a small roadside memorial to those who died in the Doo Lough Tragedy during the Famine. It's a beautiful place to stop and admire the view down the valley [53.6662, -9.7813].

CARROWNISKY STRAND
The 4km Green Coast beach at Carrownisky is a busy spot during the summer [53.7353, -9.8933]. Popular with surfers, it's one of the few consistent breaks in the area. Surf Mayo (www.surfmayo.com) is based at the beach and offers board rental and lessons.

There are lifeguards on duty every day during July and August and at weekends during June. You are advised to wear foot protection in the water due to the presence of weever fish.

CROSS STRAND
It's also possible to access the beach at Cross [53.7219, -9.8998]. Drive further south along the Wild Atlantic Way towards Silver Strand and look out for the signposted turn right for Cross Beach. As you follow the road down to the beach you will see signs for Bunlahinch Clapper Bridge to the right. It's worth the short diversion to check out this unusual foot bridge [53.7182, -9.8886].

WHITE STRAND
On the drive south towards Silver Strand there are plenty of side roads, many of which lead down to small deserted coves. Look out for signs for White Strand. This long sandy beach is worth a visit [53.6683, -9.8989].

SILVER STRAND
Finally the road ends at Silver Strand [53.6499, -9.8804]. It's the perfect place to wander, exploring the beach, rocky headlands and sand dunes while enjoying the views across the sea to Inishbofin, Inishturk and Clare Island. Thanks to the long drive this beautiful beach is rarely busy.

It's possible to walk north from Silver Strand around the headland to White Strand and then follow the road back south to the carpark (about 10km in total). This walk takes you through a remote and unspoiled area, with beautiful sand dunes, rare machair and

Silver Strand | RC

Doo Lough | Tom Byrne

Mweelrea | RC

Bunlahinch Clapper Bridge | DF

The Tale of the Tongs, Inishturk | Michael McLaughlin

interesting archaeology, including a very significant dog whelk midden from where early Irish settlers extracted a rare pigment highly valued by North African traders. The walk is best at low tide.

LOST VALLEY
Public access to the beach just south of Silver Strand, the wonderfully named Uggool, has been prevented for many years. However, a local farming family offer tours of the beach and surrounding lands. See www.thelostvalley.ie for details.

INISHTURK
The peaceful island of Inishturk lies just over 10km off the coast of Mayo. Much quieter than its neighbour Clare Island, this is a place for those looking to get away from it all. What it lacks in tourist amenities it more than makes up for in rugged beauty. The majority of the island's six square kilometres are rough and rocky hillside, perfect for exploring on foot.

Clare Island Ferry Company (www.clareislandferry.com) and O'Malley Ferries (www.omalleyferries.com) regularly make the 50 minute crossing from Roonagh Quay [53.7619, -9.9030] to the island.

There are a small number of B+Bs as well as a basic campsite. The Community Centre, which houses the pub and a restaurant, is the social hub of the island [53.7010, -10.0933].

BEACHES
There are two sandy beaches on the eastern end of the island, Tránaun [53.7005, -10.0891] and Corraun [53.7040, -10.0920], both of which have crystal clear water and are well sheltered.

WALKS
The island's two signposted walks serve as excellent starting points for getting to know the place. The Lough Coolaknick Loop (green arrows) is a short (5km) ramble following narrow roads and tracks.

The Mountain Common Loop (purple arrows) is a longer, 8km, variation of the Lough Coolaknick Loop. It crosses open ground to a viewing point overlooking the cliffs on the western side of the island. It's possible to extend this walk to include the highest point of the island, Mountain Common, which, although only 189m high, offers amazing views back to the mainland.

THE TALE OF THE TONGS
Set above the cliffs on the northern shore is the 2013 installation, The Tale of the Tongs, which was built to commemorate those who have emigrated from the island. The glass walled structure is an ideal place to take shelter and soak up the view [53.7087, -10.1066].

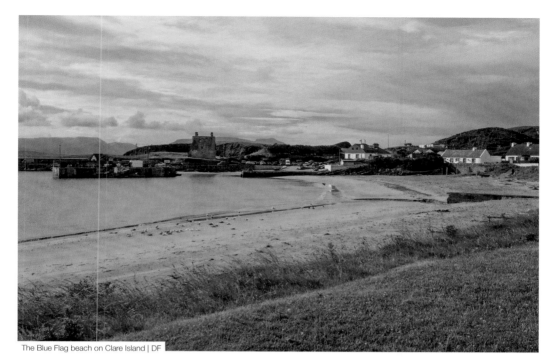
The Blue Flag beach on Clare Island | DF

CLARE ISLAND

This vibrant island is only a few kilometres off the coast of Mayo in the mouth of Clew Bay. The gentle eastern side contrasts with the impressive sea cliffs on the west coast, which is dominated by Knockmore, the highest point on the island.

The island is popular with visitors, particularly hikers and groups who are there to enjoy the nightlife.

The dramatic cliffs and inland habitats support a wide variety of flora and fauna and it is one of the most studied islands in Europe. In 1909 Belfast naturalist Robert Lloyd Praeger led an exhaustive biological survey of the island and since then it has been a focus of interest for botanists, geologists, ornithologists, marine biologists and nature lovers.

With its rich history there is much to see, including the ruined castle at the harbour (famous as the stronghold of the legendary Pirate Queen Grace O'Malley), the 12th century Abbey, the Napoleonic signal tower and The Church of the Sacred Heart, as well as many ancient archaeological sites.

Two companies - Clare Island Ferry Company (www.clareislandferry.com) and O'Malley Ferries (www.omalleyferries.com) - make the short crossing from Roonagh Quay [53.7619, -9.9030] a couple of times a day.

There are two pubs. Sailor's Bar and Restaurant, which is co-located with the hostel (www.goexplorehostel.ie), has live music on weekends during the summer. The Community Centre bar has regular traditional music sessions, set dancing and concerts. On Tuesday nights during the summer the adjacent sports hall hosts local and visiting musicians, singers and dancers.

There is a basic campsite just above the beach beside the Community Centre with (coin-operated) showers, a tap and toilets. Wild camping is not encouraged.

There is plenty of accommodation including the hostel, B+Bs, self-catering cottages and the very luxurious lighthouse (www.clareislandlighthouse.com). Food is available during the summer in Anna's Café [53.8117, -9.9656] at weekends and daily in both pubs. Note that the shop is a long walk from the main village.

Clare Island Adventures (www.clareislandadventures.ie) offer coasteering, snorkelling, rock climbing, abseiling and raft building.

For general information and details of upcoming events and festivals check out www.clareisland.ie.

CYCLING

The island is too big to cover on foot in a day so hiring a bike is a good option if you are short on time. Bicycles are available for rent at the harbour and it's also possible to take your own on the ferry. Bear in mind that many of the narrow roads and tracks that

The Lighthouse | DF

The Cove | DF

Knockmore | DF

The Green Road | DF

crisscross the island are quite rough and aren't really suitable for the narrow wheels of a road bike.

MACALLA FARM
Macalla Farm is a small, family-run retreat centre and working organic farm [53.8162, -9.9754]. They offer a wide range of residential courses on yoga, mindfulness, cooking and horsemanship. See www.ecofarm.ie for more information.

BEACHES
The sheltered, sandy beach in the harbour has a Blue Flag and is ideal for families [53.8010, -9.9526]. There is a small fishing harbour, known as The Cove, on the northeast side of the island. It's a picturesque spot, ideal for a quiet swim [53.8210, -9.9707].

WALKING
The roads and tracks offer lots of possibilities for short and medium length walks and there are two signposted walking routes on the island.

The 3km Fawnglass Loop, marked by the green arrows, is a short stroll across the hillside above the village.

The 8km Knocknaveen Loop, which is marked by purple arrows, follows the road west before heading north across the centre of the island and rejoining the Fawnglass Loop via the Green Road.

The 462m high Knockmore is the obvious challenge for the experienced hiker. Probably the best approach is to follow the road that runs west across the island to the signal tower [53.8004, -10.0463] before climbing steeply up the shoulder to the summit, which is marked by a large cairn and a trig point [53.8075, -10.0212]. Descend in a westwards direction, keeping well away from the cliff edge, and follow the zigzag track down to the road where you rejoin the Knocknaveen Loop. This is a tough 13km with a significant amount of height gain.

Bartraw Strand | DF

LOUISBURGH
This small quiet town on the edge of Clew Bay is a good place to stock up on provisions, particularly if you are heading south, as there isn't another town until Leenane in Connemara.

LOUISBURGH CYCLE HUB
Three signposted cycle routes tour the countryside surrounding the town [53.7621, -9.8100].

• Route 1 is a 19km loop across flat bog roads and then over a few hills that overlook Clare Island, Inishturk, Achill and Inishbofin.
• Route 2 is a 7km loop around the quiet back roads of Louisburgh, passing close by Turlin Strand.
• Route 3 is a challenging 26km trip through the Sheeffry Hills. Plenty of wonderful scenery and quiet roads, there are even two streams to ford!

OLD HEAD
The sheltered Blue Flag beach overlooking Croagh Patrick is very popular with families [53.7764, -9.7715]. There is a lifeguard during the summer, plenty of carparking, toilets and a café (Old Head Café and Ice Cream Parlour) and campsite (www.oldheadcaravanpark.ie) nearby.

There is plenty to be done apart from lazing on the sand. Just behind the beach is the Old Head Wood Nature Reserve, a small oak forest. Adventure West (www.adventurewest.ie) organise coasteering and pier jumping and Summer SUP (www.summersup.com) offer paddleboarding summer camps, lessons and rentals during June, July and August. There is also a snorkel trail and two kayak trails at the Old Head.

SNORKEL TRAIL
The snorkel trail starts at the beach just north of the pier and continues north for about 400m to the western headland. Best at high tide, keep an eye out for anemones, shoals of fish and shore crab.

KAYAK TRAILS
Two kayak trails start from the beach or the slipway beside the pier.

The 5.5km (each way) trail follows the shore east between Old Head and Leckanvy Pier [53.7832, -9.6900], passing a number of coves and some short sections of cliff. Only the start of this trail in the vicinity of Old Head is suitable for beginners.

A more exposed 5km (each way) trail extends west from the harbour to the beach at Calla [53.7712, -9.8219], passing some interesting caves along the way. There are no easy exit points along this route so it should only be undertaken by experienced kayakers in good conditions.

BERTRA STRAND
The long, thin neck of sand that stretches out from the foot of Croagh Patrick for 4km into Clew Bay is a 'tombolo', a landform where sand is deposited to create a narrow connection between the mainland and an island [53.7884, -9.6610]. It is a very popular beach for swimming, walking, bird-watching, kite surfing and windsurfing. There is a lifeguard in the summer months as well as toilets and plenty of parking.

CROAGH PATRICK
Croagh Patrick is considered the holiest mountain in Ireland. The tradition of pilgrimage to its 764m summit stretches back over five thousand years from the Stone Age to the present day without interruption. Its religious significance dates back to the time of the pagans, when people are thought to have gathered here to celebrate the beginning of harvest season.

Croagh Patrick | RC

The mountain is named after Saint Patrick, Ireland's patron saint, who is said to have fasted on the summit for forty days in 441 AD.

Known locally as The Reek, the mountain attracts the devout and the curious throughout the year but on Reek Sunday, the last Sunday in July, over 25,000 pilgrims climb the mountain, some doing so barefoot. At the summit is a chapel where mass is celebrated through the day. The chapel is open daily between 10.00 and 15.00 during July and August.

The view from the summit gives an almost bird's-eye perspective over the myriad islands of Clew Bay.

The pilgrim path starts from the large carpark in Murrisk [53.7884, -9.6610] and follows the steep, rocky track to the summit [53.7595, -9.6583]. It's a tough 7km climb as you are starting from sea level and the path is very badly eroded.

It's also possible to traverse the east-west ridge of the mountain, starting from the laneway taken by the Western Way near Belclare [53.7713, -9.5799] and finishing at the small road southwest of Leckanvy [53.7681, -9.7190]. This is a longer, more peaceful route, but requires a long road walk back to the car or else a two car shuttle.

MURRISK WALKS

If the weather is bad or you aren't feeling able for the tough hike up Croagh Patrick then the four short signposted walks that start and finish at the carpark in Murrisk [53.7884, -9.6610] might be of interest.

- Murrisk Abbey 0.8km (yellow arrows)
- Mountain Loop 3.5km (blue arrows)
- Murrisk Pier 3.6km (green arrows)
- Murrisk Loop 4.5km (red arrows)

CLEW BAY AND ISLANDS

The unique landscape of Clew Bay is a legacy of the last Ice Age when the retreating glaciers left behind hundreds of low, elongated hills known as drumlins. These were then submerged by the rising sea levels caused by the melting of the ice caps.

Kayaking is the perfect way to explore the sheltered bay and its many islands. The Adventure Islands (www.theadventureislands.com), who have a base on Collanmore Island, offer full and half day sea kayak tours of the bay. Alternatively give the arms a rest and take a trip with Clew Bay Cruises (www.clewbaycruises.com).

Kayaking, Clew Bay | Christopher Tierney

The steep path up Croagh Patrick | RC

The National Famine Monument in Murrisk | DF

WESTPORT
The bustling town of Westport is full of shops, pubs and restaurants and was recently voted the best Irish small town to live in. On the edge of the town is Westport House (www.westporthouse.ie) which has a campsite and an adventure centre offering a high ropes course, zip wire, archery and zorbing [53.8006, -9.5354].

CYCLE HUB
The Westport cycle hub offers three routes varying in distance from 8km to 24km, but the Greenway will probably be of more interest to most cyclists.

BURRISHOOLE LOOP WALKS
From Westport the Wild Atlantic Way follows the coast north and then west along Clew Bay. This area has twelve signposted loop walks following quiet roads and gravel tracks. Some could also be cycled on a mountain bike. For detailed maps of all the routes see www.mayotrails.ie.

NEWPORT
There are five loops that start from the village and explore the surrounding countryside [53.8834, -9.5461].

- Abbey Walk 6km (blue arrows)
- Lecarrow Loop 7km (purple arrows)
- Derryhillagh Loop 8km (purple arrows)
- Lough Morchan Loop 8km (blue arrows)
- Doogary Loop 12km (red arrows)

There are also three very short walks around the village itself.

Looking across to Slievemore on Achill | DF

The Brogan Carroll Bothy | DF

Owenduff Valley | DF

THE BANGOR TRAIL

The Nephin Beg Range is the closest thing to wilderness that we have in Ireland. A vast expanse of hills, lakes and blanket bog, it is relatively untouched by man, however there is an ancient path that has been used for over a thousand years to travel through these mountains.

The path, known as the Bangor Trail, starts in the village of Bangor [54.1405, -9.7363] in the northwest and makes its way south through the mountains before joining the road near Newport.

The trail takes the path of least resistance so there aren't many long climbs, but the terrain is difficult, wet and boggy and each step needs to be chosen with care. The route is marked by posts at regular intervals, however in many places the path isn't obvious and it would be impossible to follow in thick mist without a map and compass.

It's possible to complete the 25km walk in a long day. The alternative is to do it over two days staying at either of the huts at the southern end of the trail. The Brogan Carroll Bothy [53.9893, -9.5728] in Letterkeen Woods is accessible from the road north of Newport, while the wooden hut [54.0042, -9.6203] built by Mountain Meitheal is further north along the trail near Lough Aroher.

The Bangor Trail and the Nephin Beg mountains are covered by Wild Nephin, East West Mapping's excellent map (www.eastwestmapping.ie).

The Greenway near Achill Island | DF

Burrishoole Bridge | DF

DERRADDA
Three loops around Lough Furnace and the foothills of the Nephin Mountains. The trailhead is the Derradda Community Centre [53.9038, -9.5866].

- Lettermaghera 8km (red arrows)
- Furnace 10km (blue arrows)
- Oghillies 11km (purple arrows)

TIERNAUR
The following walks start and finish at the Newfield Inn [53.9036, -9.6895].

- Glenthomas 11km (blue arrows).
- Knockbrega 13km (purple arrows)
- Tiernaur 15km (red arrows)

MULRANNY
Two loops start from Mulranny beach [53.8976, -9.7846]. The Causeway Loop 4km (blue arrows) crosses the salt marsh and returns via the road. The 6km Lookout Hill Loop extends the Causeway Loop by climbing up to the high ground behind the village.

GREAT WESTERN GREENWAY
The 42km Greenway is the longest off-road walking and cycling trail in Ireland. It follows the route of the Westport to Achill railway which closed in 1937. Since it opened in 2011 it has been very popular, bringing an influx of visitors, with 300 people walking or cycling the scenic route daily in the summer. The route is very well signposted and traffic free so it's very safe for children. It is divided into three sections:

- Westport to Newport (11km)
- Newport to Mulranny (18km)
- Mulranny to Achill (13km)

A large number of businesses have sprung up since the Greenway opened, including bike hire, guiding, shuttle services and bike friendly accommodation. See www.greenway.ie for route maps and the latest information on bike hire. ⬚

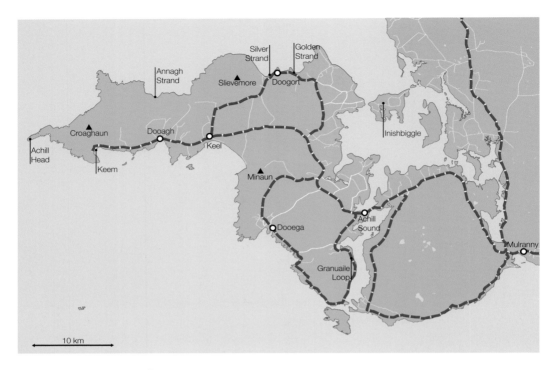

10 km

ACHILL ISLAND

Ireland's largest island, Achill, is joined to the mainland by a bridge so it doesn't quite have the same remote feel as the offshore islands. However, its position, jutting far out into the Atlantic, gives it a distinctive raw beauty all of its own.

At the northern and western end of the island rugged mountains rise directly out of the sea, while the southern and eastern shores are lined with great sandy beaches. This combination of mountains and coast in such close proximity is what makes Achill so special. It also means that the island, particularly the hills, receives more than its fair share of rain and wind, but this makes for dramatic, ever changing light that enhances the wonderful scenery.

There are two campsites on the island, Keel Sandybanks beside Keel beach (www. achillcamping.com) and Lavelle's in Doogort (www. lavellescaravanpark.com). There are also two hostels, Valley House near Doogort (www.valley-house. com) and The Railway House at Achill Sound (www. railwayhostel.ie).

INISHBIGGLE

The tiny, idyllic island of Inishbiggle lies in Blacksod Bay between Achill Island and the mainland. Some of the strongest currents in Europe flow around the

island and despite its proximity to the mainland there are times when the small community of native Irish speakers can be cut off from the rest of the world.

Access to the island is by boat from either Doran's Point [54.0053, -9.8686] (contact Michael Leneghan 087 1269618) at Ballycroy on the mainland or from Bull's Mouth [53.9969, -9.9300] (contact Joe O'Malley 086 0612482) on Achill. The crossing in currachs equipped with outboard engines takes about ten minutes.

It's possible to stay overnight on the island. Camp Biggle offers all the basic facilities in a beautiful garden setting [53.9950, -9.9107]. Email campbiggle@gmail. com to make a reservation.

There are two short signposted walks. The Gubnadoogha Loop (4km) starts and finishes at the east (mainland) side of the island and the Bull's Mouth Loop (5km) starts and finishes on the west (Achill) side of the island.

BEACHES

Achill has a great variety of beaches, from remote hidden coves to vast expanses of sand. Five have been awarded the Blue Flag, which is very impressive for one island. Keem and Keel are probably the best known but there are plenty of other excellent beaches.

Keem beach | Imagea

ANNAGH STRAND

The most remote beach on Achill, Annagh Strand, is about an hour walk from the road on the lonely north coast of the island [53.9993, -10.1335]. The beach is accessed via a steep descent through a band of cliffs that almost completely seals it off from the outside world. Thanks to its inaccessibility you are likely to have to it all to yourself (see the photo on page 10).

KEEM

The small curved strand at Keem lies at the very end of the road that traverses the island and is worth visiting for the spectacular drive from Dooagh alone [53.9673, -10.1955]. The beach is surrounded by steep slopes so it can be quite sheltered from the wind.

During the spring and early summer you may spot a basking shark. These huge filter-feeders are the world's second largest fish and can weight up to three tonnes.

In the fifties and sixties Achill Basking Shark Fishery operated in Keem Bay. The sharks, which were valued for their oil, were entangled in nets attached to the cliffs and killed by harpoons from currachs. They were then towed by larger boats to Purteen Harbour where the oil was extracted.

The southern end of the beach is an ideal snorkelling spot, suitable for beginners, that can be used at any tide. Look out for basking sharks, spider crabs and trigger fish. For further information consult the board in the carpark. Contact Keem Adventure (www.fb.com/KeemAdventure) for guided snorkelling and kayaking trips.

There is a lifeguard on duty every day during July and August.

KEEL

The 3km long beach at Keel (also known as Trawmore Strand) takes the full force of the Atlantic, creating ideal conditions for windsurfing, kiteboarding and surfing (there is also more sheltered water suitable for beginners on the lake behind the beach) [53.97360, -10.0734]. It's also the perfect place for a bracing walk on a wild winter's day.

Blackfield Surf School (www.blackfield.com) offer surfing lessons and rentals. Look out for their double decker bus that serves as a surf shop and coffee bar.

There are dangerous rip tides on certain sections of the beach so consult the lifeguards and signs before getting into the water.

DOOEGA

The fishing village of Dooega on the southern side of the island has a small, sheltered Blue Flag beach that is ideal for swimming [53.9212, -10.0184]. As it's located away from the island's most popular tourist areas it's rarely busy.

Keem Blueway | Roland Martins

DOOGORT
There are two Blue Flag beaches, Silver Strand *[54.0133, -10.0183]* and Golden Strand *[54.0122, -9.9949]*, on the north side of the island near Doogort. Both are close to the road, with plenty of parking and lifeguards during the summer.

The two beaches are linked by a 2.4km kayak trail. It's only suitable for proficient paddlers with sea kayaking experience. Less experienced kayakers should contact one of the providers listed on 167.

The Blueway should be avoided when the wind is offshore. Start at either strand and follow the rocky coastline. If you are lucky you may spot bottlenose dolphins and seals along the way. Watch out for tidal flows at the eastern headland near Silver Strand.

CYCLING
Cycling is an excellent way to get around the island and it's very popular as Achill lies at the western end of the Greenway (see page 161). There are three signposted loops, all of which start and finish in Keel. Traffic is generally light, but can get busy during the summer, especially on the main road across the island.

LOOP 1
A 44km route that travels around the coastline on the southern end of the island. The route is generally flat but there are a few short steep sections. It's possible to take a shortcut at Ashleam.

LOOP 2
This 28km loop follows quiet back roads north to Doogort, passing the beaches of Silver Strand and Golden Strand, the ideal place to stop for a swim, before returning along the main road.

LOOP 3
A pleasant 12km route with just a few gentle hills. It's worth making a short detour to visit the eerie deserted village *[53.9961, -10.0758]* on the slopes of Slievemore.

WALKING
Achill offers a wide range of walking, from gentle sunset strolls along the beach to gruelling days in the mountains. As much of the higher ground on the island is in common ownership it is freely accessible to hill walkers.

If you do venture onto the mountains you should be equipped for wet, windy weather and heavy cloud which can arrive without notice. You should carry a map (OSI sheet 30) and compass and be capable of navigating in low visibility.

Sunset from Minaun | RC

CROAGHAUN

Croaghaun (668m) dominates the western end of the island. Its northern slopes form some of the highest sea cliffs in Europe *[53.9840, -10.1964]*.

There are a few possible routes to the top. The most direct is from the carpark at Keem beach *[53.9673, -10.1955]* but no matter which route you choose it's a hard slog, but more than justified by the sensational views.

It's possible for strong hikers to do both Croaghaun and Slievemore in a day but you will need to arrange a taxi or do a shuttle to get back to your car.

ACHILL HEAD

This 7km loop starts and finishes at Keem beach *[53.9673, -10.1955]*. It's a great way to take in the fantastic cliff and coastal scenery of this, the wildest part of the island, while avoiding the hard climb up Croaghaun. See the photo on page 148.

From the beach, head in a southwesterly direction up the steep grassy slopes. Once you reach the cliffs follow them northwest (keeping a safe distance from the edge). At the point where the slender ridge of Achill Head juts into the sea turn east and follow the small stream down the valley back to the beach.

It's possible to extend the walk by following the narrow ridge to the end of Achill Head. The ridge is narrow and steep in places, and not advisable on a windy day, but experienced walkers with a head for heights will savour the sense of isolation at this lonely outpost.

DOOAGH LOOP

This gentle 4.3km signposted walk follows narrow bog roads in a loop above the village of Dooagh *[53.9750, -10.1281]*. It's ideal for stretching the legs on a day when the mountains are covered in cloud. Follow the purple arrows.

MINAUN

Minaun lies above the southeast end of Keel beach. The views from its summit are excellent and it's a great place to watch the sunset. It's possible to drive (signposted as 'Barr an Mhionnáin') to within a kilometre of the top, leaving only a gentle walk west to the summit which is marked by a cairn topped with a statue *[53.9497, -10.0396]*.

GRANUAILE LOOP

This 6.8km signposted (green arrows) trail is named after the pirate queen, Grace O'Malley, also known as Granuaile.

The walk is mainly on bog roads and some open ground (can be wet underfoot), in a loop around Derreen Hill. Part of the route follows the old funeral path to Kildownet Cemetery. Look out for the piles of rocks where the coffin was placed while the bearers took a rest.

Annagh Strand | Will Greene

To get to the start of the walk head west out of Achill Sound and after just under a kilometre turn left (signposted 'An Chloich Mhóir') onto the Atlantic Drive. Follow the road for 4km to Johnny Patten's pub which is the trailhead *[53.9030, -9.9413]*. No dogs are allowed as the walk goes through open farmland.

SLIEVEMORE
The elegant triangular profile of Slievemore rises straight from the sea at Doogort to 671m, making the climb to its summit a formidable slog *[54.0098, -10.0588]*.

The most interesting route up the mountain starts in Doogort and follows the prominent curved ridge to the summit. The view from the top, if you are lucky enough to reach it on a clear day, is one of the best along the Wild Atlantic Way.

From the beach *[54.0113, -10.0272]* follow the road west along the shore until there is open hillside to your left. Leave the road and head for the ridge. Follow an intermittent path up the left-hand side of the ridge keeping well back from the steep cliffs. The summit is marked by a trig pillar and a small stone shelter.

Return either by retracing your steps or by descending the west ridge to the deserted village *[53.9961, -10.0758]*, leaving a 4km road walk back to Doogort. ∎

Achill Head ridge | RC

Surfing at Keel | Ian Boyle

ACTIVITY PROVIDERS ON ACHILL

PURE MAGIC
Kitesurfing, stand up paddleboarding
www.puremagic.ie

ACHILL ISLAND SCUBA DIVE CENTRE
Scuba diving
www.achilldivecentre.com

CALVEY'S EQUESTRIAN
Horse riding
www.calveysofachill.com

ACHILL SURF AND KAYAK
Surfing, kayaking, rock climbing, coasteering,
www.achillsurf.com

ACHILL OUTDOOR EDUCATION CENTRE
Canoeing, kayaking, sailing, windsurfing, surfing,
rock climbing, archery
www.achilloutdoor.com

ACHILL SEA ANGLING
Deep-sea fishing
tmburke@eircom.net

TOMÁS MAC LOCHLÁINN
Walking guide
siul@eircom.net

SAOIRSE NA MARA
Sea kayaking
www.irelandwestseakayaking.com

ACHILL BIKES
Dooagh and Achill Sound during the summer
www.achillbikes.com

CLEW BAY BIKE HIRE
Westport, Newport, Mulranny, and Achill Sound
www.clewbayoutdoors.ie

WEST COAST CLIMBING AND ADVENTURE
Kayaking, rock climbing, hiking
www.westclimbadventure.ie

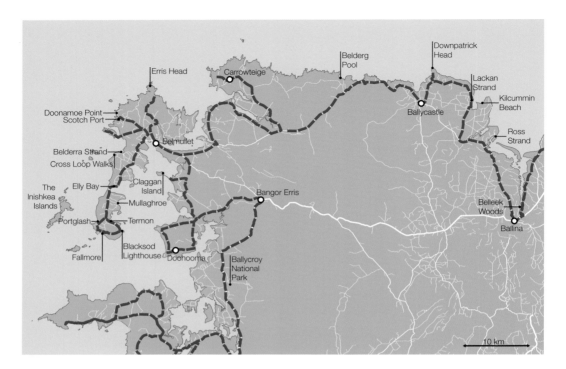

ERRIS

Erris, in the northwest corner of Mayo, is the emptiest, wildest part of Ireland. The landscape, which is characterised by vast swathes of blanket bog, and the coast are extremely rugged with some of the most impressive cliff and rock architecture in the country.

It's also one of the most overlooked stretches of the west coast, and is much quieter than the better known tourist areas like Dingle or Connemara. However that's not to say it's any less beautiful. Its beaches and coastal walks easily rival those of the more famous regions. Erris is the ideal destination for those looking to experience the wild landscape of the west coast in a quiet setting.

The sculpture trails that run along the coast of Erris and North Mayo are the most extensive of their kind in the country. They offer a unique and really interesting way to get to know the landscape. See page 177.

Erris Beo, the tourism cooperative, has created a very useful smartphone app that has detailed information on the many points of interest in the area. Once downloaded it's available off-line. See www.app. errisbeo.ie for details.

The only hostel in the area is Kilcommon Lodge *[54.2661, -9.8001]* (www.kilcommonlodge.ie). There aren't any formal campsites but there are plenty of opportunities for wild camping.

BALLYCROY NATIONAL PARK
Ballycroy National Park covers 11,000 hectares of blanket bog and mountain. The park is dominated by the Nephin Beg Range and Owenduff Bog, one of the last intact active blanket bog systems in Western Europe.

The Park's visitor centre *[54.0245, -9.8235]*, located in Ballycroy village along the Wild Atlantic Way between Mulranny and Bangor, houses an exhibition of the landscape, habitats and species found in the Park and the surrounding area. It's a good place to escape the weather on a rainy day.

There is a short (1.8km) nature trail that offers panoramic views of Achill Island to the west and the Nephin Beg mountains to the east. The trail, known as Tóchar Daithí Bán is named after the mythical giant Daithí Bán who built a fortress on the park's tallest mountain, Slieve Carr.

There is another nature trail further south along the Wild Atlantic Way between Mulranny and Ballycroy *[53.9573, -9.7926]*. The 2km loop follows a wooden boardwalk south before returning along the shore (only

Ballycroy Visitor Centre | DF

possible at low tide). If you are very lucky you may catch a glimpse of an otter.

DOOHOOMA
A quiet peninsula well off the beaten track. The long, sandy, sheltered beach has stunning views of Achill and Blacksod Bay [54.0715, -9.9630]. If you pass through the pretty fishing village of Doohooma check out the charming Sea Rod Inn (www.thesearodinn.ie) which has rooms, a restaurant and a pub.

CLAGGAN ISLAND
Claggan Island is Mayo's newest island - it was only officially declared an island in 1991 after storms flooded the narrow sandy causeway (not driveable) that links it to the mainland [54.1779, -9.9669].

The former coastguard station on the island is available for rent, as are two wooden pods. See www.belmulletcgs.com for details.

Srah Beach connects Claggan with the mainland. The 4km curved strand has a Green Coast award and is perfect for both swimming and strolling [54.1725, -9.9550].

BELMULLET
The town of Belmullet is on the thin strip of land that joins the Mullet Peninsula with the rest of the world. To the north is Broadhaven Bay and to the south is Blacksod Bay.

BELMULLET TIDAL POOL
A saltwater swimming pool is located a short walk from the town centre, in Blacksod Bay [54.2173, -9.9902]. It has a toddler's area and a deeper section for experienced swimmers. During July and August there is a lifeguard as well as swimming and safety lessons for children. Follow the coast south from the western end of the Main Street.

BELMULLET CYCLE HUB
Belmullet serves as a hub for two linear and two looped signposted cycle routes ranging in distance from 37km to 72km. Each route offers breathtaking views of the Mayo coast. Sections of all these routes are on busy roads so take care.

Two linear routes join Belmullet and Ballycastle. The more direct option is the North Mayo Linear Route (49km) which follows the busy R314. The quieter option is the 72km Rossport and Glinsk Linear Route which includes a short loop around Rossport and follows some very quiet scenic roads between Rossport and Belderg.

There are also two loops around the surrounding area. The Carrowmore Lake Loop is a gentle 37km circuit on good surfaces. There are good views from the R313 out of Belmullet, then a quiet road follows the western shore to Carrowmore Lake before returning along the R314. The Pullathomas Loop is a 50km route that keeps close to the coast and is fairly

Portglash | RC

flat following good roads with views over Broadhaven and Sruwaddacon Bay.

You can hire bikes from Belmullet Adventure Centre (www.belmulletadventurecentre.com) and Léim Siar Bed and Breakfast (www.leimsiar.com).

BEACHES

The coastline on the southern half of the Mullet Peninsula has no shortage of beautiful sandy beaches. As a rule those facing the Atlantic are wild and windswept, while those on the Blacksod Bay side are calmer.

• The Blue Flag beach at Elly Bay is clean, sheltered and ideal for swimming, sailing and other water sports [54.1623, -10.0865]. On the opposite side of the peninsula is another beach that is popular with surfers. Avoid swimming here when there is a swell as there can be strong currents [54.1593, -10.0972].

• Mullaghroe, a quiet Blue Flag beach a short drive from the main road [54.1386, -10.0768].

• Termon beach, on the east side of the peninsula, has a Green Coast award [54.1126, -10.0924].

• Fallmore is a beautiful south-facing beach, with magnificent views of Achill Island. Sheltered when there's a northerly wind [54.0959, -10.1110].

• Portglash is a very quiet beach that looks across the water to the Inishkea Islands [54.1119, -10.1211].

• Belderra Strand, which is just north of the much larger Cross Beach [54.2085, -10.0828], is well sheltered and quiet. Watch out for strong currents [54.2086, -10.0636].

• Scotch Port is a beautiful bay with a stony beach. The water is crystal clear and there is plenty of colourful marine life so it's an ideal snorkelling spot [54.2551, -10.0732].

THE INISHKEA ISLANDS

Inishkea North and Inishkea South lie four kilometres west of the Mullet Peninsula. They are low lying, with no trees and are covered in short grass and beautiful fine white sand. The sand lies everywhere and it's slowly filling the abandoned houses that face the beach at the harbour.

In 1927 the island's men went out fishing and were caught in a violent storm in which ten fishermen lost their lives. After this the inhabitants of the island, devastated by their loss, left to live on the mainland.

Now the islands lie uninhabited and are slowing returning to a wild state, home to a thriving population of seals and sea birds. They are rarely visited and there is no regular ferry service, however it's possible to charter a boat. Contact Geraghty Charters at info@bruchlannlir.com or Dive West Ireland www.divewestireland.com for more information.

BLACKSOD LIGHTHOUSE

At the southern tip of the peninsula is Blacksod Lighthouse [54.0985, -10.0604]. It is famous for the important role it played in the success of the D-Day landings. A report warning of bad weather which

The village on Inishkea South | Frank Fullard

Blacksod Lighthouse | DF

Cross Graveyard | DF

issued from the lighthouse convinced the Allies to delay the invasion for 24 hours, a decision which averted a military catastrophe.

CROSS LOOP WALKS

The Cross Loop is a beautiful coastal trail that starts at the ruins of Cross Abbey [54.2085, -10.0828]. From the walk there is a great view across the water to the islands of Inishkea and Inishglora, the burial place of the mythical Children of Lir. It's best done in a clockwise direction at low tide. There are two options, a 5.7km circuit (green arrows) and a 6km variation (blue arrows).

Both routes follow the beach south around Corraun Point before turning inland and along the track on the shore of Cross Lough. The longer variation loops around the far side of the lake.

To reach the trailhead follow the R313 south from Belmullet town (signposted 'An Fód Dubh'), after 5km turn right at the church in Binghamstown. Continue past Belderra Strand until you see the signpost directing you to turn right.

DOONAMOE POINT

With uninterrupted views of the Atlantic, this is one of the best viewpoints in Erris and is the ideal spot to watch the sun set [54.2645, -10.0753]. A large sculpture has been built around the impressive blowhole (see page 177) and on rough days sea spray and foam explode up from it.

Benwee Head | RC

ERRIS HEAD

Erris Head, the northernmost point of the Mullet Peninsula, is a remote spot with wonderful scenery and a wild feel. It juts out into the sea and takes everything the Atlantic can throw at it. The headland is home to a wide variety of wildlife. Look out for choughs nesting on the cliffs, hares on the cliff tops and seals, porpoises and bottlenose dolphins in the water below.

ERRIS HEAD LOOP

The trailhead for this 5km signposted walk is the small carpark at the end of the road [54.2886, -9.9886]. It is signposted (as 'Ceann Iorrais') from Belmullet. The walk takes a clockwise loop around the headland and the ground can be boggy in places. Keep well back from the cliff edges. This walk should be avoided in very windy weather.

At the northernmost point of the walk there is a railed viewing point where you can enjoy the spectacular views of the surrounding cliffs and the Stags of Broadhaven in the distance.

As you continue along the trail watch out for the World War Two lookout post and the faint outline of 'EIRE 62' which identified the land as neutral Ireland to pilots during the war.

CEATHRÚ THAIDHG

The cliffs near the small Irish-speaking village of Carrowteige (Ceathrú Thaidhg) are some of the most spectacular along the Wild Atlantic Way. The small village is the trailhead for four signposted walks [54.3131, -9.8128]. Download maps of the walks from www.irishtrails.ie.

There are two nice beaches in the area, the remote Green Flag beach at Portacloy [54.3312, -9.7835] and the more sheltered Rinroe Strand [54.3022, -9.8411].

CHILDREN OF LIR WALK

This is a beautiful 10km coastal walk through a wild landscape of bog and windswept mountainside. It follows surfaced roads, grassy tracks and paths and brings you past the Children of Lir sculpture, which overlooks the most impressive cliffs of Benwee Head. It is signposted with blue arrows.

This walk is named after the famous legend, 'The Children of Lir', which tells of four children who were turned into swans and condemned to wander the countryside for 900 years, with 300 of these being spent on the island of Inishglora, off the coast of Mullet. If you are short of time it's possible to start the Children of Lir loop at the carpark [54.3236, -9.8404] beside the Children of Lir sculpture.

There are two variations of this walk. The 6.5km Beach Loop (green arrows) follows the road down to

Portacloy | RC

Rinroe Strand *[54.3021, -9.8411]* and is ideal when it's too windy for the other, more exposed, walks. The other is the 13km Black Ditch loop (red arrows) which is a slightly longer version of the original loop.

If you are looking for a more challenging route then you could combine the Children of Lir and Benwee Head walks to create a 16km route along the cliffs from Rinroe to Portacloy.

BENWEE HEAD WALK

This remote 12.4km signposted (purple arrows) loop follows the dramatic coastline north of Carrowteige with some excellent views of the huge cliffs. The ground can be boggy in places. The trailhead is in Carrowteige opposite the post office *[54.3131, -9.8128]*.

BELDERG POOL

The tiny fishing port of Belderg is home to a natural swimming pool, known as Pol A Sean tSaile, that is popular with locals *[54.3119, -9.5529]*. It's a good spot for a swim when the sea is rough. Turn off the Wild Atlantic Way at Belderg *[54.2935, -9.5508]* (not signposted) and follow the small road down to the sea. The pool is behind the harbour wall.

CÉIDE FIELDS

This ancient network of stone walls was discovered in the 1930s by a local schoolteacher when he was cutting turf. It's the most extensive Stone Age monument in the world, consisting of field systems, dwelling areas and megalithic tombs. The stone walled fields, extending over thousands of acres, are almost 6,000 years old, the oldest in the world. The visitor centre at the Céide Fields explores the archaeology of the site and the botany and geology of the area *[54.3082, -9.4565]*.

The remains themselves may be a little underwhelming, but it's worth a stop to admire the view from the platform on the edge of the 100m tall cliffs.

BALLYCASTLE WALK

The Sralagagh Loop is a pleasant signposted loop with great views of Downpatrick Head. The 9.5km route follows narrow roads and tracks and is suitable for both walking and mountain biking. The walk starts and finishes in Ballycastle village *[54.2798, -9.3734]*.

DOWNPATRICK HEAD

Just a few miles north of Ballycastle village is Downpatrick Head. The spectacular sea stack, Dún Briste (The Broken Fort), which lies just off the tip of the headland, is one of the iconic images of Ireland *[54.3228, -9.3458]*.

The cliff scenery is spectacular, but the headland is very exposed to the elements so take care near the cliff edge, especially on windy days.

Dún Briste | RC

There are two blowholes close to the Head. The larger one has a sculpture/viewing platform which is part of the North Mayo Sculpture Trail (see page 177).

LACKAN STRAND

This vast sandy beach is formed in the bay where the Cloonalaghan River joins the sea [54.2741, -9.2574]. The beach is completely covered by water twice a day so make sure that you don't get cut off by the rising tide. If swimming, be alert for dangerous currents and heed the warning signs.

On the other side of the small estuary is Kilcummin beach [54.2789, -9.2318]. More sheltered and remote, it's backed by towering sand dunes. It is accessible at low tide by walking across the sand from Lackan (watch the tide) and by car via the back roads from Kilcummin village.

The picnic area beside Lackan Church [54.2741, -9.2574] is the trailhead for the Rathlackan Court Tomb Trails which explore some very quiet lanes and tracks. There are two variations, an 11km version (blue arrows) and a shorter 8km loop (green arrows).

ROSS STRAND

Ross Strand lies on the westerly side of Killala where the River Moy reaches the sea [54.2327, -9.1980]. The most northerly of Mayo's Blue Flag beaches, it has great views across the bay to the coast of Sligo. The flat sand is a great place for a long walk at low tide.

Lifeguards are on duty during July and August. Beware of the strong currents and keep inside the designated swimming areas. The best time to swim is at high tide, but at low tide there are lots of interesting rock pools just north of the carpark.

BELLEEK WOODS

Just north of the town of Ballina, on the banks of the River Moy, is Belleek Woods [54.1301, -9.1428]. A 4km long signposted trail follows a series of paths through the peaceful 1,000 acre forest. Follow the signs for Belleek Castle from the centre of town.

Sea kayaking near Benwee Head | Gareth McCormack

ACTIVITY PROVIDERS IN NORTH MAYO

Elements Kitesurfing
Kitesurfing
www.elementskitesurfing.com

BELMULLET ADVENTURE CENTRE
Cycling, surfing, hiking, kayaking
www.belmulletadventurecentre.com

WAVESWEEPER SEA ADVENTURES
Surfing, snorkelling, kayaking, powerboating, coasteering
www.wavesweeperseaadventures.com

BELLACRAGHER BAY BOAT CLUB
Sailing, powerboating
www.bellacragherboatclub.jimdo.com

UISCE
Sailing, windsurfing, surfing
www.uisce.ie

BANGOR ERRIS ANGLING
Salmon and sea trout fishing
www.bangorerrisangling.com

DUVILLAUN RIDING CENTRE
Horse riding
duvillaunridingcentre@gmail.com

TOURISM PURE WALKING HOLIDAYS
Guided walking tours
www.tourismpure.com

PADDLE AND PEDAL
Cycling and Kayak tours
www.paddleandpedal.ie

GAOL SIAR
Foraging, seashore tours and workshops
www.gaolsiar.com

The Vault of Heaven, Annagh Head | DF

Tearmann na Gaoithe, Kilcummin | DF

The Thin Places, Land Eating the Sea, Annagh Head | DF

The Thin Places, Sea Eating the Land, Doonamoe | DF

The Crossing, Downpatrick Head | Michael McLaughlin

Deirbhle's Twist, Fallmore | DF

MAYO SCULPTURE TRAILS

North Mayo is home to two outdoor sculpture trails, Tír Sáile and Spirit of Place. Between the two trails there are more than twenty sculptures scattered along the coast, many in scenic, remote locations. Seeking out the sculptures, visiting a place you otherwise mightn't have gone, adds an extra dimension to a visit to this part of the country.

TÍR SÁILE

Tír Sáile, The North Mayo Sculpture Trail, is the largest public arts project in Ireland. It consists of fifteen sculptures celebrating the wild beauty of the area and its long history of human habitation.

Most of the sculptures are well signposted (by brown signs marked 'Tír Sáile') but unfortunately some of the sculptures have fallen into disrepair. Thankfully there are plans to rejuvenate and better document the trail in the near future.

SPIRIT OF PLACE

Spirit of Place was conceived by Architect and Professor Travis Price at The Catholic University of America. The program designs and then builds in nine days, structures that reflect upon ancient folklore. Spirit of Place has built seven large structures along the Mayo coast in concert with Mayo County Council.

- A Home for the Children of Lir, Ceathrú Thaidhg (see page 172) *[54.3244, -9.8401]*.
- Temple of the Tides of Time, Belmullet *[54.2256, -9.9921]*.
- The Thin Places, Land Eating the Sea, Annagh Head *[54.2417, -10.1045]*.
- The Thin Places, Sea Eating the Land, Doonamoe *[54.2644, -10.0758]*.
- The Vault of Heaven, Annagh Head *[54.2426, -10.0894]*.
- Tale of the Tongs, Inishturk Island (see page 154) *[53.7079, -10.1067]*.
- The Crossing, Downpatrick Head, Ballycastle (see page 173) *[54.3254, -9.3467]*.

For more information about the program see www.spiritofplace-design.com. ∎

Walking the Mullaghmore headland with Classiebawn Castle and Benbulbin in the background | Gareth Wray

SLIGO
AND
LEITRIM

The Sligo coast (and the short strip of Leitrim that meets the sea) is one of the more gentle sections of the Wild Atlantic Way. Here the green fields run straight down to the shore and cattle graze on the sweet and salty grass.

A short distance inland there are mountains that are very different in character to those to the north and south, but are just as impressive. The geological foundation is limestone that has been eroded to leave vertical cliffs with flat summits, a form that is exemplified in the iconic profile of Benbulbin.

Also inland from the coast are a number of worthwhile diversions including the wooded shores of Lough Gill near Sligo Town and the beautiful valley of Glencar in Leitrim with its spectacular waterfalls.

Sligo is world famous for its surfing, with spots like Strandhill, Mullaghmore Beach, Easky and Enniscrone recognised internationally as having some of the best surf in Europe.

179

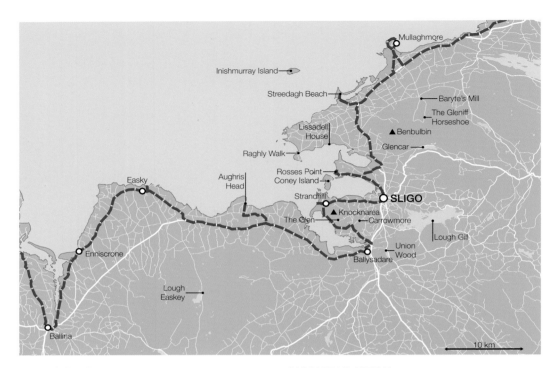

ENNISCRONE

This lively little seaside town backs onto a vast, sandy Blue Flag beach that stretches for 5km *[54.2122, -9.0972]*. There is a lifeguard on duty on weekends during June and September and daily in July and August.

The beach break is an ideal place to learn to surf. Two surf schools offer board hire and lessons, North West Surf School (www.nwsurfschool.com) and 7th Wave Surf School (www.surfsligo.com).

Harbour SUP n Sail (www.harboursupsail.com) offer paddleboarding and dinghy sailing lessons in the sheltered waters of the harbour *[54.2199, -9.0953]*.

EASKY

This small village is world famous among surfers for the wave that breaks near the mouth of the river *[54.2859, -8.9607]*. There are always a few dilapidated vans and caravans on the commonage beside the castle where camping seems to be tolerated *[54.2912, -8.9573]*.

LOUGH EASKY

Upriver from the village in the Ox Mountains is Lough Easky *[54.1594, -8.8436]*. A 6km signposted (purple arrows) trail loops around the lake. The trail is pretty flat but, as much of the ground is blanket bog, a good pair of boots is essential if you want to keep your feet dry.

AUGHRIS HEAD

Near the tip of this rocky headland is The Beach Bar *[54.2688, -8.7572]*, a well-known thatched pub that serves food and has a small campsite.

There is a short but worthwhile walk along the clifftop path on the east side of Aughris Head. From The Beach Bar walk back up the road and turn right. Just before the pier a small grassy track makes its way west along the coast. Follow this. At the far end of the rocky cove look out for the distinctive curved banks of an Iron Age promontory fort that is slowly being consumed by the sea *[54.2781, -8.7557]*. Shortly after the fort the path tapers out, and it's time to retrace your steps.

Note the beach to the west of Aughris Head, at Rathglass, is unsafe for swimming due to dangerous currents.

DUNMORAN STRAND

East of Aughris Head is Dunmoran Strand, a sheltered bay with a nice sandy Green Coast beach. The beach can be accessed from the carpark at its eastern end, or from The Beach Bar *[54.2625, -8.7245]*.

UNION WOOD

Just east of the village of Ballysadare, a few minutes from the Dublin-Sligo road, is Union Wood *[54.2135, -8.4710]*. The forest is a mix of broadleaf and

Enniscrone Beach | Discover Enniscrone

The Beach Bar, Aughris | DF

Carrowmore | DF

coniferous trees. There are great views of Knocknarea and the Ox Mountains from the top of Union Rock.

There are two signposted walks in the forest. The 4km Union Rock Trail (red arrows) has a few steep climbs. It loops around Union Rock, but it's worth making a diversion to see the views from the top. The second route is the 5.5km Oakwood Trail (green arrows) which takes a low-level route around the hill, passing through some beautiful oak forest.

From Sligo Town head south on the N4 and take the N59 exit to Carraroe. Take the first exit off the Carraroe roundabout and turn left at the church onto the R287. Take an immediate right onto the R284, signposted Keadew. Look out for Union Wood on the right after approximately 4km.

CARROWMORE

A short drive from Strandhill in the townland of Carrowmore is one of Ireland's most extensive prehistoric cemeteries *[54.2135, -8.4710]*. It is the largest group of megaliths in the country and the second largest in Europe. The monuments range from four and a half thousand to six thousand years old. The dolmens, which consist of a number of standing stones supporting a large flat horizontal capstone, are the only remnant of the burial chambers which were originally covered with earth and stones. Archaeologists have recorded over sixty tombs, of which thirty are visible today.

The view from Knocknarea towards Benbulbin | Graham Higgs

HOSTELS

The Beach Bar, Aughris
www.thebeachbarsligo.com

Harbour House Guest House, Sligo Town
www.harbourhousehostel.com

Ocean Wave Lodge, Strandhill
www.oceanwavelodge.com

The White House Hostel, Sligo Town

The Railway Hostel, Sligo Town
www.therailway.ie

Surf n Stay, Strandhill
www.surfnstay.ie

CAMPSITES

Atlantic Caravan Park, Enniscrone
www.atlanticcaravanpark.com

Easkey Caravan Park, Easky
www.easkey.ie

Greenlands Caravan and Camping, Rosses Point
www.greenlandscaravanpark.com

The Beach Bar, Aughris
www.thebeachbarsligo.com

Strandhill Park, Strandhill
www.sligocaravanandcamping.ie

The visitor centre is open daily during the summer and offers guided tours and multilingual self-guide options (admission €4).

Coming from the south follow the Wild Atlantic Way from the N4 towards Strandhill. In the village of Knocknahur take the first exit off the roundabout, the visitor centre is on the right after 1.5km.

THE GLEN

Truly a hidden gem, the Glen is a narrow canyon that runs for just under a kilometre *[54.2482, -8.5764]*. Almost completely hidden from view and difficult to find, it's a peaceful, still place with a lush, rainforest feel. The vertical limestone walls and the thick vegetation nearly completely obscure the sky.

To find it, follow the Wild Atlantic Way south out of Strandhill. After 3km take the left turn signposted for Knocknarea. Drive 600m up the hill and park in the scenic layby on the right *[54.2481, -8.5733]*. Walk back down the hill. After 300m look out for a small well on the right, the entrance is directly opposite this. The ground in the Glen is always very wet and muddy so wear Wellingtons or hiking boots.

STRANDHILL

This small seaside village has a real surfer vibe *[54.2694, -8.6102]*. The seafront, which has some very nice cafés and coffee shops, is a great spot to watch the surfers in action.

Be warned that swimming is strictly prohibited at the beach due to the very dangerous currents and rip tides. If you want to get into the water then go for a soak at Voya Seaweed Baths (www.voyaseaweedbaths.com) on the seafront.

The Glen | DF

SURFING

Strandhill has become a Mecca for surfers from far and wide. It is considered one of the best beach breaks in the country. County regulations prohibit surfboard rental in Strandhill due to the dangerous currents. But if you want to give it a go then you can take a lesson with one of the surf schools (iSurfIreland www.isurfireland.com, Strandhill Surf School www.strandhillsurfschool.com or Surf n Stay www.surfnstay.ie) who provide all the required equipment.

The beach at Strandhill is northwest-facing and picks up any swell from southwest to north, making it one of the most consistent breaks in Ireland. The beach is sand-bottomed and is surrounded by many other reef and point breaks.

County Sligo Surf Club, on the second floor above Voya Seaweed Baths, has changing and shower facilities.

CULLEENAMORE BEACH

South of the village, in the sheltered water of Ballysadare Bay, is the sandy Culleenamore Beach [54.2593, -8.6006]. It's well protected from the big waves so is a safe place to swim (though there is no lifeguard). On warm summer days look out for seals soaking up the sun on the sandbanks.

There is a nice 7km walk that follows the coast south from Strandhill around the sandy headland to Culleenamore. To return either retrace your steps or take the path through the dunes as a shortcut.

KILLASPUGBRONE LOOP

This 7km signposted walk explores the coast north of Strandhill. From the seafront head north along the dunes or through the campsite (note there is no swimming on this beach due to dangerous currents) following the purple arrows. The trail passes Sligo Airport and then swings east past Killaspugbrone Church, an early Christian site, and along Dorrins Strand before returning along the road to the village.

KNOCKNAREA

The distinctive steep profile of Knocknarea rises up behind Strandhill [54.2585, -8.5741]. At the summit is a huge pile of stones, known as Meabh's Cairn, that is believed to contain a neolithic passage tomb. Please don't climb the cairn or remove any stones from it.

The reward for the short, steep climb is the spectacular view in all directions, taking in the Ox Mountains, Lough Gill, Benbulbin, Slieve League in Donegal, and on a clear day, Croagh Patrick to the southwest.

Until recently the most popular route to the top started from a carpark [54.2532, -8.5575] on the southeast side but this has been superseded by the Queen Maeve Trail. This 2.4km route starts opposite the Sligo Rugby Club, which is just east of Strandhill

Slishwood | DF

along the northbound Wild Atlantic Way *[54.27051, -8.5848]*. A gravel path and wooden boardwalk lead through the trees to the summit. Decent footwear is recommended as the trail, particularly the wooden boardwalk, can be damp and slippery.

CONEY ISLAND

The 400 acre Coney Island is the largest and the best known of the three islands off the northern coast of the Coolera Peninsula. It is very popular with holidaymakers during the summer.

The only facility on the island is McGowan's pub *[54.3003, -8.5797]*. There are two nice beaches, a small one by the pier *[54.3020, -8.5801]* and Carty's Strand, on the west side *[54.2995, -8.5936]*. Caution is required if you are going to swim as there can be dangerous currents. Enquire locally.

Coney Island, which translates as 'The Island of Rabbits', gave its name to the American Coney Island. In the 18th century the captain of a merchant ship, a Sligo man, noting lots of rabbits on the New York island, named it after his own Coney Island back in Sligo.

Access to the island is by boat from Rosses Point, or by driving at low tide over the 2.5km causeway across Cummeen Strand *[54.2795, -8.5522]*. To find the start of the causeway follow the Wild Atlantic Way towards Strandhill from Sligo Town. After 4km take the right turn and follow the road. Be warned the crossing is rough on a car, with many deep saltwater puddles and hard, rutted sand.

LOUGH GILL

A short distance inland from Sligo Town is Lough Gill. Its beautiful, serene waters lie in sharp contrast with the more turbulent Atlantic. The 5km long lake contains about twenty small islands, including the Isle of Inishfree, made famous by the W. B. Yeats poem of the same name.

The lake is surrounded by woodland, mostly of oak, rowan and willow, but also a number of other species such as yew, strawberry tree, and the rare bird cherry and rock whitebeam. The lake supports a number of protected species of lamprey, as well as salmon and otter. Plenty of animals also live in the woods. Of particular note is the community of pine martens.

Two companies offer boat tours of the lake departing from the quays east of Sligo Town - Lough Gill Tours (www.loughgilltours.com) and Rose of Inishfree (www.roseofinnisfree.com).

CYCLE LOOP

A 40km cycle route circumnavigates Lough Gill in a clockwise direction. While the route is well signposted, some of the roads can be quite busy. En route you will pass many wonderful forests and viewing points so it's a great way to see the lake. Wild Atlantic Wheels (www.fb.com/wild.atlantic.ways.sligo) offer bike hire,

Paddleboarding on Lough Gill | SUP For All

Drumcliffe High Cross | RC

as well as lunches and minibus transfers for this and many other cycling routes around Sligo.

DOONEE ROCK FOREST PARK
A 1.2km trail follows a path through this mainly coniferous forest to the viewing point on top of Doonee Rock [54.2384, -8.4279].

SLISHWOOD
This is a stunning location between the southern shore of the lake and the Ox Mountains [54.2307, -8.4013]. A delightful 3km signposted loop passes through the remains of an ancient oak woodland. The wood is home to plenty of native wildlife including mute swans, ducks and herons, while badger, fox and fallow deer may also be seen.

HAZELWOOD DEMENSE
This beautiful lakeside forest is just 3km east of Sligo Town at Half Moon Bay [54.2580, -8.4264]. The Wynne family, who built Hazelwood House, planted most of the mature trees in this area including many species that are not native to Ireland such as beech, hornbeam, lime, rhododendron and cherry laurel.

As well as a quiet picnic area there is a 3km nature trail and a sculpture trail. Unfortunately, many of the wood carvings are in a bad state of repair.

DEERPARK COURT TOMB TRAIL
This 3.5km trail follows forest tracks over a series of hills and hollows [54.2820, -8.3756]. The court tomb, which dates back to the third millennium BC, is considered one of the finest of its type in the country. From the tomb there are expansive views over Lough Gill and the Glencar Valley.

KAYAKING
Gliding quietly across the water in a kayak is a great way to experience Lough Gill. Sligo Kayak Tours (www.sligokayaktours.com) run guided tours of the lake and some of the more sheltered coastal estuaries.

Stand Up Paddleboarding, also known as SUP, is another excellent way of exploring the lake. Two companies offer tours, Perfect Day Surf School (www.perfectdaysurfing.ie) and SUP for All (www.fb.com/SUPforall).

ROSSES POINT
The jutting peninsula north of Sligo Town is very popular with holidaymakers and gets very busy on nice summer days [54.3088, -8.5707].

The beach, which has a Blue Flag and a Green Coast award, is divided in two by a small rocky headland. There is a lifeguard on duty at weekends during June and September, and daily in July and August.

Glencar Waterfall | RC

The smaller, southern beach is more accessible and busier. The northern beach, which backs the golf course, is longer and quieter. Look out for the caves, known as the Cellars, at its southern end.

ROSSES WALK
A very pleasant 7km stroll starts from the main beach carpark [54.3088, -8.5707]. Follow the beach north skirting the golf course to the end of the long, sandy spit before retracing your steps.

GLENCAR
It's well worth diverting the short distance from the coast to visit the valley of Glencar. The valley's steep limestone walls give it an almost alpine appearance, hence its alternative name - Swiss Valley. The famous waterfall is very pretty and only a short walk through lush woodland from the carpark [54.3386, -8.3692]. The great thing about the waterfall is that it's much more impressive on a rainy day, of which we have one or two!

From Sligo Town take the N16 toward Manorhamilton. After about 8km look out for a left turn (signposted). Follow this road to the carpark at the far end of the lake.

TORMORE TRAIL
A pleasant but steep 2.3km trail leads through native woodland to the base of Sruth In Aghaidh An Aird, also known as The Devil's Chimney. Roughly 100m tall, the waterfall is one of the highest in Ireland. The Irish name translates as 'stream against the height' which refers to the fact that when the wind blows from the west the water appears to rise back up the cliff. Be warned that the waterfall doesn't flow during dry weather, however it is particularly spectacular after heavy rain.

The walk starts from the northern shore of Glencar Lough, 1.5km west of the waterfall carpark [54.3405, -8.3930].

DOONEENS WALK
A steep walk with spectacular views of Glencar Lough, Swiss Valley, and Sligo Bay. The 7km round trip is well signposted (yellow arrows) and on good roads and tracks.

Park at the small lakeside carpark [54.3408, -8.3748] west of the waterfall carpark. Just opposite this is a steep, winding road. Follow it up to the mountain plateau. Pass through a set of gates and follow the old bog road right to the end and enjoy the view.

BENBULBIN
The flat summit, steep ribbed sides, and angular corners of Benbulbin give it an unmistakable profile. Its spectacular appearance owes more to the South American tepui than the rounded hills more common in this part of the world. The distinctive peak

The Devil's Chimney | Ford Fisher

Benbulbin | Gareth Wray

was formed during the last Ice Age when massive retreating glaciers carved the landscape. Its steeper sides are limestone, while the smoother slopes are shale.

The summit plateau's unusual landscape is home to a wide variety of flora and fauna, including Arctic alpine plants, foxes, wild hares and choughs.

As there are some access issues with walking to the summit, which is not particularly memorable anyway, this incredible mountain is best appreciated from below.

GORTAROWEY WALK
This 4km walk is a pretty straightforward out and back along forest tracks, but the views of the northern slopes of Benbulbin make it very worthwhile. Driving north along the Wild Atlantic Way look out for a right turn (signposted 'Ben Bulben Forest Walk') 3.5km past the village of Drumcliffe (where Yeats is buried). Follow the road to the carpark in the forest [54.3616, -8.5021].

LISSADELL HOUSE
The beautiful house [54.3492, -8.5850] is famous as the childhood home of Constance Markievicz, one of the leaders of the 1916 Rising and the first woman elected to the British House of Commons. For a fee (€12) you get a guided tour of the house, entry to the current exhibitions as well as the beautiful alpine and kitchen gardens. The café is open daily in the summer.

RAGHLY WALK
Raghly is a tiny headland that juts out into Sligo Bay. Apparently the easy 2.2km loop around its narrow roads was one of Yeats' favourite walks. The views over Benbulbin, Knocknarea and Sligo Bay are excellent.

To get to the start, continue along the road past Lissadell House, following signs for 'Raghley' until you reach the narrow neck of land. Park here on the right [54.3311, -8.6472] and take either turn at the junction. Both will bring you in a loop around the headland.

STREEDAGH BEACH
This long sandy beach, known as the Back Strand [54.4042, -8.5598], forms a narrow tombolo which joins Streedagh Point to Conor's Island. The Green Coast beach has some good surf suitable for intermediate surfers. There is a lifeguard on duty on weekends during July and August.

This is a great spot for an invigorating walk on a winter's day with excellent views of Benbulbin, Mullaghmore Head and across Donegal Bay to Slieve League. The beach is very exposed to the elements so it can get wild on stormy days.

The beach was the final resting place of three ships and up to 1,800 men of the Spanish Armada and the

Big wave surfing, Mullaghmore | Roo McCrudden

remains of one of its smaller landing boats can still be seen at low tide.

BEACH WALK
Either park in the small parking area beside Trawgar [54.3974, -8.5668], the smaller beach west of Streedagh, or on the sand at the end of the road beside the Back Strand [54.4042, -8.5598]. From Trawgar follow the coastline north around Streedagh Point looking out for fossils in the limestone cliffs. Once on the Back Strand it's just a matter of walking along the beach to Conor's Island. The walk out and back along the beach is 6km and is best at low tide.

INISHMURRAY ISLAND
Lying 5km northwest of Streedagh, the tiny island of Inishmurray, which is just under a square kilometre, is known for its monastic settlement, wild scenery and as a wildlife sanctuary [54.4319, -8.6481].

The island served as a secluded retreat for Saint Molaise who founded a Christian monastery there in the 6th century, the remains of which are still remarkably intact. The settlement, known as a cashel, is surrounded by the remains of a 3m thick wall which houses a stone-roofed oratory, two churches, a clochán, a beehive hut and round rocks known as the 'cursing stones' [54.4315, -8.6570]. After being attacked numerous times by the Vikings in the 8th and

9th centuries, the monks were forced to return to the mainland.

Inishmurray, which had a population of 100 people in 1880, was finally abandoned in 1948. The ruined homes and schoolhouse are the only reminders of the small thriving community.

Nowadays the island is a wildlife sanctuary of national importance for breeding and wintering birds including shags, kittiwakes, terns, petrels, eider duck and brent geese. It also holds one of the largest colonies of barnacle geese in Europe.

Three companies regularly make the crossing to the island from Mullaghmore Harbour [54.4666, -8.4477], Sligo Boat Charters (www.sligoboatcharters.com), Offshore Watersports (www.offshore.ie) and Inishmurray Island Tours (www.inishmurrayislandtrips.com).

For more information about the island see www.inishmurray.com.

MULLAGHMORE
The small seaside village of Mullaghmore is popular with both tourists from abroad and Irish holidaymakers [54.4668, -8.4481]. Near the village is the harbour and a fine, sheltered beach [54.4614, -8.4527]. There is a small grassy carpark in front of the beach but more parking is available near the harbour.

Mullaghmore has an international reputation among surfers for producing some of the biggest waves on

The Birthing Stone, Inishmurray | John Lyon

Clochán, Inishmurray | Val Robus

Diarmuid and Gráinne's Cave | DF

the planet. During winter storms these waves can reach up to 15m in height.

The Wild Atlantic Way does a circuit around the headland and the 4km loop is a popular walk with locals. From the coast road there are great views of the very pretty Classiebawn Castle with its distinctive conical roofed turret (see the photo on page 178).

BISHOP'S POOL
Just off the coast road is a sheltered rock inlet that is a popular swimming spot on warm summer days *[54.4728, -8.4557]*. You will find it 1.2km north of the village, look out for the narrow inlet shaped like a bishop's crozier, hence the name.

THE GLENIFF HORSESHOE
This 10km cycling, walking or driving route in the Dartry Mountains has some of the most spectacular scenery that Sligo has to offer. As you emerge through the trees at the highest point of the loop the legendary Diarmuid and Gráinne's Cave comes into view high up on the steep slopes. It is reputed to be the last hiding place of the ill-fated lovers.

Nearby, the Benwiskin Centre (www. benwiskincentre.com) offers self catering accommodation and bike hire *[54.4126, -8.3905]*. Also nearby is Teapot Lane (www.glampingireland. ie) which has a range of yurts, a cottage, a vintage caravan, log cabin and even a tree house available to rent *[54.4458, -8.3841]*.

Heading north from Sligo Town on the Wild Atlantic Way, take a right turn 1.5km past Cliffony (look out for the signpost for the Benwiskin Centre). Continue up the road, straight through a number of crossroads. Follow the signs for the Horseshoe. At the T-junction at the end of the loop *[54.4458, -8.3841]* turn right and retrace your steps back to the Wild Atlantic Way.

BARYTE'S MILL
The site of the 19th century Baryte's Mill has been carefully re-invented as a beautiful recreational area by Ballaghnatrillick Environmental Group *[54.3979, -8.4000]*. There are a number of short trails through the woodland and plenty of picnic tables and seats. If you are following the Gleniff Horseshoe in a clockwise direction then the Mill is on the left after a short distance. ∎

Slieve League | Tony Webster

DONEGAL

The huge sprawling county of Donegal fills the northwest corner of the country. And even though it's only a few hundred miles north of the bottom tip of Cork, the change in latitude is apparent in a number of ways. The Northern Lights are seen relatively frequently, and the weather is a little cooler, as it's further from the benign influence of the Gulf Stream.

From a tourism point of view Donegal is probably the most overlooked of the counties along the west coast. As it is somewhat of a cul de sac and doesn't have quite the same reputation as other more famous regions of the country, it doesn't get the attention it deserves from visitors. Those who do visit will be rewarded with spectacular scenery and a very friendly welcome.

The peninsulas at the top (Inishowen) and bottom (Glencolmcille) of the county offer wild coastline and rugged mountainside. In some areas the terrain has forced the roads inland, away from the sea, leaving some of the most beautiful and remote coast in the country only accessible by foot and all the better for it.

In contrast the granite coast in the northwest is a little more serene. It is still rugged - but on a smaller scale - it's a landscape littered with idyllic rocky coves and grassy clifftops.

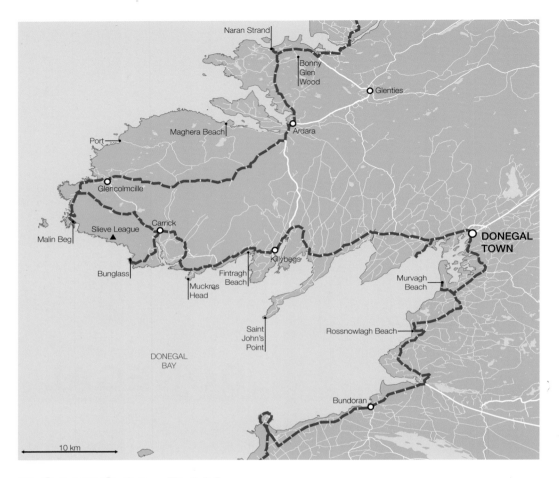

Naran Strand
Bonny Glen Wood
Glenties
Maghera Beach
Port
Ardara
Glencolmcille
Carrick
Slieve League
Malin Beg
Killybegs
Bunglass
Fintragh Beach
Muckros Head
DONEGAL TOWN
Murvagh Beach
Saint John's Point
Rossnowlagh Beach
DONEGAL BAY
Bundoran
10 km

DONEGAL BAY

North Sligo and south Donegal have much in common, with low lying coastline, lots of long sandy beaches and excellent surfing. However, as the coastline swings west there is a distinct change and the vast beaches and green fields give way to rocky hills and jagged coastline.

The peninsula of Glencolmcille is one of the remotest and wildest parts of the Wild Atlantic Way. It's also home to the Slieve League cliffs, some of the highest in Europe.

BUNDORAN

For many generations Bundoran was a traditional seaside holiday town, but recently it has reinvented itself as a surfer town [54.4776, -8.2808]. With plenty of beach, reef and point breaks in close proximity, not to mention pubs, cafés, surf shops and schools, it has

a decent claim on the title of Surf Capital of Ireland. For more information about the town see www. discoverbundoran.com.

Surf lessons and hire are available from Surf World (www.surfworld.ie), Turfnsurf (www. turfnsurf.ie), Donegal Adventure Centre (www. donegaladventurecentre.net) and Bundoran Surf Company (www.bundoransurfco.com).

MAIN BEACH
The sandy beach right in the centre of town has a Blue Flag and is patrolled by lifeguards during the summer [54.4776, -8.2808]. The narrow inlet at the east end of the beach, known as Rougey Rock, is a popular spot for diving and jumping [54.4848, -8.2805]. The jump from the highest ledge is something of a rite of passage for the local kids.

Bundoran | Miguel Silva Rodrigues

TULLAN STRAND
A short walk northeast of the town is Tullan Strand *[54.4903, -8.2675]*. The 2.5km beach is backed by a vast network of sand dunes. One of Donegal's renowned surf beaches, the consistent beach break is open to almost any swell going, with a wave for every level of surfer. High tide is best for beginners.

The water can get very busy in the summer and there is no lifeguard. Jellyfish and weever fish can be a stinging hazard in the warmer months so wear something on your feet when you are in the water.

OUTDOOR SWIMMING POOLS
There are two outdoor pools along the rocky coast beside the town. West End Pool, a large man-made seawater pool, is a few hundred metres west of the Lifeboat Station and can be accessed from the cliff path via a set of steps *[54.4779, -8.2926]*. The other pool, known as the Thrupenny Pool, lies just west of the Main Beach *[54.4806, -8.2810]*.

ROUGEY WALK
This path links the Main Beach with Tullan Strand and offers fabulous views across Donegal Bay. Look out for the Fairy Bridges, a number of precarious sea arches, and the Wishing Chair, both of which are signposted from the path. Keep a close eye on small children as there are many steep drops in this area. From Tullan either retrace your steps or follow Tullan Strand Road to the junction with the main road where you turn right to return to the Main Beach.

ROSSNOWLAGH BEACH
This Blue Flag beach is very popular and can get extremely busy on good days in the summer *[54.5529, -8.2101]*. There is good surfing, particularly for beginners. Fin McCool Surf School (www. finmccoolsurfschool.com) offer lessons and you can hire boards from Finnegan's Surf Shop (www. finnegansshop.com).

It's possible to drive onto some areas of the beach however you must be on the lookout for soft sand and the people using the beach. Drive slowly and remember the tide.

CREEVY SHORE WALK
A 10km coastal footpath links Rossnowlagh *[54.5474, -8.2133]* and the mouth of the Erne Estuary just west of Ballyshannon *[54.5077, -8.2252]*. A shorter linear route visits Creevy Head starting from Creevy Pier *[54.5299, -8.2554]*.

MURVAGH BEACH
This Blue Flag beach is a few kilometres south of Donegal Town *[54.6042, -8.1612]*. The long, wide stretch of sand has a massive tidal range so if you are planning to swim it's best to visit at high tide. Lifeguards are on duty during the summer months. While the beach itself is quite exposed, it is backed by extensive dunes and forest where there is plenty of shelter.

SAINT JOHN'S POINT
This narrow headland stretches almost 10km into Donegal Bay *[54.5693, -8.4573]*. Near the tip of the headland is a lighthouse, a nice sandy beach and

Rougey Rock | Brendan MacEvilly

Fintragh Beach | DF

Muckros Head | DF

excellent views north to the Slieve League cliffs and south across to the Sligo and Mayo coastline.

The sea around the lighthouse is popular with divers due to the very clear water.

FINTRAGH BEACH

Just west of Killybegs is a small sheltered Blue Flag beach [54.6352, -8.4886]. It was the site of a dramatic crash landing during World War 2 when an American Flying Fortress bomber was forced to ditch due to mechanical problems. Amazingly the crew of ten escaped unscathed.

To find it, follow the Wild Atlantic Way west out of Killybegs. After 4km, shortly after the football pitch in Fintragh, look out for a left turn (signposted 'Trá'). Take this turn and drive down the very steep road to the carpark.

MUCKROS HEAD

Muckros Head lies between Killybegs and Kilcar [54.6095, -8.5905]. The small headland, which juts out into the Atlantic, has a beach on either side and some impressive cliffs.

The beach on the western side, Trá na nGlór (Beach of the Noise), has a rip tide so isn't suitable for swimming but sometimes holds some surf. The eastern beach, Trá Bán (White Beach), is a popular family beach and safe for swimming [54.6145, -8.5771].

Looking towards Bunglass, Slieve League | Gareth McCormack

The steep sandstone cliffs at the end of the headland are of great interest to rock climbers and offer good views across the water to the considerably larger cliffs of Slieve League.

SLIEVE LEAGUE

The spectacular cliffs of Slieve League are one of the Wild Atlantic Way's must-sees. The summit of Slieve League mountain stands 595m above sea level and its slopes rise directly from the Atlantic. While the cliffs lack the sheer verticality of the Cliffs of Moher they are almost three times as tall. See the photo on page 190.

One interesting way to view the cliffs is from the water. The Nuala Star (www.sliabhleagueboattrips. com) operates daily boat tours from the pier at Teelin [54.6235, -8.6327] and if conditions are right it's even possible to swim beneath the cliffs.

The viewing point at Bunglass offers one of the best views of the cliffs, but on busy days the small carpark [54.6270, -8.6846] fills up quickly so you may have to park at the lower carpark [54.6265, -8.6639] and walk the 1.5km to the viewing point. The best time to view the cliffs is early afternoon or evening. This gives any cloud or fog a chance to burn off.

There are two walking routes to the summit of Slieve League, both of which should only be attempted by well equipped, sure footed walkers with a head for heights. Needless to say the cliffs are dangerous, always stay away from the edge. If you plan to attempt either of these walks, carry a map (OSI sheet 10) and pick a clear, calm day as the ridge is no place to be in a strong wind.

CLIFFTOP PATH

From the Bunglass viewing point [54.6270, -8.6846] a path runs along the ridge to the summit of Slieve League. This route is currently being repaired and Donegal County Council have requested that walkers use the Pilgrim Path while this work is ongoing. Nonetheless this route is still popular and it is definitely the more spectacular of the two trails.

The path is in a bad state, heavily eroded and very muddy. It crosses a number of intermediate peaks including one very narrow rocky rib, the Knife Edge of Keeringear (sometimes incorrectly called the One Man's Pass), and while it's an easy scramble it's very dangerous and is easily avoided by a path inland. The true One Man's Pass is the narrow ridge that forms the final section to the summit [54.6512, -8.7067].

From the summit of Slieve League it's possible to continue west along the coastline to Malin Beg. You will however need to arrange a lift back to the car but this amazing walk is well worth the effort.

PILGRIM PATH

This route is less exposed, at least until you reach the ridge, and is a better option in bad weather.

The cliffs at Port | DF

The watchtower at Malin Beg | DF

A good wide track leads from the carpark to the waterfall viewing point. After this point the path deteriorates and the going becomes a lot tougher, only experienced walkers should continue. The steep, rocky path leads to the top of the cliffs and is marked with yellow painted rocks. Once you meet the cliffs it's possible to continue along the One Man's Pass to the summit of Slieve League *[54.6512, -8.7067]*.

To get to the start take the Teelin road south from Carrick. Look out for a signposted right turn after 2.5km. Take this turn and follow the steep, narrow, winding road to the carpark, closing all gates behind you *[54.6416, -8.6604]*.

MALIN BEG

The tiny village of Malin Beg lies at the very tip of the Glencolmcille Peninsula. It's unusual in that it's one of the few villages in Ireland that doesn't have a pub, but there is a hostel (www.malinbeghostel.com) and there is also one down the road in Malin More, Áras Ghleann Cholm Cille (www.arasgcc.com).

If you turn right at the crossroads in the village the road leads down to a sheltered harbour *[54.6653, -8.7860]*. You can park here and follow the track to the watchtower where there are great views across to Rathlin O'Birne Island and down the coast to Slieve League.

Glencolmcille Folk Village | Peter Astle

SLÍ CHOLMCILLE

The Slí Cholmcille is a 65km signposted walking route that travels around the Glencolmcille Peninsula, starting and finishing in Ardara. The route is best tackled in a clockwise direction as this means the best views can be enjoyed on the descents. Highlights include the lonely deserted village of An Port and the steep valley of Glengesh.

Most of the route follows narrow roads, some of which can be busy so take care. There are also sections of bog road and open moorland that can be damp underfoot.

The walk could be done as one continuous hike over a few days either camping or staying overnight in the villages en route, or alternatively a shorter section could be done as a point-to-point day hike. See www.irishtrails.ie for detailed maps.

INTERNATIONAL APPALACHIAN TRAIL

This extension of the world famous Appalachian Trail, which travels along the spine of the east coast of the United States, links geologically similar terrain in America and Europe. The Irish section of the trail starts at Slieve League and makes its way east across Donegal and through Northern Ireland, combining existing walking trails for a total length of 485km. See www.walkni.com/iat/ for more information including maps.

DONEGAL CYCLE ROUTE

This 200km tour starts in Donegal Town and travels north keeping close to the coastline before finishing near Letterkenny. The route is well signposted and has a couple of spurs and loops which offer short scenic diversions. See www.donegalcycleroute.ie for more information.

BALLYSHANNON CYCLE HUB

The town of Ballyshannon is the start/finish point for two signposted cycle loops that explore the countryside of south Donegal.

The 39km Route 1 heads west along the shores of Assaroe Lake before turning north and then west to Rossnowlagh. After a short stretch along the beach the route follows the coast south to Ballyshannon.

Loop 2 (36km) heads south to Bundoran and passes Lough Melvin and the village of Belleek before joining Loop 1 on the final stretch into Ballyshannon.

SILVER STRAND

This beautiful beach lies at the far end of Malin Beg [54.6653, -8.7771]. Drive through the village to the carpark at the end of the road. The beach is accessed by a steep series of steps and is well sheltered by the surrounding cliffs.

GLENCOLMCILLE

The small village of Glencolmcille is a great base for exploring this remote area which is surrounded by some of the most spectacular coastal scenery in the county [54.6652, -8.7770].

On the edge of the village is Glencolmcille Folk Village (www.glenfolkvillage.com). The small cluster of pretty cottages show how life used to be in times gone by [54.7070, -8.7410].

There are two hostels in the village including the rather unique Dooey Hostel (dooeyhostel@gleanncholmcille.ie), which allows camping in the garden, and Ionad Siuil guesthouse (www.ionadsiul.ie).

GLENCOLMCILLE TO MAGHERA WALK

The 20km stretch of coast between Glencolmcille and Maghera is some of the most remote in the county.

Starting in Glencolmcille follow the Slí Cholmcille (see box opposite) to the tiny cove at Port [54.7475, -8.7023]. Continue east along the clifftops and descend into Glenlough. This wonderfully secluded valley can only be accessed on foot and is probably the most remote place along the Wild Atlantic Way.

After leaving behind Glenlough it's a matter of either sticking to the coast or taking in Slievetooey mountain before descending to Maghera [54.7624, -8.5273].

As this walk covers some very isolated, trackless ground good navigation skills and a map (OSI sheet 10) and compass are essential.

The walk could be extended by starting at Teelin and following the Slieve League ridge west to Malin Beg. This would be an exceptional two day trip with plenty of places to stay in Malin Beg or Glencolmcille.

TOWER LOOP

This signposted 10km loop (marked by the blue arrows) starts from the village of Glencolmcille [54.7086, -8.7311] and follows lanes and mountain paths to the watchtower high on the ridge. The Drum Loop (red arrows) is a slightly longer (3km) variation.

PORT

The remote townland of Port was once home to a small fishing village, however it has been deserted since the Famine [54.7475, -8.7023]. The beautiful cove is the only breach in the long line of huge cliffs that stretch for many miles. It's possible to walk the grassy clifftops in either direction and admire the amazing rock architecture beneath.

There is an off-grid cottage just above the beach that is available for rent. See www.port-donegal.com for details.

Bonny Glen Wood | DF

Portnoo | Andrew Hurley

Assarnacally Waterfall | DF

Head east out of Glencolmcille village on the R230 and after 2km turn left (signposted 'Port'). Follow the narrow road for 7km to a junction where you turn left and descend the narrow road to the sea.

MAGHERA BEACH

A vast sweep of pristine white sand on the northern side of the peninsula [54.7624, -8.5273]. At low tide it's possible to explore the caves at the west end of the beach, but be very careful that you don't get cut off by the rising tide. Swimming isn't advised as there are sudden changes in depth and very strong currents.

The steep, narrow road that climbs southwest out of Maghera is known as Granny Pass and it's a very interesting 'shortcut' to Glencolmcille. It's not suitable for nervous drivers or large vehicles.

Travelling south from Ardara on the Wild Atlantic Way turn right (well signposted) after 1.5km. Follow the road past the waterfall to the beach carpark (small fee) on the right.

ASSARNACALLY WATERFALL

This picturesque waterfall is just off the road between Maghera Beach and Ardara and is well worth a quick stop [54.7587, -8.5140].

NARAN STRAND

With its elegant curve, pale sand and clear azure water Naran (aka Tramore Strand) has a tropical flavour (on a sunny day at least) as well as a Blue Flag [54.8386, -8.4469]. During July and August there is a lifeguard in attendance.

Just to the west of the beach is the small village of Portnoo [54.8423, -8.4658]. Its tiny pier and beach are used by Tirconnell Charters (www.tirconnellcharters.com) for fishing and whale watching trips and by Rapid Kayaking (www.rapidkayaking.com) for sea kayaking.

INISHKEEL

Spring tides (which occur twice a month, around the new moon and full moon) expose a sandbar making it possible to walk across to the island of Inishkeel from Naran Strand [54.8449, -8.4513]. Be very careful, it would be very easy to get cut off. The small island was home to a monastery founded in the 6th century and there are a few beautifully decorated stone pillars that are worth seeking out.

BONNY GLEN WOOD

A small, peaceful forest with two short signposted trails [54.8317, -8.4033]. From Naran follow the Wild Atlantic Way to the R261 and continue east for 1.5km before turning right. Follow the road for 1km to the entrance to the forest. The shorter walk is a 1km loop around Bonnyglen Lough and the longer trail (6km out and back) follows forest roads and paths to Lough Namanlagh. ⬚

Maghera cave | Tobias Senger

Sea stack climbing | Iain Miller

SEA STACK CLIMBING

The coastline north of Glencolmcille is extremely rugged and home to dozens of sea stacks. These massive rock towers are formed when sections of softer rock are eroded into headlands and then arches, which ultimately collapse and leave an isolated pinnacle of rock.

Sea stack climbing is quite different from conventional rock climbing. It's much more committing and often getting to the start of the route is harder than the actual climbing.

Iain Miller has done the first ascents of over sixty sea stacks in this area, standing where no one has ever stood before. Iain is a climbing guide and his company Unique Ascent (www.uniqueascent.ie) takes people out climbing on the cliffs and sea stacks of Donegal. If you are very lucky you may even end up doing a first ascent on a day out with him!

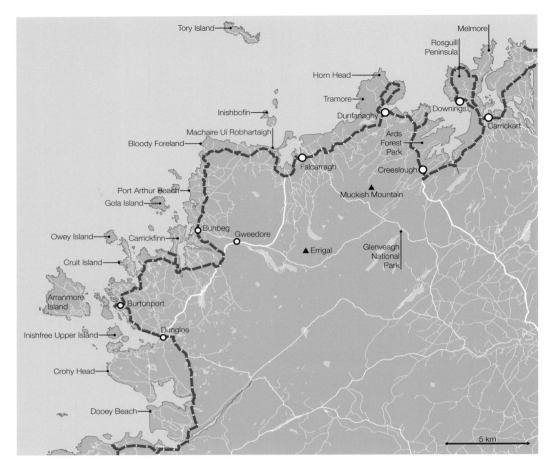

NORTH WEST DONEGAL

While the northwestern coastline of Donegal has its share of expansive sandy beaches it also has hundreds of beautiful rocky coves, hidden away, waiting to be discovered and enjoyed in solitude.

A large part of this area is Gaeltacht, which means that Irish is the spoken language.

This part of Donegal is overlooked by many visitors from overseas, possibly because it lacks a world renowned attraction like its neighbours to the north (Malin Head) and south (Slieve League). It's a great place to seek out a quieter, more authentic experience and there is nowhere quieter or more authentic than the numerous remote offshore islands, particularly Tory Island.

The area around the village of Dunfanaghy has plenty of excellent beaches and is very popular with Irish families, particularly with visitors from Northern Ireland.

Inland the ground is barren, consisting of little more than heather, rocky outcrops and peaty lakes. Two distinctive peaks lie a short distance from the coast, the sharply pointed Errigal (Donegal's highest mountain) and the flat topped Muckish. Also a short drive inland, hidden deep in the mountains, is the beautiful Glenveagh National Park.

DOOEY BEACH

This quiet Green Coast beach lies on the opposite side of Gweebarra Bay to Naran [54.8734, -8.3819]. The carpark is at the northern end of the 3km stretch of sand. Wild Atlantic Surf School (www.wildatlanticsurfschool.com) are based here and offer surf lessons and board rental during the summer.

Crohy Head | Gareth Wray

CROHY HEAD
Just offshore of Crohy Head is a much photographed sea arch *[54.9146, -8.4563]*. There is also a nice beach to the north, on the edge of Maghery village *[54.9282, -8.4437]*. In the village is the community centre, Ionad An Mhachaire, which has a café and information on many of the walks in the area.

INISHFREE UPPER ISLAND
A square mile of meadows ringed by rocky coves. The beautiful, serene island has recently been re-inhabited after lying empty for many years *[54.9552, -8.4463]*. There is no ferry to the island so you will either have to paddle over in a kayak or find a local fisherman who will bring you.

DUNGLOE RIVER WALK
A gentle 2km loop following the wooded banks of the Dungloe River and Lake. The main loop is marked with red arrows, an optional 1.5km extension is marked with green ones. The trailhead is accessed from the N56, just past the bridge *[54.9531, -8.3593]*.

BURTONPORT
The small town of Burtonport (or as it's signposted 'Ailt an Chorráin') is a good base for exploring the myriad islands and beaches in this area *[54.9848, -8.4383]*. There are three signposted walks based

around the disused Letterkenny and Burtonport railway near the town.

- The Old Railway (red arrows) 5.5km each way.
- The Kinballycrowie Loop (orange arrows) 7km
- The Crickamore Loop (blue arrows) 5km

For a map of the walks see www.therosses.ie.

BEACHES
The coastline north of Dungloe is a maze of wonderful coves and rocky islands that are well worth exploring at low tide. Look out for a left turn (signposted 'Beach') 1.3km north of Burtonport, and follow the signs to one of the numerous beaches which include An Chloch Ghlas *[54.9996, -8.4471]* and Portacurry *[55.0062, -8.4281]*.

ARRANMORE ISLAND
The largest inhabited 'proper' island off the coast of Ireland (Achill Island is bigger but is connected to the mainland by a bridge). The island is part of the Gaeltacht and the majority of its residents are Irish speakers.

The exposed west coast bristles with high cliffs, sea stacks and caves with names such as Paradise Cavern, the Moon Pool, the Grotto, the Cave of Light, the Sea Eagle's Stack and the Giant's Stack.

Arranmore Lighthouse | Ross McDonald

Diving off Arranmore | Pauric Ward

The waters surrounding the island are crystal clear with an abundance of sea life. Talk to Dive Arranmore (www.divearranmore.com) for information about diving and sightseeing charters.

Two ferry companies make the short (15 minute) crossing from Burtonport Pier [54.9835, -8.4412] a couple of times daily (see www.arranmorefastferry.com and www.arranmoreferry.com). There are plenty of B+Bs, a hotel, a guesthouse and a hostel (www.arranmorehostel.com) on the island.

SLÍ ÁRAINN MHÓR
The 14km long signposted trail Sli Áraínn Mhór takes in most of the island's interesting sights including the Beaver Island Memorial at Lough Shore [55.0023, -8.5361], the island's highest point Cnoc an Iolair [54.9909, -8.5287], and the old graveyard [54.9753, -8.4961]. The walk follows narrow roads and tracks in a loop around the island, starting and finishing at the ferry port [54.9899, -8.4969]. The 2km (each way) spur walk to the old coastguard station and lighthouse [55.0144, -8.5601] is well worth taking if you have time.

Another option is to cycle the route. Grass Routes offer electric and pedal bikes for hire. See www.grassroutes.ie for details.

BEACHES
There are a number of sandy beaches and coves on the more sheltered southern and eastern shores of the island, notably Leadhb Gharbh [54.9867, -8.4962], which is right beside the pier, and the strand at Leadhb Reannach [54.9719, -8.5228].

CRUIT ISLAND
This long, narrow island is connected to the mainland by a small bridge [55.0147, -8.4092] just north of the tiny village of Kincasslagh. The island is ringed by granite cliffs and is one of the most popular rock climbing areas in Donegal.

There are over a dozen sandy coves hidden along the coast. The most popular beach is found halfway across the island on the western side, just before the thatched cottages [55.0332, -8.4196].

The island lies just off the Wild Atlantic Way. Look out for a left turn (signposted 'An Chruit') directly opposite the Viking Bar and Restaurant.

If you want to try some rock climbing, get in touch with Unique Ascent (www.uniqueascent.ie) who are based nearby.

OWEY ISLAND
This small island lies a few hundred metres off the northern end of Cruit [55.0525, -8.4413]. During the summer months it's possible to arrange a boat to the island with Dan Gallagher (086 6013893) from the

Wild camping on Cruit Island | Claudio Raboni

Looking toward Errigal from Gola Island | Liam Moloney

DONEGAL **203**

Rock climbing on Gola Island | Michael O'Dwyer

Owey Island from Cruit | David Ardron

pier near the golf course on Cruit *[55.0481, -8.4320]*. At other times contact Saoire Mara Charters (www. saoiremara.com).

In the summer many of the cottages are used as holiday homes. The rest of the time the island lies deserted. Even though it's only a ten minute boat ride from the mainland, the island is like another world, with no electricity or services. The islanders get their water from a spring and their houses are heated by turf fires and lit by gas lamps.

The massive granite cliffs, the numerous coves and the deep caverns are of great interest to rock climbers and sea kayakers. In the past the caves were used by poitín (the Irish equivalent to moonshine) makers to hide their illegal wares when the police came to inspect the island.

The only accommodation is Owey Homestay which offers the choice of a self-catering barn or a bed in the family cottage (www.oweyhomestay.com). Campers are very welcome as long as they leave the island as they find it.

CARRICKFINN

This small headland is home to Donegal Airport as well as a number of very nice sandy beaches and rocky coves.

The long Blue Flag beach just to the west of the runway is very popular *[55.0378, -8.3468]*. There are lots of small coves south of the beach that are worth seeking out. Follow the signs for the airport, drive past the entrance and park at the end of the road.

There are also plenty of small, sheltered coves at the northern end of the headland. Trá na mBád, Boat Strand, is particularly nice *[55.0560, -8.3435]*. Find it by driving along the road parallel to the runway, turn left at the fork. The next turn left leads to the beach. Rapid Kayaking (www.rapidkayaking.com) offer sit-on-top kayak tours of the rocky coastline starting from the beach.

GOLA ISLAND

The small island of Gola lies 1.5km offshore. Now uninhabited it was once home to over a hundred people *[55.0910, -8.3582]*. Beautiful and unspoiled, the island is popular with walkers, birdwatchers and climbers. The eastern side of the island, where the cottages and pier are found, has white sandy beaches, while the western side is more rugged with granite cliffs, narrow bays and sea arches.

The Seod Gabhla (087 6607003) makes the short crossing from the small pier at Magheragallon *[55.0869, -8.3242]*, just west of Bunbeg, regularly during the summer months. There is one house for rent on the island, Portacrin Cottage (www. portacrincottage.net). The only other option is to camp on the grassy ground between the lake and the beach on the western side of the island *[55.0902, -8.3683]*.

Tory Island | Owen Clarke

SLÍ GABHLA

This 4km walk starts at the pier *[55.0910, -8.3582]* and follows the sandy roads in a loop around the eastern part of the island. It's well worth making a diversion to the western coastline. The view from Mweelmore *[55.0860, -8.3748]*, the highest point on the southwestern corner of the island, is wonderful.

PORT ARTHUR BEACH

This long, sandy Green Coast beach looks out across the water to the island of Inishmeane *[55.1016, -8.3156]*. The commonage near the beach is often used by campers.

BLOODY FORELAND

This broad, rocky headland marks the point where the coast starts to run east rather than north. It gets its name from the red hue that the cliffs take on at sunset. The viewing point on the Wild Atlantic Way is a great place to watch the sun set *[55.1372, -8.2893]*.

TORY ISLAND

Lying 11km off the coast, Tory Island is Ireland's most remote inhabited island *[55.2649, -8.2273]*. It is exposed to the full fury of the Atlantic and is often cut off during winter storms. The island is stark and treeless with some very impressive sea cliffs.

Thanks to its isolation many of Tory's ancient customs survive to this day, including the appointment of the island king, who may well greet you as you arrive. The island even has its own school of painting and gallery (www.toryislandpaintings.com).

There are a number of fascinating historical and mythological sites including a round tower that once protected monks from Viking raids, the ruins of Saint Colmcille's 6th century monastery and the intriguing Tau Cross which suggests early seafaring links to ancient Egypt.

On the highest point of the island lie the remains of an ancient promontory fort known as Dún Balair *[55.2623, -8.1938]*. A little to the east is the incredibly narrow ridge that terminates in a point known as An Tor Mór. It's possible (with great care) to walk about half way along the ridge but the outer half remains the realm of experienced mountaineers.

As it's a mere 4km long and never more than 1.5km wide Tory is easily explored on foot. The best approach is to follow the 12km signposted trail that loops around the island in a figure of eight. The trail starts and finishes at the ferry port *[55.2646, -8.2270]*.

Catch the ferry (www.toryislandferry.com) from either Machaire Uí Robhartaigh *[55.1467, -8.1743]* (1 hour crossing) or Bunbeg *[55.0869, -8.3245]* (2 hour crossing). Be warned the crossing can be rough.

There is a hostel, a hotel and a couple of B+Bs and a pub. However if you are visiting outside of the summer they may not be open, so check in advance.

Horn Head | DF

For more information about the island visit www. oileanthorai.com.

INISHBOFIN
Not to be confused with its namesake in Galway, this small island is just 1.5km from the mainland *[55.1772, -8.1764]*. With no services and only a handful of year-round occupants this quiet island is a great place to escape the modern world. The Carmel Olivia runs a ferry service from Machaire Uí Robhartaigh *[55.1467, -8.1743]* to the island. Contact handaisle1@yahoo.ie for details.

MACHAIRE UÍ ROBHARTAIGH
This elegant curve of pale sand stretches for almost 5km and shelters the sandy expanse of Ballyness Bay *[55.1458, -8.1733]*. Thanks to its exposed position the beach is of great interest to surfers, windsurfers and kitesurfers. It has a Green Coast award and there is plenty of parking at the pier where the Tory Island ferry sails from, as well as toilets and a café.

HORN HEAD
Just north of the town of Dunfanaghy, the Wild Atlantic Way does a short loop around the dramatic coastline of Horn Head. The huge cliffs, which rise straight out of the water to a height of 180m, are an internationally important colony for breeding seabirds including the European shag and the razorbill.

Be sure to make the short diversion off the Wild Atlantic Way to visit Coastguard Hill *[55.2229, -7.9790]*, the highest point at the tip of the headland. Rather than following the Wild Atlantic Way over the first cattle grid, continue straight on and park at the end of the road *[55.2149, -7.9783]*. Walk a short distance up the hill to the watchtower where you can soak up the great views to Tory Island and inland to Muckish and the Derryveagh mountains.

COASTGUARD HILL LOOP
An 8km signposted walk starting at the most northerly carpark on Horn Head *[55.2149, -7.9783]*. It's only suitable for experienced walkers, due to the rough ground, steep cliffs and number of stiles to be crossed. Dogs are not allowed on this walk as there is livestock on the land.

LURGABRACK NATURE WALK
This is an easy 5km signposted walk that visits the beautiful remote beach at Tramore and the old forest at Lurgabrack. The first section to Tramore Strand (dangerous currents, don't swim) can also be done as a shorter linear route.

To get to the start head towards Horn Head from Dunfanaghy and turn left just after the bridge. The carpark is on the left after 100m *[55.1854, -7.9870]*. Please keep dogs under effective control.

Ards Forest Park | Rob Underhill

MCSWYNE'S GUN
A short distance north of Tramore Strand is a blowhole known as McSwyne's Gun *[55.1899, -8.0242]*. During storms, water gets forced hundreds of feet into the air and the noise can be heard miles away. Take care as stones can also be launched skyward!

KILLAHOEY STRAND
Just east of Dunfanaghy is the Blue Flag Killahoey Strand *[55.1861, -7.9563]*. A quiet beach and very safe for swimming, during the summer months there are lifeguards on duty.

Access the beach via the road through the golf course, which is on the edge of Dunfanaghy. Alternatively walk along the coast from Arnold's Hotel in the town.

MARBLE HILL STRAND
This sandy Blue Flag beach in Sheephaven Bay is one of the most popular beaches in Donegal *[55.1762, -7.9018]*.

Two watersports providers operate at the beach and elsewhere in the area. Jaws Watersports (www.jawswatersports.ie) offer surfing, windsurfing, paddleboarding, kayaking and sailing and Narosa School of Surf (www.narosalife.com) run surf lessons, rental and kids camps.

Follow the Wild Atlantic Way south from Dunfanaghy, towards Creeslough. Look out for a left turn 2km past Portnablahy village. Follow the road to the beach, parking at the roadside.

HARRY'S HOLE
North of the beach is Harry's Hole *[55.1833, -7.8972]*. The small inlet is a popular swimming spot and there are plenty of outcrops of all sizes to jump off. Follow the small track north for 500m from the west side of the beach to find them.

ARDS FOREST PARK
On the sheltered western shore of Sheephaven Bay is Ards Forest Park, one of the most beautiful and varied of Ireland's forest parks *[55.1588, -7.8887]*. The 480 hectare park contains a large diversity of habitats with sandy beaches, rivers and forest. Scattered across the park you will find many features of historical and archaeological interest including the remains of four ring forts and the Mass Rock where mass was celebrated in defiance of the penal laws.

There are six signposted walks ranging in length from 0.5km to 13km. Check out www.irishtrails.ie for a detailed map.

The entrance to the park is on the Wild Atlantic Way, midway between Creeslough and Dunfanaghy. There is an automatic pay barrier at the entrance, the fee is €5 (in coins) per car.

Boyeeghter Bay | Gareth Wray

ARDS FRIARY
Adjacent to the forest park is the Capuchin Friary *[55.1583, -7.8642]*. A very peaceful place, which is used throughout the year for retreats, conferences and seminars, it has many paths weaving around its 200 acres. Travelling towards Creeslough on the Wild Atlantic Way look out for the signposted turn to the left just past of the entrance to Ards Forest Park.

WILD ATLANTIC CAMP
A nice family campsite on the southern side of Creeslough *[55.1192, -7.9045]*. It has bell tents and wooden pods for hire as well as camping and motorhome pitches (www.wildatlanticcamp.ie).

ROSGUILL PENINSULA
This beautiful peninsula has a number of wonderful beaches and great views.

DOWNINGS BEACH
A popular Blue Flag beach in the village of Downings *[55.1943, -7.8366]*. Lifeguards patrol the beach between June and September. Just to the south is another quieter beach, Trá Mór, adjacent to Saint Patrick's Golf Links.

ATLANTIC DRIVE
The Wild Atlantic Way follows a very scenic clockwise route, known as Atlantic Drive, around the peninsula.

The 12km loop is on narrow roads and could easily be walked or cycled. The views are great, particularly those across Sheephaven Bay to Horn Head and over Trá na Rosann Bay.

MELMORE
It's well worth making the short diversion from the Wild Atlantic Way to visit Trá na Rosann, the spectacular beach on the western shore of the low, flat ground that connects Melmore to Rosguill *[55.2245, -7.8138]*. Heed the warning signs and don't swim near the rocks. Not far from the beach is the An Óige hostel in a former hunting lodge (www.anoige.ie).

BOYEEGHTER BAY
On the western shore of the headland there is a beautiful beach (see the photo on page 2). Hidden from view, a short walk from the road, it's known locally as the Murder Hole, however the origins of this sinister name are unclear.

Follow the road north past Trá na Rosann and shortly after the sign marked Melmore Head park on the right beside the beach *[55.2399, -7.7918]*. A little further up the road on the left is a gate. Go through this and follow the track west, passing through a grassy field before descending steeply down to the beach *[55.2403, -7.8046]*. ∎

Glenveagh National Park | Michal Osmenda

Muckish Mountain | Greg Clarke

Errigal | Warren Campbell

ERRIGAL

The distinctive conical profile of Errigal, Donegal's highest mountain, is hard to mistake. The most popular route to the summit of the 751m peak is steep and rocky and even though it's only a 4km round trip there is serious height gain (500m). As such it's only suitable for well equipped, fit hikers.

The starting point is the small carpark on the R251 east of Dunlewey *[55.0249, -8.0899]*. From the carpark follow the boggy trail directly up the hillside. At the large cairn turn left and follow the path towards the ridge. Steep, rocky ground leads past a circular shelter and a number of cairns to the summit *[55.0343, -8.1126]*. A narrow ridge separates the two summits, the easterly one is considered the highest point. Take care on the descent, particularly on the loose scree.

In Dunlewy village *[55.0314, -8.1446]* there is an An Óige hostel (www.anoige.ie) and community centre where you can get information about Errigal.

GLENVEAGH NATIONAL PARK

One of six national parks in Ireland, Glenveagh occupies over 16,000 hectares in the heart of the Derryveagh Mountains. This vast area of mountain and bog is home to many plants and animals including a herd of red deer. At the head of Lough Beagh is a visitor centre and tearooms. The beautiful castle and gardens are a short bus ride or a pleasant 3km walk along the lake shore.

There are a number of walks in the area and at weekends the shuttle bus will drop walkers to the start of their walk for a small fee.

From Gweedore follow the R251 west. From Termon follow the R255 then R251 to the park *[55.0573, -7.9387]*. See www. glenveaghnationalpark.ie for more information.

MUCKISH MOUNTAIN

The 666m tall mountain derives its name from its distinctive flat top, the Irish being 'An Mhucais' which translates as 'pig's back'. The rocky plateau is a wonderful place but it can be very disorientating in bad conditions so you must be able to navigate using a map and compass.

The easiest route to the summit starts from the shrine at Muckish Gap on the R256 *[55.0886, -8.0023]*. A harder alternative is the Miner's Track which approaches from the north. For details of both routes see www.mountainviews.ie/summit/163/.

If you aren't up for Muckish there are three shorter signposted trails nearby *[55.1257, -7.9866]*.

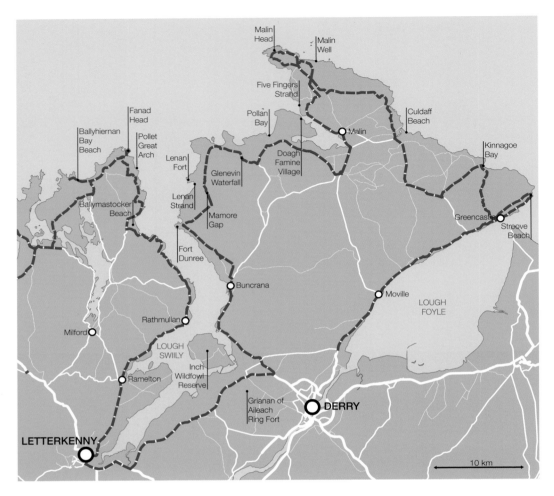

FANAD AND INISHOWEN

The peninsulas of Fanad and Inishowen are home to some of the most dramatic coastal scenery in the country as well as many beautiful beaches. The sea to the north has always been an important shipping channel and there are plenty of reminders of this as the coast is littered with forts, shipwrecks and lighthouses.

At the tip of Inishowen is Ireland's most northerly point, the wild and windswept Malin Head. It's a great place to watch the waves surge along the cliffs during a storm.

The scenery at Fanad Head is more gentle, with lots of sandy coves and of course its iconic lighthouse.

The ferries (see page 217) and the Harry Blaney Bridge, which connects Rosguill and Fanad [55.1895,

-7.7644], make it possible to move easily from headland to headland with minimal driving.

For more information about the area check out www.visitinishowen.com.

BALLYHIERNAN BAY BEACH
A long sandy beach, backed by low dunes [55.2469, -7.7274]. To the west of Ballyhiernan, either side of Ballywhorisky Point, are some smaller, quieter beaches and rocky coves.

FANAD HEAD
For centuries Fanad Head has played an important role in protecting passing ships. There has been a lighthouse here since 1811 [55.2756, -7.6345].

Fanad Lighthouse | Gareth Wray

The present lighthouse, which was built in 1886, is picture perfect with its neat whitewashed exterior and elevated position. And even though you can't access the lighthouse itself it is possible to get a good view of it from the small headland just beside it.

There are three self-catering cottages in the lighthouse complex that are available for rent. Check out www.fanadlighthouse.com for the details.

POLLET GREAT ARCH
This sea arch is one of the most impressive along the Atlantic coast [55.2576, -7.6195]. To find it drive south from Fanad Head along the Wild Atlantic Way. After 4km look for a signposted turn left, take this and park (carefully) near the end of the narrow road [55.2574, -7.6248]. Follow the track down to the beach, the arch is to the left.

BALLYMASTOCKER BEACH
This long sandy beach is undoubtedly one of the most beautiful in Ireland, particularly when viewed from the Wild Atlantic Way as it winds its way south over the shoulder of Knockalla Mountain.

The popular beach can be accessed at the northern end via the large carpark [55.2069, -7.6258] on the edge of Portsalon village, or at the southern end from a small carpark [55.1882, -7.6093]. It has a Blue Flag award and is quite sheltered, particularly at the southern end where there are a number of rocky

outcrops. There are lifeguards on duty during the summer.

Deep Blue Watersports (www.seafishingdonegal. com) offer angling charters and pleasure trips departing from the pier in Portsalon [55.2082, -7.6187].

Near the northern end of the beach is Knockalla Caravan and Camping Park (www. knockallacaravanpark.com).

Nestled in the hills above Portsalon is Portsalon Luxury Camping which has five beautiful yurts for rent from April to October. Each is equipped with wood burning stoves and fully furnished interiors (www. donegalglamping.com).

GRIANAN OF AILEACH RING FORT
This circular stone ring-fort is well over a thousand years old [55.0237, -7.4278]. Its origins are linked to the mythical Tuatha dé Danann, a race of supernaturally gifted people who invaded Ireland before the Celts. The fort's elevated position makes for dramatic views across north Donegal. It is signposted from the small village of Burt which lies on the Wild Atlantic Way 30km north of Letterkenny.

INCH WILDFOWL RESERVE
Inch Island, which is connected to the mainland by two causeways, is a birdwatcher's paradise. It is an internationally significant destination and staging

Portsalon Luxury Camping | Paul McGuckin

Pollet Arch | Michal Kostra

Mute Swans, Inch Wildfowl Reserve | RC

Grianan of Aileach | DF

Ballymastocker Strand | Philip McErlean

ground for migrating birds from three continents. There are three hides from which to observe the birds and a network of walking trails to explore.

The full loop, crossing to the island on one causeway and returning on the other, is 8km but it's also possible to do a shorter walk by retracing your steps.

Travelling north through the village of Burt take a turn left opposite the distinctive church. After a short distance the main road swings to the right but continue straight on for 1km to the carpark [55.0517, -7.4440].

BUNCRANA

The largest town on Inishowen, Buncrana is popular with tourists and day trippers. There is plenty to see in the immediate area and it's a good base for exploring the peninsula.

Tullyarvan Mill, just north of the town, is a 19th century mill that has been converted to a hostel. See www.tullyarvanmill.com for more information.

THE WHITE STRAND

The 2km White Strand or Trá Bán lies just south of Buncrana Town [55.1187, -7.4585]. A short distance further south is the Blue Flag Lisfannan Beach [55.0966, -7.4806].

THE SHORE PATH

This 3km path runs north from Buncrana to Stragill Strand. The route starts at Ladies' Bay, a sheltered cove five minutes walk from the town centre [55.1381, -7.4613]. The first point of interest is Ned's Point Fort [55.1407, -7.4739]. This Napoleonic battery is currently under restoration, but still occasionally hosts concerts and markets.

Passing by the local landmarks of Father Hegarty's Rock, Highlandman's Rock and Porthaw Beach leads to the end of the path at Stragill Strand.

Stragill is a nice, long sandy beach with great views across Lough Swilly [55.1601, -7.4901]. It is accessible from the main road and has plenty of carparking.

SWAN PARK

This small but very beautiful park runs alongside the River Crana on the edge of Buncrana. Park either at the southern end of the park [55.1381, -7.4613] as for the Shore Path or else at the northern entrance at Wilson's Bridge [55.1417, -7.4555] where the Wild Atlantic Way leaves town on the R238. A beautifully illustrated guide to the park can be download from www.visitinishowen.com. Look out for fairies!

FORT DUNREE

Originally built as a Royal Navy position during the Napoleonic Wars, Fort Dunree (www.fortdunree.com)

Dunree Fort | DF

is located on a rocky promontory overlooking Lough Swilly [55.1966, -7.5528]. It is now a military museum with detailed exhibitions, many restored guns and an old military camp. There are also displays about the area's birds, marine life and coastal vegetation as well as a gift shop, auditorium and café. Three short signposted walks explore the fort complex and the hill above.

AN PORT BÁN
The quiet sandy beach known as An Port Bán, or since Napoleonic times Crummies Bay, is a great place to watch for harbour porpoises. Just north of the point where the road to the fort meets the main road is a small parking area. Park here [55.1985, -7.5396] and follow a narrow track down to the beach.

MAMORE GAP
North of Dunree the Wild Atlantic Way cuts steeply through the Urris Hills via Mamore Gap. From the top of the pass there are great views of Dunaff Head.

At the highest point of the road look out for the holy well named after Saint Eigne and a shrine where for centuries local people have made pilgrimages [55.2339, -7.4993].

The gap is home to one of Ireland's 'magic roads', an optical illusion in which a stopped car in neutral appears to roll uphill. The spot is 100m downhill from the carpark. It is marked by a white rock on the left-hand side of the road.

BUTLER'S GLEN LOOP
This is a tough 10.5km mountain walk through the Urris Hills. The signposted (purple arrows) loop starts from the carpark [55.2434, -7.5012] on the north slopes of the Gap and follows old bog roads through Butler's Glen.

LENAN STRAND
A short distance north of Mamore Gap is this secluded and unspoiled beach [55.2397, -7.5174]. It's well off the beaten track and is an ideal spot for a quiet day by the water.

To get there descend Mamore Gap in a northerly direction, take the left turn at the junction at the bottom of the hill and follow the road until you meet the strand.

URRIS LAKES LOOP
Another tough 6.5km loop through the Urris Hills with great views down into Mamore Gap. The going is steep, with 290m of height gain, but the trail is well marked by purple arrows. The trailhead is at the southern end of Lenan Strand [55.2391, -7.5165].

Urris Hills | Paul O'Connor

LENAN FORT

Just past the northern end of Lenan Strand is Lenan Fort *[55.2458, -7.5297]*. It was one of a number of defensive forts built by the British in 1895 to defend the deep-water anchorages of Lough Swilly. The gun positions, which are linked by extensive underground passages, are still in remarkably good condition.

It is a fascinating place to explore and has a very empty, eerie feel. If you want to check it out remember to bring a torch and be very careful as there are some uncovered hatches.

From Lenan Strand continue north along the road to a junction. Turn left and after 650m is a right turn. Take this and follow the rough, pot-holed track to the fort.

GLENEVIN WATERFALL

This very picturesque waterfall lies at the head of a beautiful wooden glen *[55.2625, -7.4441]*. It is reached by a 1km signposted walking trail that follows the stream gently uphill from the carpark. There are plenty of benches and shelters along the way to stop and enjoy the surroundings.

The carpark *[55.2676, -7.4361]* is right beside the Glen House Tearoom and Guesthouse, 1.2km west of Clonmany village.

FERRIES

The deeply recessed nature of the bays on both sides of Inishowen mean that it's possible to take a car ferry as a shortcut if you are tight on time or want a break from driving.

FOYLE FERRY

Until very recently the Foyle Ferry linked Magilligan Point near Limavady and Greencastle but unfortunately the service has stopped. Hopefully it will resume in the near future as it allowed fast access to Inishowen for visitors coming from Ballycastle and the Causeway Coast.

SWILLY FERRY

The Swilly Ferry links Rathmullan on the Fanad Peninsula and Buncrana on the west coast of Inishowen. The short crossing saves about an hour of driving time. The ferry runs during the summer months. Check the website (www.swillyferry.com) for the most up to date information.

Five Fingers Strand | Davide Borghetti

Glenevin Waterfall | DF

POLLAN BAY

A popular location for water sports, particularly surfing and windsurfing. The 3km long sandy beach is just a short distance north of Ballyliffin village [55.2901, -7.3909]. Be aware that there is no lifeguard on duty and there can be strong currents and rips. There is a children's play area beside the carpark.

A walking trail runs north along the beach between the sand and the dunes. At the far end of the beach are the ruins of the 16th century Carrickabraghy Castle [55.3158, -7.3742], which is currently under restoration. On stormy days keep your eyes and ears open for the blowhole near the castle.

DOAGH ISLE

Maybe a few thousand years ago Doagh was an island but nowadays it's connected to the mainland by a wide stretch of low-lying land.

DOAGH FAMINE VILLAGE

The Doagh Famine Village tells the story of life in the Inishowen area from the Famine in the 1840s, through to the present day [55.3089, -7.3356]. While the museum isn't state of the art it's a good option on a rainy day and is very popular. Guided tours of the village last about an hour. See www.doaghfaminevillage.com for details.

Climbing out of the Cauldron, Malin Head | Bren Whelan

DOAGH STRAND

The beach directly opposite the Famine Village is great for exploring, with plenty of huge rock pools, caves and cliffs [55.3093, -7.3350]. Unfortunately it's unsafe for swimming as there is a strong current and the water gets deep very suddenly. Thankfully some of the rock pools are deep enough to swim in and as a bonus the water tends to be warmer than the open sea!

FIVE FINGERS STRAND

One of Donegal's most beautiful beaches, Five Fingers Strand is the ideal spot for an invigorating walk on a wild day [55.3240, -7.3324]. The beach, which takes its name from the five sea stacks at its northern end, is backed by massive sand dunes, some of the largest of their type in Europe. The wreck of the Twilight, which sank in 1889 en-route from Newfoundland to Derry, is visible at low tide.

Be aware that the beach is unsafe for swimming due to very strong currents.

You will find the beach just off the Wild Atlantic Way (R242) between Malin Village and Malin Head. The road down to the beach is very narrow and there is limited parking so it's best to park at the church [55.3212, -7.3242] and walk the rest of the way down.

MALIN HEAD

Ireland's most northerly point, Malin Head, lies at the very tip of the Inishowen Peninsula. It's a wild and windswept place with dramatic cliffs and crashing waves, but it also has much of historical, scientific and ecological interest.

Birds flock here, blown in by the Atlantic winds. These regular visitors from Iceland, Greenland and North America include gannets, shearwaters, skuas, and auks on their southward migration flights.

The coast around Malin Head is some of the most treacherous water in the world - it's been the site of over four hundred ship wrecks. The insurer Lloyds of London even used the signal tower on Banba's Crown to contact ships offshore, particularly during the World Wars.

The nearest villages are Malin and Culdaff but there are plenty of B+Bs and one hostel, Sandrock Hostel (www.sandrockhostel.com), in the area.

BANBA'S CROWN

The small hill known as Banba's Crown lies overlooking the cliffs at the end of the headland [55.3810, -7.3738]. The signal tower on the top of the hill was built in 1805 by the Admiralty. The carpark at the top offers magnificent panoramic views and between Easter and September there is a small mobile café serving good coffee and home-baked treats.

Ireland's most northerly point, Malin Head | Paul O'Connor

Named after Banba, one of the mythical queens of Ireland, this was also the point where people stood to wave goodbye to their loved ones as they set out across the sea to a new life in America.

On the grassy slopes below the tower you can see a series of white stones spelling out 'EIRE'. These stones were placed there during World War 2 to warn pilots they were flying over neutral territory.

HELL'S HOLE TRAIL
The signal tower is the starting point for a short trail that leads to Hell's Hole, a long, narrow chasm through which the sea surges on stormy days [55.3806, -7.3823]. Also nearby is a picturesque natural arch called the Devil's Bridge.

There are plenty of benches along the walk where you can sit and take in the breathtaking views. The official trail ends at Hell's Hole but it's possible to continue further west along the path above the cliffs. Needless to say you should be very careful near the cliff edge.

BALLYHILLIN BEACH
To the east of the signal tower is this unique raised beach system of international scientific importance [55.3795, -7.3647]. The beach has four levels that dramatically illustrate the changing relationship between the sea and the land when the glaciers began to melt 15,000 years ago. It is also noted for its semi-precious stones so keep your eyes peeled.

MALIN WELL
East of Portmore Pier is a small road that drops steeply to the coast [55.3682, -7.3174]. Here you will find the ruins of Saint Muirdhealach's Church. Beside the church is the Wee House of Malin, a small cave carved into the rock. Also close by is a small holy well that was a place of pilgrimage until very recently. The pebble beach is worth visiting in its own right with its small sea stacks and an infinity of beautiful smooth pebbles.

CULDAFF BEACH
Culdaff has been popular with Irish holidaymakers for generations. The long sandy Blue Flag beach is 2km outside the village [55.2917, -7.1450]. There is plenty of parking, toilets, a children's playground and a lifeguard on duty during the summer months. If conditions are right the beach holds some decent surf. Donegal Surf School (www.donegalsurfschool.com) offers lessons.

KINNAGOE BAY
Kinnagoe Bay is a delightful, secluded, sandy beach (see the photo on page 28). It's perfect for families and safe for swimming. Facing away from the prevailing wind and backed by forested slopes it's very

The Northern Lights over Malin Head | Gareth Wray

sheltered. A steep, narrow road leads down to the small carpark [55.2586, -7.0128].

The rocky headland at the northern end of the bay marks the point where the Armada vessel La Trinidad Valecera ran aground in 1588.

STROOVE BEACH
This small Blue Flag beach is the starting/finishing point for two interesting walks [55.2269, -6.9291].

INISHOWEN HEAD WALK
An 8.5km signposted loop follows rough roads and gravel tracks across the hillside above Inishowen Head. There are some wonderful views, and on a clear day it's possible to see Scotland. Follow the purple arrows.

PORT-A-DORAS
Not far from Stroove is a curious piece of geology that is worth the short walk. From the carpark at Stroove follow the road north. Where the road swings around to the left is a signpost and beside it is a small gate, go through the gate and walk down the field to the sea. Follow the vague path north along the shore. After about 15 minutes you will arrive at a large outcrop that appears to block the way forward. However there is a small, natural doorway in the rock that leads to a hidden pebble cove [55.2357,

NORTHERN LIGHTS
The Aurora Borealis, or Northern Lights, are caused by collisions between gaseous particles in the Earth's atmosphere and charged particles released from the sun. Variations in colour are due to the type of gas particles that are colliding. The phenomenon can be seen above the magnetic poles of both the northern and southern hemispheres.

The lights appear in many forms ranging from shimmering clouds to streamers, arcs, rippling curtains or shooting rays that light up the sky with a green or pink glow.

Inishowen is the best place in the country to view this amazing spectacle thanks to its northern latitude and the lack of light pollution. And even though the displays are relatively infrequent and rarely as spectacular as those in the Arctic it's still worth keeping an eye out.

To get an email notification of any potential auroras email DonegalSkies@gmail.com with Aurora Alerts in the subject or follow Aurora Alert Ireland on Twitter www.twitter.com/Aurora ireland.

Culdaff Beach | David Ardron

Port-A-Doras | DF

-6.9233]. This is the door, or doras in Irish, after which the area is named.

LOUGH FOYLE COAST
There are a number of pleasant seaside villages along the placid shores of Lough Foyle between Inishowen Head and Derry City before the Wild Atlantic Way starts/finishes rather abruptly at the border between the Republic and Northern Ireland.

MARITIME MUSEUM AND PLANETARIUM
The old coastguard station in Greencastle is home to the Inishowen Maritime Museum and Planetarium which could be worth a visit on a rainy day [55.2021, -6.9871]. See www.inishowenmaritime.com for details.

MOVILLE SHORE PATH
This gentle 2km stroll follows the shore north from the attractive Victorian village of Moville [55.1881, -7.0393] and has nice views across Lough Foyle to the hills of the Derry and Antrim coast. ∎

Paddling past the Stookarudden near Malin Head | Loughs Agency

KAYAKING

Inishowen is an ideal location for kayaking. The exposed headlands offer the experienced paddler a serious challenge while the sheltered bays are perfect for beginners. Donegal Sea Kayaking (www.donegalseakayaking.com), based on the Fanad Peninsula, offer tours and hire. Inish Adventures (www.inishadventures.com), who are based in Moville, offer tours, canoeing, and river rafting.

EAST INISHOWEN SEA KAYAK TRAIL

This kayaking route travels up the eastern shore of Inishowen from near Derry City to Malin Head. The trail, which is only suitable for experienced sea paddlers or in those in the company of a capable guide, offers sea caves, off-shore islands, surf, sheltered harbours and wild camping. The Loughs Agency has produced a free guidebook which is available from www.loughs-agency.org or by emailing general@loughs-agency.org.

SURFING

Inishowen has some of the most consistent surf in Ireland. Adventure One (www.adventureone.net) runs a paddleboard school and surf shop in Rathmullan and a surf school from Ballyhiernan Bay in Fanad. They also offer surf guiding for intermediate surfers. Inishowen Surf School (www.inishowensurfschool.com) run surf lessons and summer camps in Ballyliffin, Culdaff and Tullagh Bay.

CYCLING

Cycle Inishowen (www.cycleinishowen.com) offer bike hire and guided day tours. Grass Routes (www.grassroutes.ie), who operate out of Termon and Downings, rent both electric and conventional bikes. Far and Wild (www.farandwild.org) run mountain biking tours as well as a range of other outdoor activities.

INIS EOGHAIN CYCLEWAY

This 55km signposted route loops around the countryside west of Derry City. It follows a mix of traffic-free paths and quiet country roads passing many interesting spots including Grianan of Aileach, Ballyarnett Country Park and the Foyle Valley Railway Museum. A map and information booklet is available from Cycle N.I. www.cycleni.com.

ROCK CLIMBING

Instructor Bren Whelan (www.mountaintraining.ie) runs rock climbing outings on the steep cliffs and ridges of Malin Head, a mind-blowing setting.

Three **Rock** **Books**

ACKNOWLEDGEMENTS

The authors would like to thank everyone who gave advice, feedback or encouragement or helped in any way. We would especially like to thank the photographers who generously contributed their photos.

PROOF READERS
Patrick McClean, Inga Bock, Bríd Colhoun, John Creagh, June Creagh, Marius Curtin, Denis Dineen, Lorraine Doyle, Brian Flanagan, Julie Flanagan, Darina Lawlor, Ronan McLoughlin, John Murphy, Kathleen Murphy, Conor Ryan, Diarmuid Smyth.

PHOTOGRAPHERS
All photographs by David Flanagan (DF) and Richard Creagh (RC) unless credited otherwise. We would like to thank the following people and organisations for kindly allowing us to use their photographs (all reproduced with permission or with CC-BY-SA CC-BY-2.0 CC BY-ND 2.0 CC BY-SA 2.0).

Kris Acton, David Ardron, Peter Astle, Terry Ballard, Richard O'Beirne, Davide Borghetti, Jennifer Boyer, Ian Boyle, Chris Brooks, Christopher Brown, Ronan Browne, Tom Byrne, Warren Campbell, Terry Casserly, Michele Cati, Dónal Ó Cearbhaill, Greg Clarke, Owen Clarke, Paul O'Connor, Gareth McCormack, Allie Couture, Alan Cronin, Roo McCrudden, Denis Dineen, Dingle Horse Riding, Discover Enniscrone, Dromquinna Manor, Shaun Dunphy, Michael O'Dwyer, Xavier von Erlach, Philip McErlean, Brendan MacEvilly, Tom Fahy, Ford Fisher, Frank Fullard, Harvey Futcher, Matt Gillman, Will Greene, Paul McGuckin, Graham Higgs, Valerie Hinojosa, Andrew Hurley, Imagea, Olivier Issaly, Nicole Johnson, Carolyn Jordan, Michal Kostra, Michael McLaughlin, Conor Lawless, Ilaria Leschiutta, The Loughs Agency, John Lyon, Roland Martins, Julien Mattei, Dave Mention, Iain Miller, Liam Moloney, Sean O'Moore, Marcus Murphy, Seán Murray, Michal Osmenda, Todd Parker, Anne Phillips, Sigita Playdon, Pure Camping, Claudio Raboni, Nicolas Raymond (www.freestock.ca), Andreas Riemenschneider, Val Robus, Patricia Ronan, Ross McDonald, Tobias Senger, Miguel Silva Rodrigues, Dale Simonson, Janusz Sowa, SUP for All, Christopher Tierney, Paul Tomlin, Rob Underhill, Pauric Ward, Bren Whelan, Becky Williamson, Gareth Wray, Yoko Nekonomania, Féron Benjamin, Conor Ryan, Chris Cant, Dingle Horseriding, Tony Webster.

ABOUT THE AUTHORS
David Flanagan is a writer and publisher from Dublin. This is the fourth book that he has written and published under the Three Rock Books imprint. His previous books, Bouldering in Ireland, Bouldering Essentials and Rock Climbing in Ireland were all finalists in the guidebook category of the Banff Mountain Book Award.

Richard Creagh is a photographer and writer from Cork with a great love of all things outdoors. He has spent most of the past ten years living and travelling around the west of Ireland. More of his photography can be seen at www.richardcreagh.com.